D0713185

Interdisciplinary perspectives on modern history

Editors
Robert Fogel and Stephan Thernstrom

Police in urban America, 1860–1920

Frontispiece reproduced from *Harper's Weekly*, January 5, 1895.

Police headquarters — lost children waiting for parents

Police in urban America
1860 – 1920

ERIC H. MONKKONEN

Department of History
University of California, Los Angeles

CAMBRIDGE UNIVERSITY PRESS

Cambridge
London   New York   New Rochelle
Melbourne   Sydney

Published by the Press Syndicate of the University of Cambridge
The Pitt Building, Trumpington Street, Cambridge CB2 1RP
32 East 57th Street, New York, NY 10022, USA
296 Beaconsfield Parade, Middle Park, Melbourne 3206, Australia

First published 1981

Printed in the United States of America
Typeset by David E. Seham Assoc., Inc.
Printed and bound by Vail-Ballou Press Inc.

Library of Congress Cataloging in Publication Data
Monkkonen, Eric H   1942–

Police in urban America, 1860– 1920.

(Interdisciplinary perspectives on modern
history)

Includes bibliographical references and index.

1.   Police – United States – History.   I.   Title.
II.   Series.
HV8138.M65   363.2'0973   80– 16762
ISBN 0 521 23454 9

to
Pentti and Paavo

Contents

Tables and figures

Figures

Preface

This is a social history of policing. It examines the function and social effects of modern uniformed police in American cities. It explores social history by examining the behavior of a governmental agency and by tracing changes in this behavior over time. It then uses this behavior to construct an analysis of the social role of the police agency. Those concerned with the role of police, with trends in crime, with social welfare services to the indigent, and with the lives of urban children will find new information and topics of interest to them in the following pages. In dealing with these subjects, the book touches upon many problems of importance to social historians, but my hope is that it synthesizes these problems and thereby creates new sets of problems.

For the nonhistorian, this book explains the development of a now-ubiquitous urban institution, and in so doing has policy implications. Perhaps the most important policy implication is that, although we have in the police a municipal agency capable of both social service and disservice, the best and most positive role that they can play is not clear. In the nineteenth century, the police took care of the homeless and even had soup kitchens, but we cannot easily return to that century's welfare-oriented policing. If we did, this study shows that we would have to be prepared to accept the consequences of even greater class and racial bias than we now have. On the other hand, if we choose to continue with the current model of policing, which emerged between 1890 and World War I with an emphasis on crime prevention, we must accept the increasing separation of the police from the policed, a division that opened dramatically with the decline of the welfare-oriented police after 1890. Although a middle route between the two models of policing that this book delineates may be possible, we should realize it is a less consistent approach to crime, social disorder, and poverty than that of the previous two models.

Many individuals and institutions have lent me their assistance in researching and writing this book, and I wish to thank them. I am not able to individually thank the approximately 200 librarians and archivists who responded to my queries concerning police uniforms and arrest records, and lost children. Many were unable to locate any information for me, but their efforts and the efforts of those who did find information reaffirmed my faith in the quality and dedication of librarians across the country, who seem to work as well as ever in spite of shrinking budgets.

Several organizations have provided me with monetary assistance, and it is pleasing to be able to acknowledge this, although the conclusions of this study are my responsibility. The University of North Carolina at Charlotte supported this study with a summer research grant. The University of Minnesota Computing Facility and the University of California, Los Angeles, Academic Computing Service both supported this project with computer time. UCLA also supported this work more directly with Academic Senate Research Grants and two Regents' Fellowships. At a critical early stage, the American Philosophical Society awarded me a research grant that supported my first data-gathering foray. And the Social Science Research Council's award of a Research Training Fellowship gave me the opportunity to study criminology at the Institute of Criminology, Cambridge University.

Several people assisted my research at various stages, particularly Noel Diaz, Bradley Johnson, Judith Monkkonen, Beth Williamson, and David Waterhouse, whose work was invaluable.

Many colleagues and scholars have shared their ideas, data, and critical comments with me. I have tried to answer their criticisms and follow their suggestions, and am grateful for the time they shared with me. These people include: Donald Black, Jon Butler, Edwin R. Coover, Gestur B. Davidson, Lance Davis, Ellen Dwyer, George D. Green, Mark Haller, Barbara Hanawalt, Michael Hindus, Michael Katz, Roger Lane, Colin Loftin, John Modell, Paul Murphy, Gary Nash, Forest Nelson, Harold Pepinsky, Michael Polen, John Schneider, Charles Tilly, Maris Vinovskis, Nigel Walker, Eugene Watts, and M. Norton Wise. Terence McDonald gave the manuscript an extremely close and useful reading at a final stage, for which I wish specially to thank him.

I have also benefited from seminar discussions of portions of this book at the Center for Research on Social Organization, University of Michigan, at the Newberry Library Community and Family History seminar, and at the Social Science seminar at the California Institute of Technology. Parts of Chapter 2 were presented as a paper at the annual meeting of the Organization of American Historians in St. Louis in 1976; parts of Chapter 3 were read at the International Economic History Congress in Edinburgh in 1978; and parts of the Conclusion were read at the Social Science History Association's annual meeting in Ann Arbor, Michigan, in 1977.

The original data series on which this study is based is available through the Criminal Justice Archive and Information Network, University of Michigan, P.O. Box 1248, Ann Arbor, Michigan 48106.

Los Angeles
October 1980

Eric H. Monkkonen

Introduction

> Never hit a prisoner over the head with your pistol, because you
> may afterwards want to use your weapon and find it inoperable.
>
> David J. Cook, *Hands Up* (1882)

The police in the context of urban history

For us to comprehend the blundering, ignorance, inefficiency, in-
competence, and general confusion of the nineteenth-century police when dealing with crime requires an imaginative leap over a
great distance. In an age when the best forensic techniques could
not clearly distinguish the blood of a pig from the blood of a human, the art of criminal detection bore more than a little resemblance to divination. In such a world, we should not wonder that
people afraid of crime and criminals hoped that the appearance of a
man in a uniform would strike the hearts of potential criminals
with fear, just as in late nineteenth-century novels the appearance
of a cross caused vampires to cringe and shrink back. Unfortunately, neither technique worked especially well, and as a result the
police spent the most useful of their long hours on duty reporting
open sewers, shooting stray dogs, and arresting drunks. If the appearance of a uniform deterred any potential criminals, their non-
behavior left little or no mark in the historical record.

As the United States industrialized in the nineteenth century,
Americans experienced physical uncertainty and insecurity we
would find intolerable today. Steamboats blew up.[1] People
drowned in shallow water, unable to swim. Trains regularly muti-
lated and killed pedestrians. Children got run over by wagons. Injury very often meant death. Doctors resisted the germ theory of
disease. City elites responded to the horse manure that filled the
streets by banning the pigs of the poor, which ate the manure. People too poor and too decrepit to support themselves when ill or old
died in poorhouses, when fortunate. And in the midst of all, the
police patrolled – men who at best had been trained by reading

1

pathetic little rule books that gave them virtually no help or guidance in the face of human distress and urban disorder.

Throughout the nineteenth century, U.S. cities increasingly became cities of strangers – that is, they could be perceived by their inhabitants as such because of the great amount of population mobility, high number of foreign-born immigrants, and increasing numerical and physical size. Of course, Americans had always been mobile – the expectation of a person staying in any nonfarm area averaged about 50% for one decade even in colonial times.[2] In other words, for every person who stayed in town for ten years, there was another who left or died. But in an age when unprecedented numbers of migrants came from greater distances and different cultures, perceptions of transience could easily be heightened. And when cities became large, one's daily chances of interactions with strangers became certain. Urban dwellers shared the same spaces and many customs, yet they often did not know one another. Intimacy of place, experience, and attitude became radically severed from mutual trust in the second half of the nineteenth century.

Onto the streets of these complex and unnerving cities walked the newly uniformed police, semiliterate members of the working class wearing outfits that they thought looked like servants' livery, charged with duties which no one clearly understood.

This book is about these police. It analyzes their behavior and describes the organization and growth of police bureaucracies. The analysis of police behavior forms an integral part of the description of police bureaucracy, for the behavior highlights bureaucratic changes that had measurable effects. This book purposely focuses on the police as a part of city government, a part that had a unique relationship, mediating between people and the formal institutions of society. In addition to this particular focus, the analysis explicitly seeks patterned similarities among the various major cities in the late nineteenth and early twentieth centuries. This perspective does not deny that there were differences among cities and their police forces, but it does assert that the preliminary historical task is to establish a baseline of bureaucratic development and behavior and to make this baseline conceptually relevant to urban growth and change. This description and analysis of commonality will make other studies examining local change and behavior all the more useful, for no doubt police and cities exhibited diversity: The questions are from what, and in what way, and why, did they diverge.

The first section of this Introduction presents the police in the context of urban history, giving the reader a general orientation to the remainder of the book. Because this book develops a rather complex argument, its various sections and chapters are organized as sections of the argument. The subject matter of each constitutes one part of the argument instead of, for instance, tracing chronological development. The second section of the Introduction lays out some of the theoretical and abstract issues involved in the study of crime and the police in the past. The following chapters examine the modernization of urban police in the United States from the midnineteenth century onward and analyze the relationship of various institutional and bureaucratic developments to the behavior of the police, all as measured by various rates – arrests, lost children returned to parents, overnight station house lodgers, and homicide arrests.

The substantive conclusions cover a broad range. I expect these conclusions and their implications to surprise many social historians, and I think the conclusions will open up several new avenues of inquiry. For instance, solid evidence in Chapter 1 shows that the modernization of the police in various cities across the continent followed a common and predictable pattern that many other kinds of innovations followed in the period, a conclusion in contrast to current thinking, which often links modernization of the police to specific urban riots, immigration, or labor disputes. This argument is important for the specific analysis of the chapter, but it also has implications for the spread of other innovations across the United States. Generally, it implies that the focus of historical analysis, which has so often been on the specific local context of change, might for many topics be better geared to looking first to underlying nonspecific patterns of growth and change.

Chapter 2 presents new evidence on arrest trends between 1860 and 1920, showing a counterintuitive decrease in total arrests per capita over this sixty-year period of industrialization, migration, and urbanization. Our historical intuition has usually been that the turbulent urban era down to the closing of immigration saw increasing vigor in the enforcement of the public order. The arrest trends indicate that, at the very least, the police made decreasing use of the formal arrest process as a means of urban social control. One certainly should not leap to the conclusion that the police became less repressive or more tolerant, a question needing much more examination than this book can give, but these trends do raise the question of what role the urban police did perform, a question taken up in Chapters 3 and 4.

Therefore, in Chapter 3 the subject changes from arrests to other important but ignored or underemphasized police services, the taking in of overnight lodgers and the return of lost children to their parents. These two services are examined in some detail, partly for substantive reasons and partly because they both offer systematic measurement of police activities outside the criminal arrest sphere. These police services diminished greatly in the late nineteenth century, and although the police have never ceased their service activities and still find and return lost children, their involvement in the day-to-day life of the urban poor never returned to such high levels. The chapter also shows how the presence of uniformed police changed ordinary people's perceptions of the police, resulting in greater demands for non-crime-related assistance being made upon the police. In discussing the decline of these services, Chapter 3 leads into Chapter 4, which demonstrates that the nature of policing changed in the final decade of the nineteenth century from an emphasis on class control to an emphasis on crime control. This transition, I argue, was not what it appeared to be, unfortunately, for the class-control efforts of the police involved a good deal of simple welfare assistance to the indigent and temporarily unemployed, assistance that had the distinct advantage of being unencumbered, direct, and immediate. This new emphasis on crime control itself was doomed to failure, for it was the one thing at which the police had never been especially successful. Thus the police can be seen as having helped U.S. cities through an era of difficult transition. But the very consequences of this transition created forces that would change the nature of policing – social welfare bureaucracies, more formal attempts at crime control, and a specialization of city government agencies antithetical to the general purposes previously filled by the police.

The development of police historiography

Much of the current interest in the history of urban police came as a consequence of the urban crises of the 1960s. Indeed, not since the 1880s and the 1890s have such a crop of police histories been produced. The books in the Gilded Age crop were written by ex-police officers as combination potboilers and local booster efforts. One of the earliest of these, Edward Savage's *Police Records and Recollections; or, Boston by Daylight and Gaslight* (1873), consists of 100 pages of chronological clippings, followed by 300 pages of exciting incidents, and concludes with four original poems, including "Little Ragged Nell" and "My Mother's Grave."

The current crop, of which this book is one, is the product of academics with largely liberal credentials trying to figure out what urban police do and why they do it. The most prominent of these historians had their work cited by President Johnson's National Commission on the Causes and Prevention of Violence. And at least one historian of twentieth-century police began his career as an analyst of urban riots.[3] This second group of studies quite rightly link their analyses of police behavior to suffering, inequality, and injustice in U.S. cities. They also quite rightly focus much attention on the internal processes of police departments. But it remains to be seen whether the general picture that has emerged, in which police are not just symbols of everything wrong with cities but sometimes even the major producers and enforcers of these wrongs, is not only true in itself but true in a historical perspective.

Between 1967 and 1977, four major historical analyses of nineteenth-century police were published, along with a fifth analysis of police in the early twentieth century.[4] The changing focus from book to book shows how historians have moved from specific questions to much more broadly conceived analyses, each building on previous work. Roger Lane's well-known book on the police of Boston, *Policing the City: Boston 1822–1885*, published in 1967, focuses on the first sixty years of Boston's police, and follows the creation and changing position of the Boston police within the structure of urban and state government. Rich in detail, the work shows the varied nature of the duties of the police, the conceptual problems of the police within the changing and developing political structure of the city, and the interaction between the police and the communities they patrolled – from incidents of brutality to police soup lines.

When James Richardson's history of the New York police appeared three years later, his scope broadened considerably the time span of Lane's work. Covering over a century, Richardson's book, *The New York Police: Colonial Times to 1901*, takes the reader, as the subtitles suggest, from the constable–watch system to the police of the early twentieth century. Although Richardson's work covers a span of years greater than Lane's, the books closely resemble one another, each following a police force from its pre-industrial, traditional organization to a modern uniformed system in an industrially urbanized society. Richardson added important dimensions, however, in covering some of the late-nineteenth-century progressive reforms of the police, and in dealing with a city where the police formed a key part of the political machine. For while the

Boston police were nationally admired for their honesty and general progressive nature, the vice-ridden and politically corrupt police of New York, a police force constantly under investigation, were an interesting contrast. Perhaps the most striking thing the two books show is the similarity of the two cities' police departments – the distance between the best and the worst almost disappears once the practical identity of their places in the changing role of city government has been made clear by these two pioneering works in urban and police history.

Six years after the appearance of Richardson's book on the New York police, a book by Wilbur Miller comparing the police of New York and London in their formative years, *Cops and Bobbies: Police Authority in New York and London, 1830–1870,* was published. Miller's work demonstrates the great degree to which reconceptualization of the roles of police in their societies can provide useful new avenues of historical research. His comparison, more than just a blow-by-blow analysis of the similarities and differences between the two forces, uses Max Weber's notion of legitimacy to explore how the two new bureaucracies went about legitimizing themselves. The differences, Miller finds, even account for modern differences between the London and New York police. The London police eschewed any attempts at identification with the community; rather, they made an explicit identification with the rule of law and constitutional principles. In New York, on the other hand, the police identified with the local communities and tried to establish themselves as immediate arbiters of justice. The result, more than stylistic or formal, was different levels of police brutality and corruption. Whether one questions Miller's analysis or not, the publication of his book has had the positive effect of moving police history to new levels of analysis: With the works of Richardson and Lane, studies published as articles, and unpublished dissertations, the basic narrative of police history has been established. With Miller's work, new kinds of conceptually focused questions can be asked.

Only a year after the publication of Miller's book, Samuel Walker's history of police reform in the United States, *A Critical History of Police Reform: The Emergence of Professionalism*, came out. The book, whose content is broader than its title indicates, summarizes in narrative form the development of policing in the United States, including the many Midwestern cities that previous studies had ignored. Building upon the work of Lane, Richardson, Miller, and others, Walker shows how late-nineteenth-century police reform ignored the demands of rank and file police officers, eventually stranding them in a working-class subculture isolated both politically and socially. Walker's book fills in detail previously ignored – the history of policewomen and national police organizations, for instance – and, although not making analytic advances, it admirably synthesizes previous work.

The one major failing of all these works is their assumption that the nineteenth-century creation of the institution of the uniformed police was a "natural" occurrence – an outcome entirely predictable from the growth of cities and urban crime. This assumption amounts to an affirmation of the consequent, and has created a blind spot in subsequent analyses of nineteenth- and early twentieth-century police: Once one has assumed that the creation of the uniformed police was a natural urban response to crime, the related questions of what police did, both behaviorally and funtionally, and how this changed and developed, can fall by the wayside. As a result, historians have mainly examined the police in relation to external forces – political manipulation, reform, corrupting demands of vice. Many basic questions thus remain unexamined. By building on the the work of my predecessors, I hope this book answers some of these basic questions, or at least formulates them so that the issues surrounding them can be clearly delineated. In so doing, this study should both broaden and sharpen old arguments, and create several new ones.

Compared to work on the police, studies of crime in the nineteenth-century United States, with a few exceptions, have been brief and disappointing. The best-known article, by Roger Lane, asserts that serious crime dropped in nineteenth-century cities and that police forces concentrated more on minor, public-order offences: Cities, he concludes, "civilized" their inhabitants.[5] My own work, concentrating on the relation of urbanization to crime and poverty, asserts that cities had no effect on the production of either crime or poverty, but that they did change the nature of certain offences; for example, theft involving deception and duplicity increased with urban anonymity. Neither analysis, it appears, could account for either the creation or extension of the uniformed police, although one could argue that the very presence of the urban police controlled crime to such an extent that serious crime declined, and that therefore the specifically urban component of crime creation could be deterred. Neither Lane nor I make such an argument, however. In fact, the explicit relating of police to crime rates has only been a subject of analysis for recent time periods in the twentieth century. For instance, studies relating police expenditures to crime rates have recently been conducted, as have several highly controversial studies attempting to relate the deterrent effects of capital punishment to homicide rates.[6] Thus, relative to the study of the development of urban policing, the study of nineteenth-century crime has much room for work, ranging from the establishment of empirical rates to the causal analysis of the rates.

The study of police and crime in the nineteenth and early twentieth centuries consists, both substantively and conceptually, of more than simply a narrow analysis of low-status subgroups and urban bureaucracies. In the past decade, historians have begun to ask questions about social bureaucracies in a new way, and although the specific institution or bureaucracy under analysis varies, this new way of looking at the past usually comes out with predictable results, fitting under the heading of social control.[7] The discovery of social control as a hidden institutional goal has been a subtle theme that historians have threaded through works on hospitals, prisons, mental institutions, schools, philanthropic ventures, social welfare agencies, and even lexicography. Almost always, it appears the controllers were the middle and upper classes, who controlled the working class, immigrants, the "dangerous class" – paupers, criminals, children of the poor – and any other group conceived as a threat to the social status quo. Unfortunately, this historical work has often been characterized by a naïve accusatory manner, with the accusation of social control intentions standing as a kind of historical indictment. The notion that not all social control must be bad, or that social control and positive virtue can exist in a complex relationship, has only begun to enter this corpus of historical writing.[8] Ironically, the study of police as social control agents has been neglected, yet a systematic examination of the police demonstrates that even in its boldest forms, social control is more complex than it has appeared to historians. It still remains for a study of an institution that has, as one of its explicit purposes, the social control of a specific group of people, to deal with this aspect of institutional behavior in a sophisticated manner.

Given this broadly shared set of assumptions concerning social control, one might confidently predict studies of police to utilize this perspective. Yet few do so. One recent article shows how local capitalists manipulated the police of Buffalo in order to control the city's working class.[9] In a straightforward but overly simple argument, the authors claim that the police were the sole creation of industrialists with the singular purpose of disciplining workers.

Perhaps because this perspective is almost too easy to adopt for those studying the police, a more intriguing opposite point of view has also been put forth. Sociologist Bruce Johnson, for instance, argues that the police responded more to working-class demands than to those of the class-control-oriented elites.[10] Both sides base their evidence upon the social origins of police personnel, thus both have support for their points, for police commissioners were upper class and rank and file police officers working class.

Three well-known studies epitomize the positive and negative aspects of the more broadly defined social control approach to the study of society: Kai Erikson's seminal study of deviance in the colonial era; David Rothman's study of prisons, mental hospitals, and other asylums in the early nineteenth century; and Anthony Platt's study of the creators of Chicago's juvenile justice system during the late nineteenth and early twentieth centuries.[11] Erikson, using Emile Durkheim's notion that society needs deviance in order to define boundaries of acceptable social behavior, applies a version of the labeling perspective to the study of three crime waves – the Antinomian controversy, the Salem, Massachusetts, witch hangings, and the prosecution of Quakers. The genius of his study is that it locates deviance and the criminal justice system within the values and change processes of a social system. Subsequent studies of witchcraft, for instance, although going far beyond the Durkheimian framework of Erikson, continue to follow his model of locating witchcraft practice and prosecution in its larger social space and context.

Rothman's study of hospitals and prisons explicitly focuses on the ideology of the creators and administrators, showing how this ideology related to the broader Jacksonian ideology. He attributes to the creators of these institutions a kind of optimism about their own abilities to control society by remaking individuals. Like Erikson, he locates the institutional ideology in the context of larger social thinking and change. Unlike Erikson, Rothman tends to lose his sympathetic understanding of the prison administrators and turns his study into a critique of their social control efforts. By implication, he says that all large bureaucracies have totally negative consequences in their control efforts, that the very attempt at social control is in itself wrong.

The work of Platt makes Rothman's view more explicit. Platt portrays the women who worked to separate juvenile justice from adult justice systems as agents of the upper middle class with nothing better to do than punish the children of the poor. These efforts, part of a larger effort to control working-class and immigrant children, resulted in a denial of any real justice or opportunity to children. Platt thus sees social control efforts as having totally negative consequences – social control apparently can only be bad. Although many social control efforts may have indeed had negative consequences, the tendency of historians has been to simply demonstrate that a group of people or an institutional bureaucracy has had social control as one of its implicit goals or, as Robert Merton put it, latent functions. Again, historians seem to expect this demonstration alone to morally condemn and discredit the group under study. Thus, the study of social control has too easily drifted into sloppy judgments, respecting neither the controlled nor the erstwhile controllers in their complex historical situations.

One of the goals of this book is to apprehend the social control function of the developing police system in its several manifestations, both just and unjust. It accepts society's need to arrest criminal offenders, without assuming that all arrests were or are fair. It also interprets the many non-arrest-related police activities as a part of their social control function, whatever their immediate positive benefits. The police, I argue, controlled the "dangerous class" both through the negative power of arrest as well as through the positive ability to dispense lodging and sometimes food to the indigent. The social control scope of the police also extended to the control of the problem of anonymity in the growing cities, a problem that the poor probably faced to a greater extent than the wealthy, through several means, the most important being the returning of lost children to their parents.[12] Therefore, although this study conceives the uniformed police as the front line of the formal, urban social control system, it tries to employ the concept with as much value neutrality as possible. Further, by exploring the role of the police as social control agents, the nature of nineteenth- and early twentieth-century social control itself can be explored, for the activity that a society controls tells us much about the society.

U.S. cities adopted the uniformed police as formal social control bureaucracies as a part of their shift from class-based politics to liberal, pluralistic politics and professional urban administration. When urban elites abandoned positions of power, and class-based political representation shifted to ethnic representation, the administration of city business could no longer work on a personal, particularistic basis, and the modern bureaucratic notion of rule-based, universalistic standards began to become the urban goal.[13] The uniforming of police and their reorganization into a quasi-military command hierarchy was only one part of this administrative change. The process, however, did not occur in a straightforward, predetermined manner from beginning to completion: In the case of the police, their reluctance to accept the rule of law and implement decisions made higher in the command hierarchy has become proverbial. The pressure to achieve uniform and uniformed law enforcement came from the efforts of newly powerful urban governments to legitimize themselves. As the English historian Douglas Hay has pointed out, the rule of law, whether fair or not, depends upon its uniform application.[14] In a sense, then, the legitimization of city government's new and growing bureaucracies depended on the police system, from the appearance of officers in their uniforms to their regular enforcement or ignoring of laws. It comes as no surprise that the first thing urban reform governments did to police departments was to concentrate on uniforms and martial drill – appearance and order within the police showed that the larger city government based its rule on appearance and order.[15]

City police, through their daily activities, helped shape and control much of urban life in public places. Thus the study of the police and their behavior is the examination of the interface between a formal part of the urban structure and the informal actions of most city dwellers. Considered this way, the structural position and action of the police helps to illuminate a parallel problem of urban historians: how to conceive the relationship between social structure and geographical mobility and thus reconcile the development of cities as physical and bureaucratic forms with their highly transient populations. The major social fact that historian Stephan Thernstrom and those who have followed his lead keep coming up against is the "dizzying rate" of movement in and out of American cities throughout the nineteenth century. For these historians, the premier speculation has concerned the subsequent careers of those who left the city, who disappeared from the historian's sample. Thernstrom and Peter Knights speculated about the existence of a "floating proletariat" – a constantly moving substratum of workers and their families drifting from city to city finding unskilled day labor.

This large class of floaters had significant implications for the city power structure – all else being equal, those who stayed in a city had access to power more than those who didn't. Richard Alcorn's brilliant study of a small nineteenth-century town in Illinois bore out this contention by rank ordering the most important characteristics distinguishing the town's leaders from its nonleaders. Simple length of persistence came first, followed, as one might have also expected, by wealth, occupational, age, and ethnic differences. And, Alcorn speculated, across the country urban political power tended to concentrate in what he called "value islands," a modification of Robert Wiebe's suggestion that the late nineteenth-century urban environment was filled with "island communities," communities that resisted the waves of urban innovation sweeping the country. Alcorn's notion is more satisfactory than Wiebe's, for it weaves the findings of the "new urban historians" concerning mobility together with the historical problem of understanding how urban power and values persevered and became more articulated throughout the century.[16]

This picture of urban places, where local social and political structures and power were maintained by a less mobile segment of the population, supplements the analysis of the structure of nineteenth-century cities made by Sam Warner in his two influential books, *The Private City* and *The Urban Wilderness*. In these two works, Warner described the change in cities from places where private and public interests were interlocked to places where they were separated. Commercial elites, for instance, took part in political affairs because they saw their own economic interests as parts of the city's interest; they assumed their private fortunes depended upon the city's fortunes.[17] This changed in the nineteenth century, partly as a consequence of the growth of regional and national urban hierarchies as well as the development of regional and national economies. Cities became places where private economic interests – what Warner called "privatism" – could be satisfied without direct involvement in public life or long-standing commitment to one city. In fact, public interests began to be determined by private interests. Their institutional and bureaucratic structures worked to implement this development. Migrants, the "floating proletariat," fitted into this new urban scene, both in fulfilling fluctuating labor demands and in creating cities with flexible, adaptable work forces. The very flexibility and fluidity of population upon which the growing cities rested required visible, depersonalized, predictable social control in order to facilitate population movement from place to place and to ensure a truly stable and adaptable social structure. The uniformed police answered this need perfectly. They responded to service demands of the mobile Americans, yet exerted social control for the urban power holders, those people who stayed in town, not necessarily the same as the economic elites.

Thus, as the cities become places where the goals of public policy were to facilitate private gain, the role of the police should have been to help articulate this policy. But this put the police in a situation of conflicting demands – on the one hand, they simply needed to make the city a good place in which to do business and work; on the other, the social service demands of the mobile population called for far broader activities. As a structural consequence, the police mediated between the conflicting demands of the privatistic cities described by Warner and the mobile cities described by the "new urban historians."

Issues in studying crime and the police in the past

To deal with crime is the primary purpose of government.

Frederick H. Wines, *Report on the Defective, Dependent, and Delinquent Classes* . . . (1888)

Although most contemporary students of crime and the police would agree in principle that the two phenomena should be studied as a whole, or even as part of a larger whole, in fact, very few such studies have been produced (Jerome Skolnick's *Justice Without Trial* being the best known[18]). What is true for the contemporary study of crime and police is also true for historical studies, but historical studies of the police are still in their infancy and have not approached the conceptual and methodological sophistication that should be demanded of them. As this book, in its broad and conceptual terms, examines both an urban bureaucracy (the police), the people it controlled (the "dangerous class"), and analyzes their relationship, the importance of conceiving the police and the people they arrest or otherwise deal with as two parts of the same phenomenon must be kept in mind. Although we can imagine police without arrests and criminal offenders without police, to do so is rather like discussing the sound of a tree falling unheard in the woods.[19] Thus, whereas the descriptive sections of this book focus on the police and the "dangerous class" separately, the analytic portions yoke the two, leaving only the offenses that did not receive police attention undiscussed.

The epistemological problems of studying police and crime in the past, although no different from those of other historical studies, are more eye-catching and hence more worrisome. One wants to know about those offenses that did not meet with arrest. What about the arrests that were unjust, uncalled for, or fraudulent? What about police corruption? What about the behavior of police on the street, important for neighborhoods, yet hidden from official and unofficial records? There are many things that we can never know. If they are crucial things, we must depend on our theories, hypotheses, and concepts to alert us to their locations. But if there are no records and logic cannot reconstruct the features of the missing evidence but can determine only that it is missing, we are simply reminded that all historians suffer similar deficiences and that all must proceed with some humility and acknowledged uncertainty. It usually seems to be the case that trivial questions can be answered completely and important questions only conditionally. This may well be what separates the historian from the antiquarian: The historian provisionally solves a problem of some import, whereas the antiquarian absolutely solves a problem of little extensive significance.

Facts, contrary to cliché, can never speak for themselves; they take on meaning and significance only when embedded in theory. For the historian, theory is doubly important, for it tells where to look for facts and what kinds of facts are useful. If there were only one theory and one set of concepts, there would be little difficulty in getting on with unearthing historical facts. But there are competing theories of almost everything, and it is up to the historian to arrive at a comfortable and consistent theoretical perspective within which to work on historical problems. In subject areas of current controversy, the historian must be especially careful, for besides the competing theories there are innumerable ad hoc theories and generalizations that tempt both historian and reader into inconsistency and contradiction.

This chapter presents a brief summary of the available theoretical perspectives on crime and police, social disorder and social control, stating which ones guide the analysis in this book and showing why they hold the best means of ordering facts for historical analysis. Because theoretical assumptions and hypotheses generate both the questions deemed important and the best methods to answer them, this chapter provides a rationale for the chapters that follow. Because theoretical problems can be settled by reasoning, and empirical ones by research, this chapter clarifies how questions raised in the following chapters should be answered or even whether or not they are answerable. Such matters are important: A strict Marxist, for example, might view the growth of the uniformed police as the inevitable consequence of capitalism, whereas a bourgeois liberal might instead see the police as a creation forced on

fore, is inherently and by definition political, for the essential difference between crime and private wrong is the victim – in one case, the private person; in the other, the state. This means that all prisoners are political prisoners and all criminal violence is political violence – as opposed to common parlance, where a "political prisoner" seems to be a person who is imprisoned for political opinions or actions, not for criminal behavior.

One might argue that there is no visible or even comprehensible threat to the political system in certain offenses against the public order or the peace and that, therefore, such minor victimless offenses are not political. Although today there can be little disagreement that such offenses should not be criminal, what we mean when we say this is that these offenses are no longer offenses against the state and should be decriminalized into the category of rude behavior. Originally, in Anglo-American legal traditions, the concept of an offense against the peace was highly political – in fact, all crimes were conceived as offenses against the "king's peace." As James F. Stephen explained in 1883: "The foundation of the whole system of criminal procedure was the prerogative of keeping the peace, which is as old as the monarchy itself, and was, as it still is, embodied in the expression, 'King's Peace,' the legal name of the normal state of society."[22]

Originally, an offense against the king's peace constituted a serious, felonious violation with a rather narrow meaning – offenses against the king, his house, or his servants – but the concept had inherent flexibility in both the place and the persons covered.[23] As the concept of the state, embodied in the person of the king, expanded after the Norman conquest, so did the concept of the king's peace, while felonies remained defined as serious violations. According to Pollock and Maitland, "the king's peace spread itself until it had become an all-embracing atmosphere . . . [so that] a breach of the king's peace may do no perceptible harm. . . ."[24]

For the historian to adopt any definition of crime other than the conventional one, crime as behavior violating the criminal law, would be pointless, for the conventional definition has remarkable clarity and historical specificity. If the historian is interested in deviance, in bad or disorderly behavior, then the easiest procedure is to call it so. To use the conventional definition of crime has great strength, for this definition not only tells us about social behavior, what people did in the past, but it tells about the political context of that behavior and about the state that saw the behavior as criminal.

What causes crime?

The answer to the question of what causes crime follows simply once crime has been defined: The State causes crime.[25] For it is the state that decides which private wrongs should be elevated to offenses against the state.[26] Although this answer is correct, it is also unsatisfying, for when we ask what causes crime, we really are asking another question: Why do people behave the way they do when they know that their behavior is dangerous at least to themselves, if not others? Rephrased this way, the question shows why answers are difficult and why experts continue to disagree: To be able to answer this question is to explain implicitly all human behavior.

There are five different theoretical perspectives on human behavior relevant to the explanation of criminal behavior: Strictly constructed, they are mutually exclusive but, in practice, any one perspective will adopt elements of another when convenient. All five have adherents today, and the elements of all were available in the nineteenth century, though some have been developed with more specificity and care in recent times. There is no consensus among criminologists today on theory, a warning for historians to proceed with caution. I will discuss the five theories in the order that approximately parallels their chronological periods of greatest popularity: the religious theory, the physiological or evolutionary theory, the social structure theory, the social conflict theory, and the recent Marxist theory.[27]

From the religious perspective, the existence of crime is a result of the presence of evil in the world: Crime is equated with sin, and criminals are bad people, or at least sinful people. Such a view informs the statement of a nineteenth-century prison reformer, who concluded that the reason there were so few women in prison was because they were not as bad as men.[28] This view has certain aspects to recommend it: It sees the criminal as uniquely human and inherently the same as the non-offender. Although harsh in its judgmental aspects, in its conception it also is relatively clear and unambiguous. In practice, most regimes with sacred criminal law end up adopting secular law because of its greater flexibility and creative powers. That the religious view maintains some viability may be seen in the continued equating of bad behavior and crime.[29]

Although the religious view has never held much appeal for criminologists, a physiological or evolutionary theory of one ver-

sion or another has been held for the past century. Its most sophisticated and current empirical evidence concentrates on the genetic
heritability of behavioral traits: The most developed work has been
done in the Scandinavian countries, where the quality of social records allows detailed research, especially on twins. A classic work
of this school in the United States is Robert Dugdale's *The Jukes*,
published over a century ago.[30] This fascinating study of the kin of
a rural New York family purports to show that criminal and deviant
tendencies are inherited, although a modern-day reader may find
in the study more evidence for the heritability of syphilis than of
criminal tendencies. Dugdale's study is interesting for its conclusions concerning the social control of such defective families: In
spite of his evidence, Dugdale suggests that the manipulation of
environmental variables can change criminal behavior. Another
variant of the physiological theories, one that influenced the police,
is the famous theory of Lombroso and his adherents in Europe and
the United States.[31] Lombroso felt that crime was produced by individuals who were flaws in the evolutionary process – atavistic
throwbacks to man's presumably savage state. In its concentration
on the physical characteristics of offenders, this approach caused
police to begin to use positive identification of offenders, through
photographs and cranial measurements. Today, most criminologists file these physiological theories, with the exception of specific
genetic studies, with the religious theories, mainly because the theories assume a universal and moral definition of crime, rather than
a specific historical one. (That is, because the definition of crime
varies from state to state and society to society, through time, it is
unreasonable to explain the differing violation of criminal laws by a
non-culturally specific variable.)

The environmental control of crime advocated by Dugdale implies
another theory of criminal behavior, the social structure theory,
usually miscalled ecological theory. Probably the theory with the
widest circulation in contemporary society, it implies that criminal
laws are consensual, that they reflect widely agreed-upon and public standards. This theory further implies that society itself is consensual, that its members all have the same rules of behavior and
the same goals. To explain the causes of crime in such a society, one
must look at the social and physical ecology of the offender – including housing, family size and structure, income, education, social status, and so forth. Certain combinations of these ecological
variables – subnormal housing, deviant families, inadequate edu-

cation, and the like – produce individuals incapable of measuring up to the demands and constraints of society.

The strengths of the social structure approach are in its ability to encompass other theories, like the physiological one, and in its ability to swing with social change, engulfing new variables, ignoring old ones: It is a bottle for any kind of wine. The weaknesses of the social structure approach are of two kinds. First, from the classic point of view, one examines regions or neighborhoods with a high proportion of criminal behavior and then finds what variables the neighborhood has or lacks to an unusual degree. The problem here is of the ecological fallacy, attributing group measures to individuals.[32] Second, if the study avoids the ecological fallacy and focuses on individuals, comparing the criminals to the noncriminals, the results are almost always disappointing, trivial, or even lend support to another theoretical perspective.[33] Because of its amorphous and all-inclusive nature, the social structure approach continues to dominate research in criminology, as a glance at the pages of any scholarly criminology journal will make clear.

In contrast to the social structure theory, the social conflict theory denies that criminal laws represent consensus; it denies that society itself is consensual, and sees it as the container of conflict over power. This perspective includes subcultural theorists, who discuss deviant or criminal subcultures in conflict with the larger society, and labeling theorists, who claim that criminal behavior is created by the rule enforcers.[34] For the extreme labeling theorist, criminals are created by various rule makers, from schoolteachers and parents to police officers and judges, who act from a social need to find deviants – once an individual has been labeled a deviant, the deviant behavior is "amplified" and escalated until the deviant is forced into a criminal role. Ironically, the strongest recent empirical support for the labeling theory comes from a statistical ecological study.[35] The great strength of the conflict theorists is their emphasis on the essential nature of the production of crime as an interaction between individuals and bureaucratic representatives of the dominant society, and their contribution to criminology has been a focus on the institutions that process the individual offenders.

An obsolete nineteenth-century theory of criminal behavior, one that was never fully articulated or concretely elaborated, is of interest for its blunt and rather cruel prevision of both conflict theory and the "new criminology" – that is, the idea of the "dangerous class." In this theory, crime was produced by a specific class of people, the dregs of society, what Marx called the lumpenproletariat. In the nineteenth century, the "dangerous class," made up of paupers, criminals, the underemployed, and tramps, was not always viewed as particularly dangerous, as indicated by its sometimes being referred to as the "perishing" class, or the "desperate" class.[36] The danger it posed was not so much from crime and violence as from its generally demoralized nature and parasitical dependence on the dominant society. Marx echoed the sentiments of his day when he described the "dangerous class" as "the social scum, the passively rotting mass thrown off by the lowest layers of the old society." When he did not describe it as the bottom of the bottom, he saw it as an amalgam of the worst parts of all social classes: "This scum of the depraved elements of all classes, which establishes its headquarters in the big cities, is the worst of all possible allies. This rabble is absolutely venal and absolutely brazen. . . . "[37] In some ways, the "dangerous class" analysis of crime is a precursor of the contemporary conflict theories and, although obsolete, it may be useful for the understanding of crime and police in the past.

The fifth theoretical perspective on criminal behavior is the Marxist "new criminology," which uses the perspective of the conflict theorists but tries to place conflict theory within a larger social theory.[38] Although as yet the "new criminologists" have failed to produce much in the line of substantive work, and some traditional Marxists claim that there is no such thing as Marxist criminology, the "new criminology" has two great strengths.[39] First, it recognizes that the understanding of criminal behavior and/or the institutions dealing with it cannot be divorced from the larger society, that without a social theory there can be no criminological theory. Second, it offers a resolution to the conflict/consensus argument by looking at the historical origins of cultural diversity, an approach appealing to most American historians.[40]

None of these twentieth-century theories of criminal behavior discusses a person called a "criminal"; rather, they seek to explain a kind of behavior. To the modern criminologist, there is no such thing as a "criminal," just as to the sociologist there is no such person who is a "father" and nothing else, a "worker" and nothing else, or a "collector of parking tickets" and nothing else. The vast majority of criminal offenders fulfill multiple roles, with the criminal offense occupying a small and often nonessential part of their lives. To employ the concept of a "criminal" is to engage in a kind of labeling activity, even for the historian. Yet throughout this book I employ the term "criminal," just as I use the concept of a "dangerous class." I do so semiironically, partly to avoid more subtle yet equally damning terms and partly because up to the decade of World War I both terms were used by those who discussed crime and the police.

This study uses a modified version of the labeling perspective, combined with that obsolete nineteenth-century notion of the dangerous class. This theoretical perspective is designed with the problems of historical research in mind, and does not have crime control as its objective, as does most modern theory. This modified labeling perspective views the police as agents of the law-making dominant society, as public enforcers of the criminal law, and is not concerned with the microprocesses of deviance amplification.[41] Police officers bring into the criminal justice bureaucracy persons whom they have defined as perpetrators of criminal events: Because the "dangerous class" produces the crime in the society, these offenders represent the "dangerous class" by the official social definition. The police officers' job, vis-à-vis crime, is to label criminals.

This study initially assumes as a heuristic position that the amount of crime in society, both detected and undetected, holds constant. I feel one should begin with this assumption because in many instances historians will never have available to them any evidence to the contrary, especially as regards unreported offenses. [Murder is one exception, because the use of coroners' reports suggests a measure dependent on bodies.[42]] This assumption may seem unwarranted, and perhaps even shocking, yet it should not be so, for we know that only a small proportion of crimes, with the exception of murder, meet with arrest today. Starting from this assumption of stable rates of actual offenses, each inference of changed rates of actual offenses must be critically examined, with the burden of justifying the empirical assertion. Because the arrest rate does change over time, our preliminary assumption that the amount of actual crime remains the same forces us first to examine the variations in the arrest rate that came from changing police behavior rather than changing criminal behavior. From a modified labeling perspective, this primary assumption about measuring crime parallels the obverse and more common opinion that the arrest rates represent a constant index to criminal behavior, except that the nonlabeling view gives no credit to police actions. To see why, let us return to the original definition of crime, which states that the political system defines, and in so doing, creates, crime. The first place to look, then, for changes in crime is to the political system, to those who daily apply the law, the police.

It should be made clear that this way of discussing crime and the police has several strengths for the interpretation of historical data. As opposed to most social scientists, the historian has to confront large gaps in the records – some events simply never left records. Such is the case with the presumably large number of unrecorded criminal offenses. In the face of this problem, a modified labeling position maintains that the missing information is irrelevant; the perspective's only concern is in looking at labeled crime, for it is labeled crime that tells us about both social–bureaucratic interactions and how the society defined its criminal problems. Thus, this theoretical perspective relates to larger questions, rather than smaller ones such as why a specific individual became drunk and disorderly. In helping to explain crime and police behavior, it gives more understanding of the larger society. Its implications are broad, and in some ways it fulfills the objective toward which the "new criminologists" aim, of placing criminal behavior in social context.

My position, then, is that the "dangerous class" provided a constant source of criminal events, into which police dipped to produce criminal arrests. Murder arrests provide one partial exception to this perspective because murder today is a crime usually "cleared" by arrest, and because murder produces hard-to-conceal evidence.

What are the police?

The modified labeling perspective has given us a conception of the police as agents of the dominant society whose job it is to label criminal members of the "dangerous class." Although the major role of the police that this book focuses on is crime control, it should be stressed at the outset that labeling the "dangerous class" meant much more than crime control. It also meant class control, and the police dealt with all the things that made the "dangerous class" dangerous – crime, disease, poverty, their roving animals, and homelessness.

There are several important conceptual issues concerning the police. First is the question of what branch of government they can be conceived as belonging to, administrative or judicial.[43] If the police are a part of the judicial system, then presumably they have responsibility to those bodies whose job it is to determine what laws mean and whether or not specific actions violate the laws. On the other hand, if the police act as a part of administration, then they have a responsibility to the higher administrative bodies of government, using both positive and negative sanctions to ensure that legislation gets carried out. Unless these distinctions are kept clear, both theoretically and practically, confusion is bound to result in any analysis of the police.

A second conceptual distinction must be made between community-based and municipally based policing. Because the police use statutes and laws as the basis for their activities, it seems logical that the legislative jurisdiction should provide the base, and because the smallest legislative base that has policing is the urban government, it makes sense for police to have a citywide basis.[44] Therefore, to conceive that policing be community based, that is, be responsible to a community smaller than a city, contradicts the political basis of policing. A legitimate police cannot have a base other than its political base; to change the base of policing it would be necessary to change political jurisdictions. To analyze police from another base than the political one would be to misconceive the nature of policing. As a part of city government, police legitimacy depends on responsibility to the governmental base; police responsibility to limited constituencies within the city always represents a violation of legitimacy.

For historians, there is a third conceptual issue of great importance: The historian must preserve a radical doubt as to the need for police, thus insuring that the proper energy goes into accounting for their existence. As we know and conceive them, police are rather new on the urban scene, appearing in London in 1829 and in the United States about two decades later. Before this, British and American cities were policed by a hodgepodge of traditional civil officials and private individuals. By the end of the nineteenth century, police were ubiquitous in U.S. cities, and by the end of World War I they had reached the bureaucratic and behavioral development that we all recognize. Any historical analysis of the police that does not question the necessity of the police may well be assuming an answer to a problem of crucial significance, leaving only trivial questions to be resolved. It is not the intention of this book to promote alternatives to the police, but its aim is to understand why they came about and what they did. Yet to assume that the police are the only imaginable bureaucracy to do what they do is akin to the medieval biologist assuming that plants took their shape from an immutable heavenly essence.

Some philosophical implications

Just as the historian must harbor doubt as to the necessity of uniformed police, so must a deeper questioning of crime be allowed. Why does the state have crime? Is one morally compelled to obey the criminal law? We know what the definition of crime is, but what does crime mean? For a discussion of these questions, social science theory is of little use, and we must turn to philosophy. Even though the philosophical perspective may not give us theories and concepts, it does help us to begin to understand the less ephemeral nature of crime in society.

Most of the analysis that follows in this book is concrete and historically specific; however, its broader implications move in two abstract directions. First, the relationship of the "dangerous class" and the police provides an example of how an urban bureaucracy influences a highly transient lower stratum of society and how that stratum sometimes influences the bureaucracy. In a sense, the police exemplified an operational part of the concept of city. They defined parameters of behavior and class structure in a world whose inhabitants moved about with a frequency that alarmed more stable city dwellers. The existence of rapid population turnover leads one to wonder at how the social structure worked. The police–"dangerous class" relationship should thus be seen as one example of the banks that channeled the swiftly moving river of population, what Knights and Thernstrom termed the "floating proletariat."[45]

Second, this study leads toward philosophical reflections on the nature of crime and social justice. Understanding crime helps us understand society and the restrictions on liberty its members have accepted, theoretically in order to assure social stability, justice, and equal liberty. The recent well-known analysis of the philosophical basis of justice by John Rawls, *A Theory of Justice*, provides a rationale and perspective from which to determine whether or not specific criminal offenses have been justly defined.[46] Rawls's analysis rests on a philosophical tradition reaching back through Kant and Rousseau: This tradition examines the philosophical foundations of society by using the fiction of a social contract, pretending that societies have as the basis of their institutional and ethical behavior an agreement among the members of the society, including future generations, which is a kind of public contract. This contractual base has publicly agreed upon rules and principles, duties and obligations, which determine, under specific material conditions, what makes a just society. To figure out what the principles of justice are, Rawls uses the fiction of an original position where representative persons from a society agree upon principles of justice. The representative persons are prevented from acting out of selfish or class interests by what Rawls calls the "veil of ignorance," by which he means that the persons in the original position do not know the specifics of their actual social condition. Rawls demonstrates that two principles would be reached in the original position, the first more important and lexically prior to the second. First, all persons must have equal liberty, maximized as fully as possible without injuring the liberty of others. Second, the social and material benefits of the society must be distributed so that if they are distributed unequally the greater benefits to some increase the lesser benefits of others (his controversial "difference principle"). Rawls argues that we should think of these principles as being implemented through a constitutional convention, where the veil of ignorance would be partially dropped in order to allow specific institutions to be established, and then through a legislative process, where the veil of ignorance might be totally dropped and specific laws enacted. Although ahistorical and abstract, this approach to thinking about justice helps explain why society defines certain behaviors as criminal and also shows how some behavior, although bad, unkind, or offensive, is not or should not be criminal.

There is no such thing as crime in a society without a political state, if such a society is dependent on the existence of a defining political body.[47] Crime is an act of any responsible person within a state that usurps an exclusive privilege of the state. In a just society, Rawls would argue, these exclusive privileges of the state would have been given up by the individuals in the original position in order to insure the implementation of justice. The definition of person here includes individuals, groups of individuals, corporations, and other organized bureaucracies up to the scale of, but not including, the state. The importance of defining a culpable person comes from the conceptual difficulties created by the first early corporations to be organized to make money rather than to serve the public good, as in the eighteenth century: It took a Supreme Court decision to decide that corporations were persons, thus making them liable to prosecution and punishment.[48] In a sense, the substantive list of criminal offenses constitutes the boundaries of behavior differentiating the person and the state.[49] As the purpose of the state, in a Rawlsian view, is to implement justice, its powers are those that allow the implementation of justice: Crime, therefore, is behavior the ultimate consequence of which hinders the implementation of justice.

Let us examine this view through three differing examples. The crime of murder asserts that no person may unlawfully take another individual's life, for this power is the ultimate coercive power reserved to the state, as in military conscription. In Anglo-Saxon law, the intentional differences of murder and manslaughter were not distinguishable – only murders in secret were seen as different from murders in the open. It was not until after the Norman conquest and concomitant with the increasing complexity and power of the state that intention became a part of criminal homicide.[50] The uncompensated taking of another's property, theft, is reserved to the state, most familiarly in the form of taxation. The state has reserved these privileges to itself as basic to its coercive powers, which insure its perpetuation and functioning. Discovering the same order of argument for the crime of public drunkenness is difficult if not impossible: One can argue that the state reserves the right to regulate behavior in public space, but it is unclear how this is necessary to the functioning and survival of the state. One can also argue that behavior in public must demonstrate individual responsibility, as nonresponsible persons are not, by definition, capable of committing criminal offenses. But neither argument convincingly demonstrates how public drunkenness can be defined as criminal in a justly constituted society.

Thus, a crime occurs when a person breaks hypothetical promises, the grounds to which the person would have agreed in the original position. The importance of the offender's intent comes from the state's need to determine whether or not the offense represented a conscious usurpation of power promised to the state – after all, victims of offenses care little about the intentions of the offenders. When a person breaks the criminal law, the state retaliates and protects itself, usually in terms of removing some or all of its guarantees granted in the original position to the offender.

So far this argument has assumed a just society: What about the reality of a partially just society? There are two kinds of partially just societies. In the first, the public conception of justice and the laws to insure justice are both just, but the state only partially implements justice. Rawls differentiates another way in which a society can be partially just, a society in which the laws themselves do not conform to the public conception of justice. (And a totally unjust society is one where the public conception of justice is itself

Table 1. *The obligation of victims of injustice to comply with criminal laws*

	Nature of the partially just society	
Kinds of victims	Laws untrue to conception of justice	Failure to implement just laws
Specific persons unjustly treated	Not comply	Comply
All or randomly selected persons unjustly treated	Comply	Comply

unjust.) Each of these two partially just societies can affect its members in one of two ways: Specific groups of persons or individuals within the society may suffer, or all of the society may suffer (see Table 1). Examples of the first kinds of victims of injustice include discriminated-against racial, ethnic, sex, or generational groups. Examples of the second more random victims include those affected by pollution or environmental health hazards, or perhaps the whole society through economic disaster caused by unjust economic policies.

In the case of the society with an unjust conception of justice, the person has no moral compulsion to obey any criminal law. On the other hand, in a society with random victims of injustice, the criminal laws should be obeyed. Also, in a society that only partially implements the means of justice and where the victims are specific, the laws should be obeyed. But in a society where the victims are specific, and whose partial justice is from poor legislation, bad laws should not be obeyed. Rawls argues that unjust laws (or institutions) should be conformed to unless the burden of injustice imposed is, in the long run, unevenly distributed or if the first principle of justice, equal liberty, has been violated. The reason to obey unjust laws, otherwise, derives from a public obligation to keep promises in order to "initiate and stabilize forms of cooperation," without which the society could have no means of ensuring even a modicum of justice. An exception occurs when the state, either by bad implementation or bad laws, destroys the basis for a sense of justice in individuals: Without this, the offenders cannot be said to be responsible persons. An example of the person who has no duty to obey the criminal law, then, is someone in a society that is partially just by virtue of bad laws, not poor implementation, and that has specific victims of the bad laws. Thus, if the law were that an Irish person or Indian should not be drunk in public, no moral for compunction to obey this law exists. But if the bad law states that no persons shall be drunk in public, then the law should be obeyed.

Of course, in a society with an unjust conception of justice, the moral duty is to rebel, but it should be remembered that every state will have privileges exclusive to itself and that criminal behavior, while it usurps privileges reserved by the state, is not inherently rebellious. Political, yes; rebellious, no.

All these ethical and theoretical issues inform our approach to the study of crime and police in the past in subtle ways: Part of the purpose in discussing them is to make implicit assumptions explicit, so that readers holding differing views may still profit from the analysis that the rest of this book pursues. Of course, ethical and theoretical perspectives influence the outcome of any analysis, as well as determining what questions are asked. It is hoped that the reader will be persuaded to try out the book's perspective, for this perspective has determined my ordering and analysis of the mass of information available to historians about crime and the police. Not only does an explicit ethical and theoretical stance help to analyze what we know about crime and police in the past, but this stance also shows us the gaps where more research needs to be done. I will be satisfied if this book stimulates such informed research and gives the nonresearcher a framework within which to interpret and understand our past.

1   *The historical development of the police*

> To prevent the commission of crime is a paramount object, and if
> the appearance of the police, in a dress distinguishing them from
> other citizens, will tend to this result, it is well worth the experi-
> ment . . .
>
> Boston, *Annual Report of the Chief of Police* (1857)

The urban locus of policing

Because the details of the development of the criminal justice system, and especially of the police, in the nineteenth and early twentieth centuries have inherent interest, it has been relatively easy for
historians to avoid a deeper, more analytic view other than that
which comes from narration and description.[1] This is not to deny
the value of such description and chronicling, for it is valuable, but
to demonstrate the difficulty of understanding underlying relationships in the urban police across the United States in the nineteenth
century. We know that, with only slight variations, police forces
have evolved into much the same model across the nation today,
but we need to know if each police system followed the same developmental path and if each evolved from the same starting point.[2] If
the police in different cities began from completely different points,
converging only with the completion of the moves into uniform,
the police must have been shaped by similar external forces. If,
however, all cities had the same kind of pre-uniformed police that
followed the same evolutionary path to the uniform, then it is unclear what kinds of pressure shaped the change – internal, external,
or both. I argue that the first situation obtained: Starting from diverse institutional arrangements and following diverse patterns,
external forces and constraints created modern urban police forces
in virtually the same mold.

The desciption and analysis that follows is based on the work of
various scholars who in the past ten years have each added a piece
to a puzzle that has begun to show its outlines, even though much
more work remains. It has taken a decade for a comprehensive picture to be fashioned because the details themselves have either

been ignored by historians interested in the broader aspects of social and urban history, or because the police, from the point of view of many scholars, have been and remain an unanalyzed part of the historical social structure. In the late nineteenth and early twentieth centuries, police histories functioned as a form of company history, assembled to show a glorious origin, often with conscious intent of instilling contemporary police pride: Even the title of Augustine Costello's *Our Police Protectors* (1885) shows this aspect of the book's purpose. Recent historical studies, however, show a more critical attitude toward policing in the past, but tend to convey the impression that the history of policing has been the story of progress away from the barbarism of the nineteenth and early twentieth centuries.

A specific political change underlies the more visible change in policing between 1800 and 1920: the shift of policing functions from a traditional, if vague, attachment to the judicial branch of government to a firm lodging in municipal administration. The change in the nature of the police from an informal, even casual, bureaucracy to a formal, rule-governed, militaristic organization mirrored this deeper political shift. As the nature of the police organization changed, so did its specific duties, which moved first from a general concern with the orderly functioning of cities, a small part of which was catching criminals; to the function in the mid and late nineteenth century of controlling the dangerous class, with a growing emphasis on crime control; and finally to the form of social control that we recognize today, emphasizing crime and traffic control. The criminal arrest power has always been the ultimate power underlying the police, but we must keep in mind that this in no way expresses the totality of police behavior, either in the past or today. Indeed, one of the minor points of this chapter will be to show the diversity of things the police have done, and the main task of the chapter will be to describe how this diversity has changed. Thus, although the most visible function of the post – World War I police is crime control, we must remember that today the average officer spends a good deal of time in non-crime-related activities, a situation that, incidentally, creates a frustrating inconsistency between the image and actuality of police work.

English origins

In the pre-uniform era, the constable and watch, a system with origins reaching back into thirteenth-century England, policed cities and villages. The specific office of constable as a part-time peace keeper had evolved by the late fifteenth century, but formal codification had occurred much earlier with the Statute of Winchester (1285), which had also codified the watch and the hue and cry. The constable, subservient to the justice of the peace, arrested those who broke the "king's peace," raised the hue and cry, and arrested persons responsible for the "common nuisances of the ward," which could range from bakers cheating on the weight of bread to the whole community neglecting to provision the poor.[3] Although the position of constable, an elected one in the American colonies, was compensated by fees assigned by the court or justice of the peace, the night watch began as an uncompensated, voluntary position. In its thirteenth-century origins, the uncompensated night watch was a method of community self-protection, a responsibility of all adult males. By Shakespeare's time in England, the development of a money economy and greater urban complexity had reduced the watch to a decrepit force of unemployables, paid a minimal wage that had begun as a fee-based scheme of buying substitutes for watch duty. Once the watch had changed from a voluntary position to one dependent on paid substitutes, it became the constant butt of jokes both in England and America, and whatever the effectiveness it had possessed disappeared. In 1808, for example, the *Louisiana Gazette* commented on the New Orleans watch: " 'Since substitutes have been allowed, the patrol is composed principally of the most worthless part of the community, not to use a more appropriate term. It is like setting wolves to guard sheep'."[4]

The reason for the watch's feebleness, although usually blamed on the poor pay and ineffective, defective or ancient personnel, in fact derived from its earliest English conceptual basis, which was shared by the constable and best exemplified in the hue and cry and *posse comitatus*. The two legal obligations of the posse comitatus, theoretically composed of all males over the age of fifteen in the county as called up by the sheriff, and of the hue and cry, the shout of the victim of a crime or a constable, which legally bound all males hearing it to pursue the offender until caught, formalized community law enforcement.[5] As the broadest level of community enforcement, these legal obligations concretely specified the ultimate interest of all community members in the preservation of order and law enforcement. However, that the voluntary aspects of community law enforcement had been defined as a legal obligation by the Statute of Winchester should make us suspect their truly voluntary and organic nature.

Indeed, if we step back to the era prior to the Statute of Winchester, before the codification of community law enforcement, we discover that from the time of the Norman conquest until the thirteenth century the Anglo-Saxon inhabitants of Britain, ruled by the Normans, had been under the compulsory social control system of *frankpledge*. Frankpledge, described by its historian as a " 'system of compulsory collective bail fixed for individuals, not after their arrest for a crime, but as a safeguard in anticipation of it'," forced the community to accept responsibility for the behavior of its individual members, to produce offenders for trial, or, if unable to discover the offender, to pay the fines.[6] Thus, frankpledge demanded that the conquered Anglo-Saxons preserve Norman-defined law and order within the community. Exemplifying community law enforcement at its most basic level, frankpledge provided the conceptual basis for the law enforcement scheme in the Statute of Winchester. However, it is clear that the nature of frankpledge was not voluntary community self-defense, but rather a simple way of conquerors controlling the conquered. Community policing, therefore, developed not out of any organically evolved system of social self-control, but from an expedient means of social control by alien conquerors. It is no wonder that this means of law enforcement never developed into an effective or just system, whether in England or America, for it was based on a faulty concept.

In translation from Britain to America, certain changes in the office of the sheriff came about. Originally an executive of great power in England, the sheriff had become the officer in charge of the court's business in the United States by the beginning of the nineteenth century. Although sometimes responsible for the enforcement of criminal law, the sheriff and his deputies or marshals never had a patrol responsibility like that of the watch. The term *marshal* in the nineteenth century did not always refer to an officer of the court. In the territorial West, especially in the mid nineteenth century, local police officers and their underlings were called marshals and deputies, the marshals corresponding to head constables and the deputies to constables. For instance, in Denver the city's first charter under a territorial government defined a marshal as an official who could " 'do all the acts that a Constable may lawfully do'."[7] Unlike his constabulary counterpart, however, the marshal had no night watch formally established; conceivably, the marshal's deputies could function as a watch when necessary. The lack of a watch system in the West suggests that its well-known reputation for ineffectiveness had created no reasonable substitute short of a uniformed police, and the new governments simply dropped the watch provision.

Although the specific duties of the watch and constable (or marshal) varied from place to place and time to time in the United States, the general duties covered a broad range of police functions. The night watch preserved order, broadly defined to include reporting fires, raising the hue and cry if they discovered criminal offenses, and arresting or detaining for arrest suspicious and disorderly persons. In Boston, for example, the watch had a statutory obligation to " 'examine all persons, whom they have reason to suspect of unlawful design' "; to " 'walk the rounds in and about the streets' "; to report fires and suppress riots and disturbances; and to light and maintain the streetlamps.[8] Although such duties sound straightforward enough, the implementation often proved unsatisfactory. In Cincinnati, for instance, in the 1850s each ward elected its watch members. The watch, because of its ward-based loyalties, reported only those fires within the ward. Even worse, when various volunteer fire departments clashed, the various ward watches, which had powers of arrest equal to those of the constables, arrested mainly firemen from other wards, thus coming to the battle aid of their neighborhood fire department.[9]

Responsibility for order more broadly defined to include eliminating health hazards and road obstructions, as well as executing court orders and catching criminals, fell upon constables. Compared to the watch, the constables' or marshals' duties were even more varied. Not only did they work for the courts, arresting offenders, bringing in witnesses, and serving papers; they also had to keep an eye on suspicious persons and places in the city, plus act as health officers. In Denver, for instance, in 1860 the city marshal used his authority to order the removal of a slaughterhouse and a tannery, both located in the center of town.[10] Further, and more distastefully, the Denver marshal had a constant battle with stray dogs, pigs, and other livestock; but while the hog and livestock problem had begun to abate by the 1870s, the stray dogs continued to be considered a problem. Marshals dealt with dogs by shooting them, and during the 1880s, wounded, maimed, and dying dogs, their entrails trailing, howled through the streets of Denver. Not until 1883 did this attract any negative comments, a newspaper editor finally proclaiming that " 'There is something essentially cruel in filling the hind quarters of even a dumb brute with buckshot and sending him mourning noisely up the streets, with his liver and lungs and other absolute necessities intact and quivering with pain'."[11]

It must be emphasized that all these duties did not result from a conception of the various officers of the police as preventing crime, discovering criminal offenses, or regularly intervening in the criminal process before a complaining victim or a witness appeared.[12] Those offenses that officers were obliged to discover on their own initiative were only the ones that affected the public health and welfare as a whole: All other activities resulted from some kind of formal request, whether to arrest an offender or to care for an insane person.[13] Thus, whereas the duties of the constable and watch were varied, they were precise in their general conception. They took initiative in preserving health and order rules that affected the community as a whole, and they responded to requests from individual victims of criminal offenses.

It is difficult to judge the overall effectiveness of the constable – watch system, other than to observe its ability to persist for 600 years.[14] Its main failure seems to have been its inability to protect property and control riots, for alternative means of social control developed for both these – the thief catchers and the militia or military. Thief catchers existed in England at least as early as 1534, and the system did not end until the uniforming of the police and the development of insurance in the mid nineteenth century. Thief catchers did not actually catch thieves, but rather recovered stolen property; functionally, they resembled fences in that they acted as marketing agents for thieves. The most famous thief catcher in England, Jonathan Wild, managed to act as a broker between thieves and the owners of stolen property; the owners paid a ransom fee for the property while Wild carefully avoided actually coming into possession of the property.

Although no individuals in the United States operated on such a large scale as Wild, American cities did have prominent thief catchers. Roger Lane cites the example of George Reed, both a constable and a thief catcher in Boston in the 1820s: According to a contemporary, "'The secret of his [Reed's] wonderful success, so it was said, was in his having in his employ parties who were in his power, whose liberty and in some cases, it was intimated, their permission to ply their vocation, depended on the value of the information they were able to furnish him'."[15] The constable/thief catcher, like Reed, and the commercial thief catcher like Wild, differed mainly in the greater bargaining power of the constable with his legitimate power of arrest; the passage cited by Lane suggests that the constables, like police detectives today, bargained with thieves, trading freedom for information. But unlike modern detectives, the constable/thief catcher then traded the information with the victim of the theft for a reward.

In the thief-catching system of returning stolen property, the individual property owner took the risk, as opposed to the more recent insurance system where a large group of property owners distributes the risk. Furthermore, in the thief-catching system, the thief catcher returned the actual stolen property, but today the insurance company returns a proportion of the money value.[16] A third systematic difference now allows somewhat neutral third parties, the police, rather than some kind of criminal receiver, to be involved in the transaction: Thus the insurance system breaks the material connection between thieves and property owners. The thieves and criminal receivers market the stolen goods and the insurance companies bear the compensatory cost. The police do not have to negotiate with thieves as did thief catchers, and therefore need only to define the goods as stolen. Because the change from thief catching to insurance lagged behind the unification of the police, for a period in the mid to late nineteenth century police detectives functioned as thief catchers, negotiating between thieves and property owners for personal profit. In New York, for instance, during the 1850s, the return of a stolen watch could cost a payment of seventy-five dollars to the police.[17]

The second weakness of the constable–watch system, its inability to control mobs and riots, also resulted in the use of alternate control systems. This should not be interpreted as the systematic failure of the constable–watch system, but rather as showing the inherent inability of any civil police force to deal with mass actions. Although civil authorities still make the attempt, the control of mobs has never been successfully or totally transferred from the military to the police. For instance, in 1842 in Cincinnati the constable–watch type police failed to suppress a riot, and the militia had to be called in. As a result, the city council created the "Police Guard," a militia/police reserve unit specifically for riot control.[18] In the late 1850s, Philadelphia also created a reserve corps for riot control, wearing the first police uniforms in the city.[19] In both cases, the reserve corps demonstrated the failure of traditional police systems and the need for some kind of militia. The unification and uniforming of the police did little to increase their riot control

ability. For example, a decade after the New York police had been
unified and uniformed, the draft riot of 1863 erupted. This riot,
often cited as an example of successful police protection of blacks
from hostile Irish rioters, in fact demonstrated the inability of the
New York Metropolitan Police to control determined rioters. The
riot continued until the army successfully quelled it. The police,
although relatively well organized and coordinated, and demonstrating remarkable discipline, simply lacked the power and tactics
necessary to win.[20]

One can understand the meaning and details of the change from
the traditional constable–watch means of policing to the uniformed police by looking briefly at the origins of the Metropolitan
Police of London. Created by Home Secretary Robert Peel in 1829,
the Metropolitan Police provided a model for the earliest uniformed
police forces in the United States. Peel's prior experience in policing had been the creation and administration of the police of Ireland. In subduing the continually rebellious Irish, he had learned
how to overcome the political and philosophical resistance to a uniformed police as well as how to structure this new kind of police.

Ireland, a nation of unwilling subjects ruled by a loyal English lord
lieutenant and his secretaries, had parliamentary representation
only through Irish Protestants loyal to England. Peel became chief
secretary to the lord lieutenant of Ireland at the age of twenty-four,
just three years after his father had purchased him a seat in the
House of Commons. A rising talent among conservatives, Peel
found his new position in Ireland both difficult and challenging, as
it amounted to administering a hostile country and representing its
interests in Parliament. Peel's biographer described the position as
"a combination of Prime Minister, Home Secretary, First Lord of
the Treasury, President of the Board of Trade, and Secretary for
War."[21] Peel's previous experience as an under secretary in the War
and Colonies Office had prepared him somewhat in the management of alien, poverty stricken, and rebellious populations. Moreover, his staunch Protestantism and unwillingness to grant political
rights to Catholics made him ideologically perfect to run the affairs
of Ireland, at least from the English point of view.

Irish rebelliousness against the English, Protestants, and land-
lords had been endemic since at least the mid-eighteenth-century
peasant rebellions known as Whiteboyism. By the time Peel came
to Ireland, the behavior of the Irish resembled that of ghettoized
people anywhere. He wrote to the Prime Minister, "You have no
idea of the moral deprivation of the lower orders in that country. In

fidelity towards each other they are unexampled, as they are in their sanguinary disposition and fearlessness of the consequences."[22] As the native Irish constables were uncooperative and corrupt, the peasants refused to assist in criminal prosecutions, neither coming forward as witnesses nor even reporting offenses, partly out of fear of reprisal and partly out of hatred of the English. Peel recognized the ineffectiveness of the repeated use of military force to preserve order, for the traditional English dependence on " 'the frequent use of soldiers in that manner made the people look upon them as their adversaries rather than their protectors'," and to be effective a police force had to become permanent and legitimate.[23] Peel's "Peace Preservation" Bill, which he introduced and guided to passage in Parliament in 1818, when he was twenty-six years old, provided the legislative basis for a permanent uniformed Irish police.

This new police force did not come totally unprecedented to Ireland, as the English had introduced an earlier system in Dublin in 1785. The policed areas bore the costs of the new police through taxation purposely designed as a negative sanction on rebellious counties, reminding one of the Norman frankpledge – a kind of externally imposed community law enforcement. The officers in the new police, former military men, wore wildly varied uniforms: "some in scarlet cloaks with plumed brass helmets bearing the inscription 'Waterloo,' some in hussar uniform with short cloaks, others attired as riflemen riding pillion."[24] Peel's Irish police succeeded in reducing the costs involved in continual military intervention; he also gained experience in allaying English fears of a French-style military police by the use of euphemisms like "Peace Preservation" rather than "police." As he wrote to a friend in 1822, " 'I was more inclined to the establishment of a Body of Gendarmerie (to be called by some less startling name). . ."[25]

A decade after the establishment of the Irish police, Peel, who had risen to become home secretary for England, successfully guided through Parliament the bill establishing the Metropolitan Police for greater London, the police force that to was to become the model for the United States' police system. There was an important parallel in the origins of both the "Peelers" or "Bobbies" and the constable–watch system that they replaced: Both were designed to control dissident and rebellious local populations by ethnically different conquerors. Peel's genius lay in his ability to see both the need for legitimacy of some sort and the ineffectiveness of continual military presence as a successful means of social control. His police created a new kind of bureaucracy, located in a social space midway between an outside military force and the group of people to be controlled. The semi-military uniform of the Metropolitan Police carefully symbolized this position of the new police – neither civilian nor military – the uniforms avoided the traditional military red, using blue, and followed the civilian fashions of the time.[26] Equal thought went into the design of the first American uniforms in New York: James Gerard, the "man who did the most to put the force in uniform," once wore a London Metropolitan police uniform to a New York dress ball, emphasizing the fashionable appearance of the uniform over militaristic associations.[27] In a sense, then, the uniform symbolized the inherently ambiguous position of the new police, for by their very appearance, it was impossible to say which side they were on, the state's or the community's. Peel, to create a "softer" means of social control than the military, had established an institution that would be at the center of social conflict for the next 150 years.

Historian Wilbur Miller has argued that the public relations efforts by which the new police systems legitimized themselves differed between Britain and the United States.[28] In London, the Metropolitan Police emphasized their legitimacy as representatives of the English Constitution, their behavior and demeanor bound by rules of law and decorum, and by ostentatiously avoiding political factionalism. In New York, rough and ready democratic principles legitimized the police to represent justice on the street – officers individually dispensing justice. This attitude is best seen in a statement attributed to New York officer "Clubber" Williams: "There is more law in the end of a policeman's nightstick than in a decision of the Supreme Court."[29] Miller sees the differences between the two modes of legitimization as arising from the two historically different conceptions of authority in the United States and Britain. English political philosophers conceived of Parliament as representing the interests of all persons "virtually"; that is, all members of Parliament stood for the good of all Great Britain. Americans, on the other hand, conceived of representation in a more literal sense: For specific interests of places to be represented, one needed "actual" representation. This notion accounts for the careful design of a per capita–based House of Representatives, requiring a census, as opposed to Parliament, where some MPs represented boroughs with few or no members. In terms of policing, these differences appeared on the street, individual American police officers representing "actual" authority.

Miller's argument makes the conceptual basis of the transition from the Metropolitan Police of London to the earliest U.S. police, consciously modeled on the English precedent, more sensible. Up until the modeling of the early U.S. uniformed police on English precedents, one must maintain an Anglo-American perspective on policing, but after the establishment of the first few American departments, the paths of the police of the two countries diverged, those in American cities looking at each other rather than to London. Nevertheless, even though police in the United States were legitimized in ways different from their English model, they inherited the basic ambiguity of loyalty and authority so neatly symbolized by the uniforms.

Although Peel's London police provided a workable model for innovation in American policing, it is important to realize that the model only came to be used after much controversy and resistance. As a result, the process that unified the day constables and the night watch, and then uniformed the police, took almost two decades to complete in those U.S. cities that innovated first. However, with each successful unification, the next came more quickly, so that by the end of the century the transition from constable–watch to uniformed police had become a simple overnight matter of legislative fiat. The arguments over accomplishing the change tended to follow the same pattern, whether in London or New York or Boston. The proponents of the new police argued that the traditional system could no longer adequately cope with crime and disorder because of its inefficiency, lack of central control, incompetent and/or corrupt personnel, fragmented organization, and inability to prevent disorder and crime. Opponents argued that the new police threatened traditional civil liberties and freedom, the English pointing at the evil French police of Fouché and the Americans at the monarchical and antidemocratic English.

The creators of the new police introduced a new concept in social control: the prevention of crime. We can see in retrospect that both the proponents and enemies of the new police had valid points, but on an issue that neither recognized. Taking an argument of the Italian criminal law reformer, Beccaria, they claimed that regular patrolling, predictable detection of offenses, and rational punishment would deter potential offenders.[30] They even extended Beccaria's argument, claiming that the sight of the police uniform itself would deter potential offenders.[31] The opponents of the police had a mixed reaction to the idea of the uniform: On the one hand, the visibility of the uniform would keep police from skulking and spying; on the other, the uniform seemed to confirm the suspicions of those who feared that police forces would evolve into standing armies.[32]

By arguing that uniforms would make the police a standing army, most civil libertarians overlooked the conceptual shift involved in prevention, and in so doing insured that their worst fears would be realized. As we have seen, the constables and thief catchers acted after offenses had occurred, with the hope of catching the offender and restoring the stolen property; the criminal justice system did not become involved until a prohibited behavior had occurred. But the notion of deterring potential offenses implied a new attitude toward social control, diverting attention from illegal behavior to potential offenders, from act to actor. In so doing, the emphasis necessarily implied the forecasting ability of the police, especially to explain and predict criminal behavior, thus rendering it amenable to control. From the civil libertarian point of view, this implied the ability and right of prior restraint, of stopping people from doing what one expected them to do. By accepting the notion of prevention, both the proponents and the critics of the new police opened the Pandora's box of controlling potential behavior, dealing with what might happen. Of course, if successful, the effectiveness of such control would be unmeasurable, for the predicted and thus forestalled behavior would never occur.[33]

The American adoption of the London model

James W. Gerard presented a closely reasoned argument for reorganizing and uniforming the New York police in early 1853, following a visit of his the previous year to London, made with the intent "of observing the institutions of England and their working on the masses of people." Gerard's main argument focused on the "efficiency" of the London police compared to the constable–watch police of New York. This efficiency was twofold – moral and physical. The physical efficiency came from better organization and greater numerical strength per capita, but the moral efficiency came from the character of the police, symbolized and actualized by the uniform. "The great *moral* power of the policeman of London in preventing crimes lies in his coat." This moral power operated by striking fear and dread in the hearts of the "criminally-disposed population . . . by their well-known intelligence, activity, unflinching firmness, and incorruptible *honesty*."[34] The important point to be noticed here is that the preventive power of the police operated on potential offenders through the symbolic medium of the uniform. Prevention, in Gerard's thinking, depended on creating among potential offenders moral fear and certainty of apprehension and punishment. As all three affected individuals, his very conceptualization depended on his vision of potential crime producers. Once the notion of preventing crimes had supplanted the notion of catching offenders, the focus of police actions on a "dangerous class" became assured.

The nebulous idea of preventing criminal behavior found the perfect means of implementation in the concept of an identifiable, crime-producing "dangerous class"; for only by focusing on crime producers could criminal behavior be prevented, and the "dangerous class," by definition, produced the criminal behavior. Thus, although it is erroneous to see the new police as originally created with a purposeful class-control function, class control resulted from their efforts to prevent crime,[35] one of the major reasons for creating the new police. The third chapter of this book examines certain aspects of the class-control activites of the police in more detail, but it must be emphasized that the goal of class control followed as an unintended consequence of the new idea of preventing crime.

The changing arrest powers of police compared to citizens in the mid-nineteenth century paralleled the new focus on prevention. Jerome Hall has shown that just two years before the reorganization and uniforming of the London police by Peel, the difference between citizen and police arrest powers that held through the rest of the nineteenth century in England and the United States became established.[36] Although citizens could only arrest an offender after a crime had, in fact, been committed, the police could make an arrest if they thought a crime had been committed. If the moral aspect of the uniform did not succeed in striking fear and dread into the criminal heart, the arrest power certainly would.

The complete transition from the constable–watch system to the uniformed police took two decades in Boston, 1838–59; a decade in New York, 1843–53; and eleven years in Cincinnati, 1848–59; yet fifteen years later in Denver, in 1874, it happened virtually overnight. Clearly, the early police unifications took quite a long time, but the lessons learned in each made the subsequent unifications in other cities go more quickly.

Factional political struggles, both within cities and between cities and states, also deterred early unifications, because all kinds of policing systems represented both methods of controlling votes and sources of patronage. Probably the ironic epitome of such struggles occurred in New York in 1857: The Republican, nativist-dominated state legislature created the Metropolitan Police for New York City in an effort to gain political control of the city from the Democrats, whose Municipal Police had helped to assure Democratic election victories within the city. The Municipal Police, following the leadership of Mayor Wood, refused to give up their posts, and an armed battle took place between the two departments when the Metropolitan Police tried to arrest the mayor at city hall. No one died, and the battle lasted less than a day due to the fortuitous presence of the Seventh Regiment, which joined the battle on the side of the Metropolitan Police. The battle between the two forces did not end the conflict, and both forces patrolled the city in parallel for two months until Mayor Wood dissolved his police following a State Court of Appeals decision in favor of the Metropolitan Police.[37] The new Metropolitan Police, governed by a nativist Board of Commissioners appointed by the governor, took their support from city taxes levied by the state, unexpended portions of which went to the state treasury, a situation reminiscent in some ways of Peel's Irish police. The subtle differences between the two stemmed from their political contexts – the Irish police were consciously designed to insure domination of the Irish by the English, whereas the Metropolitan Police represented a political faction within the city that used state aid to gain control from another political faction.

A battle similar to that in New York almost occurred in the "City Hall War" of Denver in 1894. Again the strife concerned political control of the police, but this time with the additional element of reform: The Republican Board of Commissioners refused to resign for the anti-gambling populist board appointed by the governor. As the battle shaped up, the state militia supported the governor while the police, sheriff's deputies, and strong arm representatives of Denver vice businesses barricaded themselves in the city hall – armed with dynamite and whiskey. Though the forces faced each other, nothing happened because the governor suddenly called the militia to Cripple Creek to suppress a strike. For a short period after this, Denver had two police boards and three chiefs, but ultimately, as in New York, the incumbents yielded to a court order and the populist police took office.[38] After the resolution of the conflict, one of the new populist commissioners candidly explained the source of the conflict: " 'All we want is a fair share of the patronage, and to keep the department in men who will do their duty honestly'."[39]

Conflict over the new police departments, exemplified by the New York and Denver police battles, occurred because the police were one of the earliest urban bureaucracies to unify communications and control of the city.[40] This unique position helped the police provide patronage, social control, electoral control, and vice control. The latter generated bribes and protection money. Only a portion of this money stayed in the hands of the police, the remainder going to political parties that forced police officers to contribute to campaigns. The support and control of the police insured dominance of competing political factions, whether the challenges came from reform efforts, state versus local control, ethnic versus nativist control, or Democrats versus Republicans. Thus, the major obstacles that actually delayed unification were not the issues of uniformed police versus traditional police, but conflicts over which established political elite would reap the benefits. The New York conflict in 1857 – which wrapped up three sets of issues: partisan politics, ethnicity, and the question of which political faction governed the city – prompted New Yorker George Templeton Strong to write in his diary that the issue was merely over "'which horde had the legal right to be supported by public plunder'."[41]

Therefore, in the most important sense, the uniformed police did not emerge out of political conflict, but rather the process of unification attracted existing conflicts. The crucial ideological problems of social control never really surfaced after Gerard's perfunctory discussion in New York. In the U.S. cities that provided the models for the rest of the country, the deepest issues, at best, met perfunctory treatment from reformers like James Gerard. Gerard saw an almost mystical power in the uniform, making it a moral agent, which affected the wearer as well as thieves and felons. Discussing the potential power of the uniform on police officers, he said:

> The dress *is* respectable, and they *feel* respectable. . . . Their costume is a sure guarantee that they will never disgrace it; they know that they are known by it and, therefore, while they are watching others, that they are watched themselves. They take good care, therefore, not to enter tipling shops, or visit any places or do any acts which will disgrace their uniform.

Thus Gerard's argument had a practical side to it as well as a mystical, moral side – in case the police officer did not feel the moral power of the uniform, it would make him stick out like a sore thumb, and the pressure of public censure would force him to behave properly. Gerard argued as though the moral power of his analysis alone would make the police sensitive to the uniform – "They ought to, and will be proud to wear it."[42]

When articulated, arguments against the new police often focused on their uniforms. These arguments had three elements: (1)

the high costs of the new system compared to the fee-based traditional system; (2) the fear of a standing army; and (3) the American
lack of respect for uniforms, considered servantlike and undemo-
cratic. The fear of a standing army seems to have been the heritage
of pre-Revolution ideology, for not until the Civil War did this argument subside and more positive feelings about uniforms become
dominant.[43] For instance, the arguments against establishing a uniformed police for Washington, D.C., took two forms, the first at-
tacking the unnecessary costs and the second the quasi-military
nature of the proposed force. Senator Ambrose Sevier (Arkansas)
called the police bill, "'nothing more nor less than a proposition to
establish a little standing army'."[44] But it seems to have been Jacksonian egalitarianism relating to matters of dress that fueled the
most vehement attacks on the uniforming of the police. Historians
agree that the uniforms for the Boston police encountered the least
resistance of any pre–Civil War department, and even there they
attracted ridicule for making the police look like "'popinjays'."[45]

In other cities, the uniforms created far more antagonism and
resistance, especially among police officers. In a protest meeting in
front of the chief's house in 1854, New York City police officers
claimed uniforms "'conflicted with their notions of independence
and self-respect'" as well as being "'expensive and fantastical'."
Further, "'this infraction of the usage of society in the matter of
dress, was but the commencement of the establishment in the City
of a standing Army'."[46] In 1855, a Chicago newspaper editor, horri-
fied at the idea of a uniformed police force, doubted that "'any
man, claiming the proud title of American freeman . . . will lay
aside his ordinary dress as an American citizen to strut about the
streets of Chicago decked out in livery furnished at public expense'."[47] And in 1855 in Philadelphia, a councilman called the uniform a "'badge of servitude'" as fifteen police officers resigned,
refusing even to wear a hat, with one officer announcing: "'I hereby
present my resignation, as an American citizen – not wishing to
wear anything derogatory to my feelings as an American . . .'."[48]

Philadelphia's Mayor Conrad apparently recognized the officers'
resistance to this innovation for what it was, a combination of tradition, pride in democratic nondifferentiation, fear of greater control on the beat by ranking officers, and, perhaps as much as all
others, simple inertia. Therefore, in 1856, he strategically started
uniforming the police "with the head, hoping to work down with
less opposition, as the men became accustomed to the idea." With
this clever approach, the resistance still took four years to stamp

out, and even at this point officers resisted the final completion of uniforming. Some police officers, "who were not proud of their new clothes," appeared before patrol duty at the station house in uniform, then went home, changed, and patrolled in civilian clothes, changing back into uniform before reporting to the station house at the ends of their shifts.[49] This incident illustrates how uniforms could take on such importance, both from the point of view of the public as well as from the police perspective. Uniforms were what people actually saw in their daily business on the streets or with the police; and, for the officers, the enforcement of personal appearance destroyed the sense of autonomy inherent in their situation – working away from co-workers and bosses for most of the time on duty.

In sharp contrast to these pre–Civil War departments, the newly organized postwar Denver police department announced the arrival of its new uniforms, in 1873, with great civic pride. These uniforms, carefully modeled on the uniforms of the New York City police but made in Denver, elicited approving, if semi-humorous, comment in the newpaper. "'The uniform is durable and hand-some, and with the belts [imported from New York] and shields will make a policeman look about as well as an editor or minister' ." During a police reform in 1895, the Denver chief hired a tailor to put permanent creases in the uniforms, a policy implementation of the moral hope James Gerard had found in uniforms forty years earlier in New York.[50]

Although it is most important to understand the symbolic and political meaning of the change from the constable–watch system to the new uniformed police, we must also look, at least briefly, at the organizational changes involved. For this purpose, Boston provides an ideal example, as the transition there took so long to ac-complish, compared to those of other cities, that each change stands out clearly in the gradual unification of the police.[51] A simplified narrative looks like this: In 1822, Boston became incorporated as a city, maintaining the constable–watch system it had had for almost 200 years; in 1837, in addition to the traditional system, separate day and night police forces were created; in 1854, the watch was abolished; and by 1859 the council unified the whole system under one chief, putting the men in uniforms. In a sense, the new system slowly grew and overshadowed the old system, the city consciously copying the London police, yet maintaining the traditional consta-ble and watch.

At the time of the city's incorporation in 1822, constables had responsibility for both civil and criminal matters; their income came from fees for attending court and serving papers. Although in theory part-time jobs performed by citizens, in actuality by this time the positions had become full time and the constables had achieved job stability and annual reappointment. The watch, a responsibility that in theory fell upon all males over eighteen, had in fact evolved into a part-time job paying fifty cents a night. Each watchman patrolled the city looking for fires and disturbances, reporting back to one of four watch stations hourly. Each man carried a loud wooden rattle that he could use to call for help or, according to critics, warn felons of his approach in order to avoid trouble. Each watch house had a constable, and a captain, whose job was also considered part-time, headed up the watch. The captain also took charge of lighting lamps, even in the early nineteenth century a traditional means of crime control. The watch patrolled from 10:00 P.M. until sunup, leaving an unpatrolled period in the early morning. This system remained virtually unchanged until the city abolished it in 1854; however, in the year before its abolishment, the city ordered witness fees, which the watch had earned for attending court in the day, diverted into the city treasury and a commercial enterprise contracted for the streetlighting job.

Shortly after city incorporation in 1822, the city council created the position of city marshal. The marshal, in effect the head constable, took charge of all that " 'affects the health, security, and comfort of the city.' "[52] These broad responsibilities constituted a traditional part of the police power of the city, usually given to the constabulary. The Acts of Incorporation for the city of Washington, D.C., for instance, gave the city power to " 'prevent and remove nuisances; to prevent the introduction of contagious diseases within the city; and to establish nightwatches, or patroles'."[53] The only change in the power of the Boston marshal came in 1837, when the city created a separate department of sewers, run by a former deputy marshal.

Until 1838, the city police consisted of the night watch, with its own four watch houses, and a day constabulary and marshal, both centrally based. In 1838, a year after a volunteer fire department and funeral procession riot had forced the intervention of the militia, the council established a different police system: Six police officers, with all but the civil powers of constables, were assigned to the marshal. These six received regular salaries rather than fees and took day police duties, but the constables remained. Within months, the council created a small separate night police. By 1851, the police had grown – forty-four in the day and twenty-two at night, with a small detective division. With the creation of the detective division, the prosecution of vice increased, and both the detectives and night police began to develop the modern relationship of police to vice and illegal business – a system of paid informers, the control of vice through protective payoffs to the police, and police (especially the night police) involvement in burglaries.[54] The late 1840s had also seen the official budgetary recognition of the police welfare services to the destitute and ill – monies specifically allotted to food and medical care. Concomitant with these developments, Boston got its first popular police officer, Marshal Tukey, whose antics, as reported in the newspaper, characterized popular police officers throughout the nineteenth century. Media-popularized officers like Tukey manipulated the detectives to control vice and crime in the city, producing spectacular arrests and vice raids as kinds of media events. Thus they publicly portrayed themselves as the individual bulwarks against the underworld, with which they were in fact in illegal collusion.

When the mayoral candidate backed by Tukey's police lost, a reform process began. Tukey lost the next election, and the city abolished the corrupt night police in 1851, while continuing the watch. The health authority moved from the marshal's office to a newly created superintendent of health in 1853, and in 1854 the council created the "Watch and Police Department," with the former watchmen given a salary of two dollars a night and the arrest powers of police officers. The police, which continued to operate in the day, were divided into eight divisions to correspond with the watch; both systems were given a para-military command structure of captains and lieutenants (the lieutenants, among other things, patrolling beats as "roundsmen" to ensure that the police kept patrolling), and all time gaps in patrol periods that had existed were eliminated. The position of constable, which had been turned into a civil court position when the day and night police had been created, disappeared. In 1856, the city brought the "special police," still not quite unified, under its control. Although privately paid by merchants, the special police, who had had the regular powers of other police since 1838, were required to report to the captains. In 1857, the new position of sergeant assumed the roundsman duties of the lieutenant, and finally, in 1859, the police began to wear uniforms. Thus ended two decades of change away from civil police and toward a military model. The goals of a preventive police system spelled out twenty-two years earlier by Mayor Elliott – " 'to imitate, as far as may be, the system of London' " – had been achieved.[55]

The spread of uniformed police forces across the United States

Although not perfectly imitated in every city, the sequence of the changes in the Boston police departments sums up the variety of duties and organizational forms that could occur in the transitional period between the constable–watch system and the uniformed police. Of course, if one examined only Boston or New York or Philadelphia, one might conclude that the final form the police took represented a unique result of particular evolutionary forces. But this would distort a process of conscious communication and imitation, for in actuality each city looked carefully at its neighbors, or London, and one cannot help but be struck by the constant intercity comparisons of departments that appear in police reports. For example, in 1850, a committee in Boston, corresponding with the London police, asked for information that London had just recently sent to New York.[56]

Although it would be repetitive and tedious to summarize the development of the unified police in many cities, the dating of the emergence of the many uniformed police departments across the United States has critical importance.[57] That is, did subsequent policing innovations come from a single, constant source?[58] Or did each city have to go through a developmental crisis, reaching a critical mass of some sort, before it was compelled to follow the lead of larger places? Were there regional lags or advances, as Richard Wade has claimed?[59] Did industrial cities with heavy immigrant populations and a need for factory discipline use uniformed police before cities with more homogeneous populations? Or was there a simple random process at work, uniforms spreading like cholera or measles from city to city – a "contagious" diffusion?[60]

Some of these questions are presupposed by the three explanations for the creation of the police that have been previously advanced by police history scholars and criminologists. It is important to examine each of these three explanations carefully, for each emphasizes one of the many variables that we associate with nineteenth-century urban growth, and commits a kind of ecological fallacy.[61] These also tend to be ahistorical explanations, which assert that the consequences of the creation of the police were the same as the original intentions and reasons. Such post hoc reasoning confuses the analysis of the nineteenth-century police.

The first explanation claims that crime – or, in some of the more sophisticated analyses, the perception of crime – rose to such an unprecedented extent that the traditional constable and watch were incapable of controlling it to the satisfaction of the public. This explanation has several problems, not the least of which is an implicit argument appealing to a "natural" sequence of causal events. That is, when crime reaches a certain level, the "natural" social response is to create a uniformed police force. This, of course, is not an explanation but an assertion of a natural law for which there is little evidence.[62] Certainly the controversies that accompanied the earlier uniformed police systems suggest that contemporaries were unaware that uniformed police were a part of nature's plan. If anything, the Western means of dealing with crime waves in previous centuries had always turned to changes in penal policy, not arrest techniques.[63]

Even if we accept, for the sake of argument, the logical necessity of uniformed police arriving in the wake of rising crime, further problems arise. There is the empirical necessity of demonstrating that crime, in fact, rose prior to a police innovation. And the fact of rising crime must remain an assertion, for if the rising crime rate was measurable by historians, it would have to have been through records generated by the arrest process; but if the rising crime had been met with rising arrests, then there could have been little wrong with the constable–watch system. A slightly more complex account might claim that while rising crime did indeed meet with arrests, uniformed police were created to prevent crime from rising even further, rather than apprehending criminals after the offense. Although an interesting alternative, this explanation needs more empirical verification, for it requires a measurable crime wave preceding the creation of the various urban police departments.

If, on the other hand, the historian claims that the perception of rising crime, not necessarily the actual rate of offenses, was the operative causal element, we again have the empirical problem of finding some indicator of these rising perceptions: How do we know who held these perceptions, how strongly were they held, and why did they change? More to the point, what made these perceptions more efficacious than previous perceptions of rising crime? Why, exactly, should some perceptions of rising crime and not others lead to the creation of the uniformed police? Why not to a standing army, an intensified constable–watch system, or more executions and deportations instead of a new departure that, according to its opponents, violated the basis of Anglo-American liberty?[64]

Allan Silver implies a second explanation for the creation of the uniformed police.[65] He points out that civil disorder and riots had been grudgingly tolerated by urban dwellers prior to the nineteenth century; this tolerance was replaced by demands for social control when the targets of riots changed from symbolic ones to property. The creation of a para-military organization that made its presence continuous and visible throughout society resulted from the increased demands of property owners for more rigidly preserved urban order. In a sense, disorderly urban dwellers had violated the informal conventions of riotous behavior and by so doing provoked the creation of a far more formally controlled society. Silver's ingenious and appealing analysis stands or falls on empirical evidence, of which precious little exists. No doubt more incidents will come to light, but I have found riots mentioned as a clear precipitating element in the creation of uniformed police in only four to six cases out of the fifty-seven examined for this book – Philadelphia, Baltimore, Washington, and, perhaps, Indianapolis, Boston and Detroit. The question of whether these riots had property targets rather than symbolic targets I have left unexplored, for it seems clear that although the riot explanation for the creation of the police is more satisfactory on a logical level than the crime explanation, it too lacks conclusive evidence.

A third explanation for the creation of the uniformed police argues that they were not created in response to disorder of the type cited by Silver, but because of elite fears of the rising proportions of poor immigrants in cities.[66] The growth in the number of immigrants, maintains Allan Levett, accompanied a decrease in the ability of urban elites to control the social order of the cities informally, and they responded by creating the police to control the "dangerous class." "The police departments," he claims, "were not created to reduce crime or control increasing riots. . . . They were established to control strangers and the poor in the main."[67] Levett's argument, although it has much to recommend it, is flawed in its post hoc assertion that what the new police did reflected the reasons for their creation, a problem in causal analysis to which historians are particularly sensitive. There is good evidence to support Levett's assertion that the uniformed police had a class-control function. But he produces little evidence to show that this was the original intent behind the creation of the police.

All three of these accounts of the uniformed police founder on the supposition that because the police, once established, performed certain activities, these activities represented the conditions that gave rise to their creation. It is equally plausible to argue that the police were created because of the increase in lost children, open sewers, or tramps needing overnight lodging.

Much of the confusion and disagreement over the introduction and spread of the uniformed police has come from a narrowly localistic approach, which when generalized moves abruptly from specific locale to grand theory – for example, from Buffalo to a Marxist or Durkheimian model of society.[68] A far more useful way to seek to understand dramatic changes in the police is to reconceive the process as one of innovation and the subsequent diffusion of that innovation. In this way, we gain analytic tools to examine each part of the process discretely and, of equal importance, can employ a technique of analysis that has a large and well-established literature in the social sciences, dating at least from Gabriel Tarde's *Laws of Imitation* in 1903.[69]

Sociologist Everett M. Rogers has broken the process of innovation and diffusion down into four "crucial elements": (1) the actual innovation, (2) the communication of the innovation, (3) the nature of the social system within which the communication occurs, and (4) the time that the diffusion takes.[70] Most analyses of innovation in policing focus hardly at all on the innovations, concentrate heavily on the social system, and virtually ignore both the communication processes and time lags involved. All too often, the innovation has been examined as though the actual consequences were the intended consequences, and as though the intended consequences can be readily inferred from the nature of the social system. Both the notion that the capitalist-industrialist state needed to create an agency to control the working class and the notion that urban growth created a rising crime rate that forced a defense reaction in the creation of the police exemplify this kind of confused thinking.

Let us accept for the moment that both the reasons for and the innovative nature of the uniformed police came from the two desires of city elites to prevent crime and control the police and move to the second and fourth aspects of the process, the diffusion over time. We will return to the nature of the social system or city system through which the innovation diffused once we have examined the diffusion through time. Finally, when the process has been examined, the reasons for uniforming the police will become clearer.

Determining the dates of unification and formalization of police departments involves several practical and conceptual problems. For the sources here I have depended both on secondary materials – local histories, urban biographies, and, wherever possible, police histories – and on newspapers and city records. Although each department followed a basic pattern of change, there were local variations enough to make date assignment difficult. Some departments, like Boston's, moved from a day constabulary that was at least nominally responsible to the courts, and a night watch responsible to the constables, to separate day and night police forces, and finally to a unified day and night police force – the whole process taking a decade or so. Other departments moved directly from a constable–watch system to a unified and uniformed police force responsible to the mayor.[71] To provide consistency in assigning dates, I have taken the date of the adoption of uniforms, whenever possible, as the starting point of the new kind of policing.

The uniform concretely symbolizes the changed system of social control represented by the new police, asserting publicly and unequivocally the difference between the old and the new. It is not surprising that both police officers and the public sometimes resisted and mocked the first uniforms, for they depersonalized the wearer, made obvious the para-military nature of the new system and, as Allan Silver observes, visibly demonstrated the "continual presence of central political authority throughout daily life."[72] Uniforms remain important today, both to the police and the public. A recent study of a state police department claimed that "probably no single symbol was of greater importance to the role of *policeman* than the uniform." The study quoted a corporal whose thoughts echoed those of James Gerard's over a century earlier: "'There is something about a uniform that makes a man different.'"[73] Whether the presence of a uniformed officer provokes public reactions of fear, hatred, anxiety, relief, or security is not a crucial matter; what counts is that the uniform is a statement of power. And when in the nineteenth century a city took the step of uniforming its police, it clearly stated its power to control its inhabitants. Thus the corporal's observation that the uniform makes a difference is wise, for the content of the difference can vary, but the ability of the uniform to make that difference is its importance.

Taking the 100 largest American cities in 1880 as my initial target group, I found precise data on 57 (see Appendix A). The model best describing the diffusion of the innovation of uniformed police through the 57 cities over a half-century period is often referred to as one of *contagious diffusion,* to be contrasted with a model of *constant source diffusion.*[74] The latter model presumes the diffusion of an innovation from one stable source, whereas the former describes a process whereby each new adopter of the innovation becomes a source for further diffusion. The S-shaped graph of contagious diffusion, displayed in Figure 1, shows the cumulative number of cities uniforming their police forces over time.[75] When regressed against a contagious diffusion model, a startling 99% of the adoptions can be accounted for, whereas only 13% can be fitted against a constant source model. Thus the graph displays the speed of the innovation process – the slow, scattered adoption at first; a quick acceleration over a two-decade period; and then a trailing off as straggling cities or those that had grown from nothing during the period (like Denver) create their police departments.

Although Figure 1 and the regression below it demonstrate clearly that the speed of the diffusion of uniformed police forces across the United States conformed to a simple communications

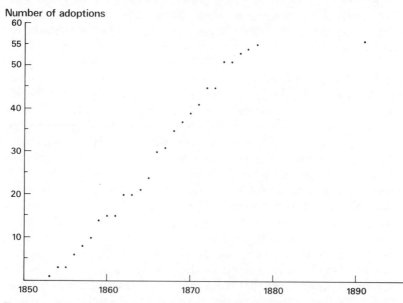

Figure 1. Cumulative number of cities adopting uniformed police, 1850–1900. (Contagion model, R^2 = .997. Straight line model, R^2 = .850.) *Source:* Data compiled from histories of individual cities. See Appendix A for complete citations.

process, this does not tell us why some cities made the innovation while others resisted it – the specific order of adoption remains to be explained. In other words, the close fit of the actual police uniform dates to the contagious diffusion model tells only that we are examining a communication process that followed a predictable pattern – a process that need not have involved more than random communications among pairs of potential adopters. We need now an explanation to account for this apparently orderly process.

The explanation I advance here to account for the creation of the uniformed police subsumes previous ones and places them in a more complete context. The growth of uniformed urban police forces should be seen simply as a part of the growth of urban service bureaucracies. The police provided the specific service of controlling an increasingly anonymous and threatening "dangerous class," but this was not the reason for their creation. The new police did represent an important and dramatic change in the nature of urban life, but their introduction and dispersion throughout the country was not a function of elite demands for class control, changing urban riots, or rising crime. Its speed and pace determined by a contagious diffusion process, the spread of the new kind of police conformed to a simple rank-order dispersion model. The innovation of the police, copied first by the largest Eastern cities from the model of the London Metropolitan Police, swept down the size hierarchy of U.S. cities, from large to small, in a forty-year period. Absolute size made little difference: Thus, when New York uniformed its police in 1853 it was a metropolis of over 600,000 people, but Taunton, Massachusetts, reorganized and uniformed its police in 1890 when its population numbered only 25,000.

The causal sequence runs thus: American urban administrations in the last half of the nineteenth century began to provide a growing range of rationalized services – police, fire, health, and sewage – which previously had been provided on an entrepreneurial basis by various organizations. For the largest cities, the conspicuously successful Metropolitan Police of London served as a policing model to be adopted when any one of several precipitants occurred. Once adopted by larger cities, the new model of policing spread from larger to smaller cities, spurred not by precipitating events any longer, but by the newly developing service orientations of city governments. Each city's position in the size hierarchy of U.S. cities determined the point at which its uniformed police force was created, with other influences – ethnic composition, industrial base, and location – operating only as minor determinants. Although city officials may have looked with horror at crime and disorder, they looked at the municipal operations of slightly larger cities for practical suggestions to urban governance.

The timing and pattern of police dispersion through the country shows that city governments seized the innovative scheme of uniformed police as a convenient and fashionable means of social control without regard for specifically threatening situations. Although in the instances of some of the larger cities, riots or perceptions of rising crime and disorder may have been precipitating factors, it is clear that as a general causal explanation such analyses have confused precipitants with preconditions.[76] For an account of the rise of uniformed policing to be adequate, it should have a large degree of applicability across the range of U.S. cities, and none of the previous models meets this condition. Each can explain the origins of only a handful of city police. My explanation, although less dramatic, directly ties the police to municipal change within an urban network, allowing more unity and complexity in the analysis of the services that the police provided by separating origins from functions. Just because the police were created for one reason does not mean that they actually did not do other things: We must be prepared to accept the idea that the actual functions of the police were unintended consequences of their reorganization. To show this, it is first necessary to locate each newly created department in the urban hierarchy, as well as in the time of total adoptions.

My hypothesis, which has been tested and tentatively confirmed, is that each city's position in the national hierarchy of cities directly determined the order in which it adopted a uniformed police force. That is, larger cities adopted police forces first, with smaller ones following quickly. The scatterplot in Figure 2 demonstrates this visually – each point represents a city, located by its rank and date of uniform adoption (city one, for instance, is New York City, which uniformed its police in 1853). As the legend below the scatterplot states, the rank-order correlation of city and police dates is a high .69, significant at .001, for fifty-nine cities. When the twelve cities located in the Southeast and West are excluded from the correlation, R declines slightly for these regions and rises for the Midwest and Northeast. This decline in R is probably the result of the scantier and poorer data for the Southeast and West, and should not be viewed as conclusive. We should look, rather, at the overall results, for in confirming the rank-order hypothesis, the previous explanations for the creation of the police can be subsumed.

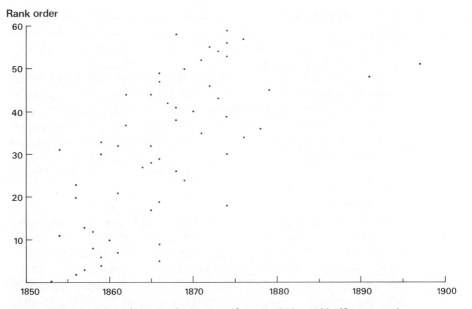

Rank order

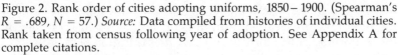

Figure 2. Rank order of cities adopting uniforms, 1850– 1900. (Spearman's R = .689, N = 57.) *Source:* Data compiled from histories of individual cities. Rank taken from census following year of adoption. See Appendix A for complete citations.

That city rank determined when a city adopted a uniformed police force indicates that local decisions concerning the means of social control, sometimes precipitated by local situations, were not
unique but were part of a national trend in urban governance.
Cities looked to other cities of similar size for ideas. If each city had
adopted a uniformed force only after a riot, changing crime rate, or
the need for a new kind of class-control agency, many places would
not today have a uniformed police force. Instead, by following the
examples of larger places, by 1890 cities as small and as different as
Auburn, New York; Lynn, Massachusetts; and Saint Joseph, Missouri, had created their own uniformed police forces. The process
of communication down the urban hierarchy, from major to minor
places, occurred not only with regard to governmental innovations.
A recent study of cholera, for instance, shows how the cholera epi-
demic of 1832 spread from city to city along major transport routes;
however, by 1866 cholera spread down the urban hierarchy from
big to small places, jumping the major transport routes.[77] This comparison demonstrates that the system of communications and eco-

nomic relationships of cities structured change and innovation by structuring information flows. Just as larger cities received more cholera carriers earlier than smaller ones, the same cities also received more information about policing innovations.

To analyze the institutional meaning of this pattern of police adoption, we must move out of the narrower focus of police history and examine the broader patterns of institutional change. In an important and suggestive article on the House of Representatives, Nelson Polsby sets up several ways to measure and describe institutional changes.[78] Although his propositions and measures are designed to apply to legislative bodies, they transfer almost without modification to bureaucracies like the police.

There are three descriptive characteristics of what he calls an "institutionalized bureaucracy" – and for bureaucracies to be viable they must be institutionalized. The first characteristic of an institutionalized bureaucracy is its clear "differentiation from its environment"; second, it has a "complex organization"; and third, it is run on "universalistic criteria." Polsby operationalizes these three characteristics into more concrete criteria, almost all of which are satisfied by the changes in policing that accompanied the adoption of the uniform. The clearest indicators of institutionalization met by the uniformed police include: (1) easy identification of membership – the uniform, of course; (2) the recruitment of leadership from within the organization – the uniformed police saw the beginning of this principle in police organization; (3) explicit separation of internal functions – the para-military command structure and the creation of detective divisions; (4) noninterchangeable roles – matrons, patrol, and chiefs, for instance; and (5) internal business conducted by universalistic, nondiscretionary, meritocratic, and impersonal codes – a goal that the police tried to implement with varying degrees of success throughout the nineteenth century.

Although none of these features was perfectly or instantly achieved in the newly formed police departments, they were the *desiderata* and neatly summarize the internal goals of the new police. Polsby lists one criterion that the new departments did not meet successfully and that has only in recent years become a demand of police departments – difficult membership requirements. Although it was relatively easy to become a police officer in the nineteenth century, departments stressed their high degree of personnel selectivity, anxiously showing that their police officers were literate people who had been recruited from skilled occupations, even to the point of distorting personnel statistics.[79] But above all these criteria of an institutionalized bureaucracy stands the uniform, differentiating the police from other citizens, visibly symbolizing the complex inner hierarchy of the police department through the differences between the uniforms of the patrol and ranking officers, and stressing universalism over individual idiosyncracy.

The development of police bureaucracies paralleled closely, both in time and form, the movement of the House of Representatives toward a thoroughly "institutionalized bureaucracy." According to Polsby, the turning point for the House came in the 1890–1910 period, the same period when police departments began to free themselves from factional local politics. Usually the defactionalization of police departments at the turn of the century is conceived only within the context of the individual department's history or as an externally imposed progressive reform.[80] But Polsby's model offers an interesting alternative. He shows how one of the predictable consequences of institutionalization is the development of "professional norms of conduct," implying that once the new departments had been established, their moves toward professionalization became almost automatic. Seen in this way, the defactionalization of the police was simply an aspect of the growth of police professionalism, which was itself a built-in consequence of the move to rationalize and uniform the police.[81]

The process of the reorganization and regularization of the police can be explored with special clarity in the twin cities of Minneapolis and Saint Paul, for both cities converted their police forces from simple organizations with one chief and a dozen or so patrolmen to uniformed para-military organizations in the 1870s. This same decade saw intense competition between the two cities as both experienced physical growth and population expansion while fighting for commercial and manufacturing advantage, their competitiveness stimulated by physical proximity and ethnic and religious rivalry. The upstart rival, Republican, Scandinavian, WASP Minneapolis, threatened the older and more established city, Democratic, Irish, Catholic Saint Paul. In lieu of comparable annual censuses, the cities estimated population on the basis of votes (one vote being considered to represent six people), each trying to outrank the other.

The two cities' concerns for population accurately reflected reality, for Saint Paul had 20,030 people in 1870 while Minneapolis had only 13,066; at the end of the decade both cities had grown considerably, but the ranking had dramatically reversed, Saint Paul standing at 41,473 and Minneapolis at 46,887. This reversal occurred at about the same time Minneapolis put its police into uniform, 1876, for in 1875 the state census showed Saint Paul still leading slightly at 33,178, with Minneapolis only 457 people behind at 32,721. Yet in spite of the intense boosterism of and rivalry between the two cities, and in spite of the tendency of the newspapers to comment on items even marginally related to the competition, the subject of the police is strangely missing from their dialogue. One searches the newspapers and city council minutes in vain, expecting to find intense argument about these visible symbols of urban modernity. In both cities, the only issue of note concerning police uniforms was whether or not the city governments should pay for them (they did). Saint Paul easily outdistanced Minneapolis in the uniform movement by four years, 1872 as opposed to 1876, timing that corresponded to the rank order.[82] But it is wrong to see any competitiveness here: The only contrast between the police of the two cities that even came close to competition occurred in 1874, when the *Minneapolis Tribune* ran a humorous note concerning the attractiveness of the Saint Paul police uniforms for women.[83] Otherwise, Minneapolitans seemed to accept complacently a smaller and more ragtag police, arguing that the city was "one of the most quiet and orderly of towns."[84]

The status of uniforms was such a non-issue that neither city even had the appropriate terminology. When the Saint Paul city council voted to pay for the new uniforms in 1872, it simply called them "outfits."[85] Equally laconic, the Minneapolis council discussed "uniform overcoats."[86] Minneapolis Alderman Bassett made this relaxed attitude clear when, in an 1872 council discussion over whether or not to reorganize the police (which consisted of a chief and handful of patrolmen) to include a captain or two, he allowed that he "was ignorant as to the duties of policemen, but had no objection to all being captains if it didn't cost any more." He then moved that the department have one chief, one captain, two lieutenants, two sergeants, and four corporals, but no patrolmen. His motion failed and the force then gained a captain.[87]

When Minneapolis finally caught up to Saint Paul in uniforming its police four years later, the adoption occurred with little commotion and almost no comment. If uniforms were discussed before the city council, the minutes failed to record the discussion. The mayor, in his inaugural message of April 11, 1876, asked for "uniform stars, belts, clubs and hand cuffs . . . as it is proposed to have all the officers in full uniform while on duty."[88] This is the first formal mention of police uniforms in Minneapolis, and the police appeared three days after the mayor's message in full uniform – in a small note, the *Tribune* said "the improvement was noticeable."[89] A month later, the chief appeared "in a nobby new blue uniform with buttons all over him."[90]

The actual mechanism and impetus for police uniforms in Minneapolis remain unclear: The entire force had petitioned for uniform overcoats in October, 1875, and the chief may have been the prime mover behind the uniforms.[91] In the case of the uniform overcoats, he apparently placed the orders and had the men wearing them long before the council could decide on how the city might pay for them.[92] And it is clear from the chief's report of 1879 that he kept abreast of police developments throughout the United States, as he included a table comparing the Minneapolis police to those in other cities.[93]

Neither crime nor public disorder figured in the reorganization of either the Minneapolis or Saint Paul police. Although there is some suggestion that the chiefs expected uniforms to help maintain the discipline of the police and the warm overcoats to keep them out of bars, it is also apparent that the police expanded numerically to keep up with the population growth and physical expansion of the two cities. The only recorded reasoning of a city official on the subject of the police came when the mayor of Saint Paul explained in 1871 that the city needed more police because it was growing and because more police constituted, in the long run, a greater economy than few police. "Disorder," he claimed, "seldom arises where an officer is at hand – his mere presence or contiguity generally prevents the offense from which follows the arrest, trial, conviction and consequent support of offenders for a term at the public expense."[94] Cost, not crime, was the concern of these two booming cities building new police forces; questions about the civil libertarian issues of standing armies, police spying, or social control did not arise, for policing had simply become an urban service to be taken for granted, like sewers, sidewalks, and streets.

It has been difficult for historians to capture descriptively the bureaucratic change from the constable–watch system to the uniformed police, and it has remained for a sociologist, Allan Levett, to come up with what I think is the most engaging presentation of this change. He calls the pre-uniformed police "entrepreneurial police," emphasizing their non-rule-bound behavior and dependence on fees rather than salaries. Because of their fee dependence, the entrepreneurial police engaged in activities generating large fees and rewards, such as the recovery of stolen property. The uniformed police he argues, were a "politicized bureaucracy": Although the new departments had rule-governed internal structures, thus meeting the definition of a bureaucracy, the rules were subject to the demands of the local political power. Of course, the entrepreneurial police were, legally and traditionally, agents of the courts, which is why they depended on fees and emphasized catching criminals rather than preventing crime. But the uniformed police, moved from control by the courts to an administrative branch of city government, became a constant and regular feature of urban life.

The gathering of the police into the administrative branch of city government paralleled the fate of a similarly entrepreneurial urban service, the volunteer fire department.[95] Both reorganizations were part of a larger change, the rationalization of urban governmental services. This must be kept in view as we analyze policed society in the nineteenth century, for this larger change in urban governance provided the necessary precondition for the creation of the uniformed police. Within the context of this precondition, several different precipitants were sufficient to move the police into uniform – that is, riots, perceptions of rising crime, sensational criminal offenses, or the demand for class control.

Although the rank-order dispersion model indicates that the unification of the Southern urban police followed the dictates of a national urban hierarchical system, there is some evidence that before unification there were regional differences caused by slavery. Historian Richard Wade cites the observations of travelers who found the Southern police efficiently repressive. Although these observations reflect, at least partially, what the travelers wanted to see – that is, evidence of the totalitarian aspects of a slave society – they still have some merit. One only wonders if acute observers could not have found similar repressive policing of the poor in Northern cities of the constable–watch era. Visiting Charleston, South Carolina, Frederick Law Olmsted found " 'police machinery as you never find in towns under free governments: citadels, sentries, passports, grape-shotted canon, and daily public whippings . . . . I happened myself to see more direct expression of tyranny in a single day and night at Charleston, than in Naples in a week'." In Richmond, Virginia, William Chambers came upon an armed police guard in the early evening patrolling the capital (when, it should be remembered, the Northern cities often had no police, the constables having gone home for the day and the night watch not yet on duty). For him, seeing the officer " 'had the startling effect of an apparition; for it was the first time I had seen a bayonet in the United States'."[96] Although the idea of guarding the capital may not seem too surprising to us, it had not been common practice even in the national capital: In 1840, a drunk was able to wander into the White House and spend the night unnoticed. And Booth shot Lincoln while the police officer assigned to guard Lincoln's box sat drinking in a local bar.[97]

Not all historians agree on the efficiency of the Southern police, for a study of the Savannah, Georgia, police by Richard Haunton describes a system remarkably like its Northern counterparts, with the exception of a much larger watch, at least on paper. In 1854, with a population of about 17,000, the city had 5 constables and 100 watchmen. The next year the police changed, declining to a watch of 60 with 20 mounted constables, and by 1860 the watch had been eliminated in favor of 56 police officers, 2 "sentinels," and 10 reservists. The Savannah jail, like jails throughout the country, contained blacks, whites, women, children, lunatics, and witnesses detained for trial. In this thriving port town with many immigrants and sailors, the city jail contained twice as many whites as blacks, perhaps because slave owners paid fines and free blacks were more apt to receive corporal punishment than whites. A newspaper editorial in 1853 mocking the watch probably would have been appropriate anywhere in the country: " 'We are really at a loss to know what to make of our up-town neighbor lately – does he mean to say that there is such a thing as a police force in this city! Brother, beware how you draw such long bows! You'll impare your credit for veracity if you put such rumors afloat. 'Watch' in Savannah! Capital joke. We just begin to see the cue, our neighbor refers to time pieces in jewelry stores'."[98]

If Southern police in the pre-uniform, pre–Civil War era were more efficient and repressive than police in the rest of the country, then the situation had certainly changed after the war, when the Southern constable–watch system evolved into police forces as inefficient and politically factional as in the North. Eugene Watts traced the development of the Atlanta police from uniforming and unification in 1874 through depoliticization in 1904 and showed that the major differences between them and Northern police were somewhat higher per capita strength and more explicit race control efforts. As in the North, police harassment kept the "dangerous class," defined mainly in terms of race in Atlanta, contained in certain parts of the city. The chief purposely allowed black "dives" to remain open to provide a convenient place for a suspect pool when arrests were needed – a practice still continued by police throughout the United States.[99]

Thus, the composition of the "dangerous class," mainly black in the South, more heterogeneous in the North, determined the regional differences in police organization North and South. After unification, whatever regional differences that may have existed had disappeared. As George Ketcham, in his study of the unification of five police departments in the North, Midwest, and South, discovered:

> Urban law enforcement agencies came to share a variety of common characteristics in their personnel and procedures. Regardless of region, a striking similarity existed in police practices and even the repeated shifts between metropolitan and state control did little to alter the mode of operations. The distinctive character of municipal police grew as much from the routine practices used in recruitment, training and law enforcement as from its statutory definition.[100]

By the end of the nineteenth century, the uniformed police in U.S. cities had assumed the form and roles with which most Americans have become familiar. To be sure, there were many technological changes to come, both in weaponry and communications, but the bureaucratic system had been firmly established. Future technology would represent fine tuning on the basic system, which had changed from a broadly conceived reactive institution to a more narrowly defined preventive and control-oriented bureaucracy. As a part of similar changes in the role and political structure of U.S. cities, the uniformed police represented a new way of ordering, administering, and controlling the city, a way substantially different from the traditional constable–watch. Although the reasons for the creation of the new police came from the new kind of city government and from new kinds of social control for physically large and diverse populations, the actual timing and adoption of the system followed the more basic communication structure of the city system. Significantly, the new police spearheaded a nonreversible and unintended process of social control in the city. Original intentions and expectations fell by the wayside as city dwellers took initiative in putting the new police to new uses in which criminal arrest activities, at least for a long time, figured only peripherally.

2   *Arrest trends, 1860–1920*

> To my own mind the entire subject |defective, dependent, and delinquent classes| is one. The causes at work in our modern society . . . affect the growth of all of them.
>
> Frederick H. Wines, *Report on Defective, Dependent, and Delinquent Classes* . . . (1888)

Previous studies of arrest and crime trends

By establishing a new national data series for arrest rates and police strength, this chapter answers some of the questions and clarifies some of the issues, definitions, and problems involved in the study of urban crime and police from before the Civil War until after World War I. For in spite of increasing scholarly attention to crime, violence, and the police, several simple yet critically important historical questions remain unanswered. Significant social change occurred between the Civil War and World War I. Wars, depressions, vast population movements, and an economic transformation all affected the behavior of persons who produced crime and disorder – the "dangerous class." The same broad social and economic forces also affected the urban bureaucracy created to control the "dangerous class," for the uniformed police grew increasingly strong, specialized and bureaucratized. There are broad questions to ask about crime during this period. As the United States changed from a booming agricultural nation to an industrialized world military power, did crime increase or decrease? Did its growing social and economic complexity demand more or less public order? What about "serious" crime, that is, offenses with suffering victims: Did the violence of the frontier give way to urbane civility? Did the police themselves mirror social and economic change, as they became more bureaucratic? Did the growth and increased sophistication of urban police work successfully repress crime?

Because the conclusions of this chapter contradict most popularly held opinions about the nature and amount of crime in the nineteenth century, a brief historiographic overview is in order to present a synthesis of the previous studies of nineteenth- and twentieth-century crime. The best-known discussion of nineteenth-century crime is Roger Lane's provocative article, "Crime and Criminal Statistics in Nineteenth-Century Massachusetts," which appeared in 1968.[1] In this article, Lane makes the challenging assertion that cities "civilize their inhabitants": He bases his assertion on evidence that shows a decrease in "serious" crime (defined only by the imprisonment of the convicted offender) between 1834 and 1901, with a corresponding increase in "minor" crime (defined by the jailing rate). He claims that the growth of cities produced new demands for order in public places, demands that resulted in increasing arrests for offenses against order. In other words, Lane asserts it was not so much public behavior as standards of the law-enforcing society that changed, growing more rigid and decorous.

Lane is not the only scholar to discuss nineteenth-century American crime rates. In fact, the subject has had a surprising number of studies, but with surprisingly few conclusions, useful empirical generalizations, or even mutual recognition. There have been, in fact, almost a dozen such studies, but none with national orientation or with measures of crime similar enough to invite cross-state or -city comparisons. When one tries to bring together all statistical research on nineteenth- and early twentieth-century crime, the results frustrate clear analysis. Not only have the various studies used differing crime categories, but they have also used several different measurement methods, ranging from imprisonments and arrests per capita to raw numbers and unique scaling systems. All these function usefully within the context of the specific study, but discourage comparisons across time or space. And when one finally reduces earlier studies to their lowest common denominators for comparative purposes, at best there can only be a vague sense of trends of idiosyncratically defined "serious" or "petty" offenses, with a few crime waves of varying periodization. Lane, for instance, defines seriousness of the offense by the court in which it was heard or by punishment, that is, by whether those defendants found guilty were either jailed or imprisoned. Sociologist Theodore Ferdinand, on the other hand, uses a different set of definitions in each of his four articles on crime and the police, ranging from specific categories (rape, murder, and the like) to popular nineteenth-century catchall definitions (crimes against property, person, or statute).[2] Thus the two best-known authorities have generated at least five noncomparable measures of crime.

Although one must come to grips with and try to summarize the previous scholarly research in historical crime data, all attempts at synthesis based on this earlier work must remain tentative because of the lack of comparable measures from study to study. For this reason, I have not attempted to present the data graphically, as to do so would give a false impression of precision. Thus, a qualitative and verbal synopsis must suffice.

Of all the states, the nineteenth-century crime rates of Massachusetts have been the most scrutinized. Looking first at those offenses usually considered most heinous, we find that various degrees of murder (as measured by the rate of indictments per capita) declined between 1871 and 1892 throughout the state; however, murder declined more in Boston than in other cities, with rural areas experiencing the least decrease.[3] On the other hand, overall arrest rates in Boston climbed from 1703 through 1967; within that broadest category, drunkenness arrests fluctuated a bit more, rising until 1890, dropping for a decade, rising again to a peak in 1917, and falling off thereafter.[4] Also, as measured by arrest rates, "major" offenses in Boston climbed from 1849 through the late 1870s, stayed fairly steady until the 1920s and then declined.[5] In Salem, as contrasted to Boston, drunkenness rates (arrests) declined steadily from 1853 through the 1920s, with the exception of two peaks around 1880 and 1910.[6] Simple assault and larceny rates (again, by arrests) in Salem also declined, with the exception of a peak for each in the early 1870s. Throughout the state, "serious" offenses (as measured by the indictment and imprisonment rates) decreased between 1834 and 1901, whereas "minor" offenses (as measured by the jailing rate) increased. To add a final complexity and contradiction to the picture, another historian, in contrast to Roger Lane, found a rise in prison commitments for the whole state from 1836 to 1873, with a serious peak in the 1850s.[7]

For Philadelphia, a sociologist comparing the period from 1791 to 1810 to the single year of 1937 found no increase in the per capita rate of all cases coming to the various criminal courts, including thereby both misdemeanor and felony offenses, but found that a higher proportion of the cases in 1937 were for offenses against the public order.[8] As an analysis that creates the image of a trend from but two points in time, it is very likely, of course, that this result obscures a pattern of great fluctuation in public order offenses similar to that of Boston. Farther west, Buffalo between 1856 and World War I saw the arrest rates for "minor" crimes and all male arrests climb to a peak in the 1870s, after which both remained stable past World War I. The arrest rates for more serious crimes of personal violence and crimes against property also peaked in 1870; after this, property and personal offenses diverged, property offenses dropping until 1885 and then stabilizing, violent offenses declining until 1900, then beginning to climb again.[9]

In Ohio, murder rates (as measured by cases coming to court) remained constant between 1867 and 1891, while felony theft quickly dropped from a post–Civil War peak in 1867 and then began a slight climb through 1891. For Franklin County, Ohio, which contains the state capital, Columbus, the overall rate of felonies coming to court between 1859 and 1885 showed remarkable stability, with the exception of a peak during 1863, followed by a dip and then another peak just after the Civil War. With the exception of the war years, murder rates also were stable, but assault and battery and theft had slight peaks in the 1870s.[10]

Farther west in Rockford, Illinois, arrest rates for "violent" crimes increased from 1880 to a peak in 1902 and then began a gradual decline through the 1920s, while vice and petty crime arrest rates stayed steady through the period. Offenses against the public order also peaked around the turn of the century, and then began a general decline.[11] Concomitantly, in Iowa between 1860 and 1920, felony conviction rates ran high during the Civil War and between 1875 and 1885, otherwise remaining stable until 1910, when they began to rise. Although the overall amount of crime per capita was greater in Iowa's urban counties, interestingly enough the trends and peaks were the same for both urban and rural counties, suggesting that the urban setting allowed for greater vigilance but that ubiquitous social forces really determined trends.[12]

Showing a trend contrary to those in Ohio and Iowa, total prison commitments for Missouri rose steadily from 1850 through 1920, with only the peak years 1860, the mid 1870s, and the last half of the 1890s conforming to patterns elsewhere.[13]

Finally, on the West Coast, San Francisco's overall arrest rate fluctuated wildly, showing a general climb from 1863 through 1880, a decline to the beginning of World War I, and an upswing during the war. The proportion of arrests for offenses against the public order climbed until 1905, then fell off rapidly.[14] Across the bay, in Oakland, arrests and arrest rates differed, the total number of arrests climbing slowly from 1870 until 1905, then soaring until the 1920s. The per capita rate varied considerably, however, with peaks in 1875, 1890, and 1920, and a deep trough in 1900.[15] That both cities had differing peaks until World War I indicates their growing similarity. But as the Oakland police often blamed offenses on persons from San Francisco, it appears that the rates of the two cities, while differing, formed part of the same phenomenon.

Generalizing about national trends from these previous studies is most frustrating, synthesis difficult, and analysis nearly impossible. Crime statistics have always been a little murky for any researcher to work with, usually having been generated for specific reasons that dictated differing compilation strategies; thus we must not blame researchers for such problems. The clearest generalizations we can make from these various studies are: Total annual offenses, or annual petty offenses (a numerically large category that approximates and dominates the total offense category), held stable in Buffalo, Rockford, Columbus, Ohio, and Iowa. Apparently at the same time, they climbed in Boston, the rest of Massachusetts, and Missouri. In San Francisco, they rose until 1880, then declined. The only points of agreement among these studies are that there was a crime wave in 1863, another wave during the 1870s, perhaps one in the 1890s, and one after World War I. It is highly possible that the conflict in these previously analyzed trends has more basis in collection methods and categorization techniques than in reality. The following section explains how a more rationally created national arrest data series reorders this confusing picture.

New data from old sources

The noncomparability of previous studies led me to design the research for this chapter specifically to produce urban data with as broad and comprehensive a base as feasible, utilizing clearly defined sources, definitions, and limitations, so that a reliable statistical series would result, making reasonably valid generalizations possible. My decision to use arrests rather than court data or convictions came partly from an interest in getting criminal data at the point closest to their generation, but more from a desire to measure the earliest and least exclusively manipulated part of the criminal labeling process. However, only on exceptional occasions should arrests be considered a substitute for a measure of crimes or bad behaviors actually occurring.

Most major American cities published annual arrest and police personnel data. The reports of police departments usually began soon after their establishment, so although no systematically comparable data from the period of the constable–watch system ever existed, there are data for uniformed police systems. Many cities issued the annual police reports as a separately bound volume and also bound in a larger volume with other city reports. When bound with other city reports, the content was usually the same as when bound separately. Occasionally, the reports contained no arrest data, only financial information, but more usually they included a complete breakdown of arrests by charge; and a tabulation of arrestees by age, sex, race, literacy, ethnicity, and occupation. The reports also gave data on the size of the department, its expenditures, and its personnel. Finally, the reports contained information on other work of the department, including numbers of lost children returned, drunks taken home, stray dogs shot, and number of lodgers accommodated. The Library of Congress holds the most complete and extensive collection of police and city reports (often referred to as the "mayor's report").[16] The major difficulties in working with the annual reports come from changing categorization and occasional, inexplicable lapses, sometimes creating situations where all information for a decade is missing – or, even more frustrating, data on arrests but not lodgers or number of police officers.

To deal with the problems of missing data and inconsistent reporting, I selected for this study the twenty-seven largest cities in the United States in 1880, and found data for twenty-three of these (see Appendix B). These twenty-three cities had 99.15% of the population in cities over 50,000 in 1880, and 50.24% of that in cities over 2,500. (The smallest city in the study, Lowell, Massachusetts, had a population of 59,475 in 1880.) To establish the four different rates – arrest, murder, police, and lodgers – I calculated the yearly population increase for each city using straight-line interpolation. Data pairs – a population of sets of cities with complete data on each specific variable and the data on the variable itself – were created for each of the four categories for each year between 1860 and 1920, with each data pair based only on those cities not missing data for the relevant variable. For example, twenty-one cities had total arrest information for 1880, while twenty had murder information, twenty had number of police personnel, and sixteen had lodging information. The purpose of this method of aggregation was to minimize the effect of errors and include as many cities as possible in the analysis at all times, creating a national data set, rather than one dependent on local or regional idiosyncrasies. The inclusion of varying numbers of cities broadened the data base and also extended the time period, alleviating such problems as five scattered years of vanished reports for Philadelphia. The maximum number of cities included in any calculation was twenty two, the minimum four, the average about fifteen. Had a city been excluded every time one piece of information was missing, it would have been impossible to establish any reasonable data series. The relative smoothness of the plotted data visually attests to the consistency of the resulting data series.

One can expect that arrest behavior for offenses without complaining victims – the "on view" or initiative arrests where an officer must view the offense and decide to arrest – differed between cities and small villages or rural areas, that is, between places with regular, uniformed police and places with less intensive and less rationalized policing. Therefore, I limited my data collection base to large cities with uniformed police. By confining the data sources to cities with established police bureaucracies, the possibility of aggregation across all the cities became a realistic goal. The use of arrests (instead of, for instance, court cases) made this goal more reasonable, for arrests do not reflect the vagaries of the differing urban adjudication processes and, more to the point, have the advantage of large numbers. With large numbers and many cities, the calculated rates will tend to have randomized error sources. The use of arrest rates rather than convictions, jailings, or imprisonments makes explicit my perspective that measurable crime is as much the result of police activity as bad behavior. And the very process of lumping together drunkenness, assaults, burglaries, and other offenses, as in the data creation, is informed with the notion that the act of labeling by arrest has social significance. Distinctions in what kind of labels were applied, although perhaps important, do not match the primary importance of the first step in labeling, which is to be defined out of the law abiders and into the "dangerous class." Without the very recently conducted victimization studies, there is little point in debating the nature and amount of bad behavior that has not led to an arrest.[17] When arrest rates soar or decline, one must make only the most qualified observations on the relationship of arrests to actual bad behavior – precisely speaking, 1863, the 1870s, and 1890s had arrest waves, not crime waves. With this caveat in mind, there is every reason to begin a systematic look into the nineteenth- and early twentieth-century arrest rates and trends.

Trends in urban arrest rates

This section analyzes four categories of arrests. Each is designed to yield the maximum amount of reliable information from data that tend to be imprecise except as counts of rather broad categories. By keeping categories broad, we can be assured of reliability across cities and can avoid any false sense of precision. Nevertheless, because there remains the possibility that even the broad categories contain miscounts, this analysis focuses on the clearest and largest trends and deviations. Of the four categories of arrest, the first, overall arrests, ranged from "scorching" on bicycles to assaults and homicides. The second group, arrests for crimes without victims, which most often required police initiative and can be viewed as attempts at enforcing public order, made up about one-half of all arrests. The slightly smaller third category, arrests for offenses with victims, mainly assaults and thefts, was estimated by simply subtracting initiative arrests from total arrests. The fourth category, homicide arrests, came from a combination of all arrests for homicide, from negligent to nonnegligent.

The discussion that follows examines the plots of the arrest rates in the four categories, looking at both long-term trends and the peaks and dips that exceeded the normal annual range of fluctuation. Those fluctuations that exceeded two standard deviations from the mean are called large, and those that fell between one and two standard deviations from the mean are termed moderate. Figure 3 plots the annual per capita arrest rates of all crimes, including those numerous crimes that require police initiative – various drunkenness offenses, disorderly behavior, being a suspicious person, being a vagrant, corner lounging, or similar statutory offenses attaching more to a person's condition than to offenses with suffering and complaining victims. The graph shows three-year running averages, but all peaks referred to come from unsmoothed data. Police initiative arrests account for the majority of all arrests and, depending on one's perspective, may be thought least indicative of the totality of criminal behavior with victims. That is, it seems to many people that such victimless offenses do not belong, logically or ethically, to the class of behavior called criminal. This view is not unique to current reformers. For instance, during a short period of

Figure 3. (a) Total arrests per 1,000 city population. (Three-year moving averages plotted. Slope of regression line = −.508. Significance = .00001.) (b) Initiative arrests per 1,000 city population. (Three-year moving averages plotted. Slope of regression line = −.492. Significance = −.00001.) (c) "Crime" arrests per 1,000 city population. (Three-year moving averages plotted. Slope of regression line = −.06. Significance = .09.) *Source:* Compiled from annual reports of twenty-three police departments. See Appendix B for list of cities and detail on data and sources.

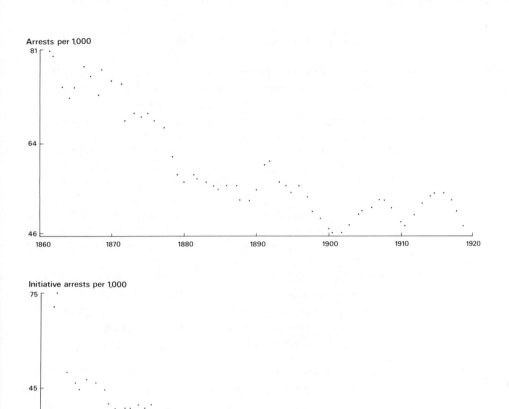

Arrests per 1,000

Initiative arrests per 1,000

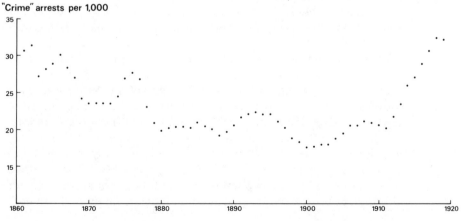

"Crime" arrests per 1,000

progressive reform, the police chief of Cleveland, Fred Kohler, adopted the "Common Sense Policy or Golden Rule," a policy, he explained, "of not making arrests where the arrests would do more harm than good, in cases of minor offenders . . . . This policy has given the department more time to prevent crime and work on and make arrests in cases of a more serious nature."[18] Although critics had claimed that the "Golden Rule" policy produced negative effects, causing the release of hardened criminals along with first-time offenders, and giving Cleveland the reputation of being an " 'easy town' " for criminals, arrest data show otherwise.[19] The policy's main effect was almost to end arrests for drunkenness and drunkenness-related offenses, which plummeted from 35.4 per 1,000 in 1907 to a low of 1.5 in 1912, and which still remained low at 3.8 in 1915. The overall arrest rate in Cleveland followed suit, dropping from 60.0 per 1,000 in 1907 to 11.6 in 1912. Homicide arrests, not surprisingly, did not reflect these policy-related changes.[20] This fluctuation demonstrates the sensitivity of overall arrests to changes in policing policies, for those arrests that require police initiative dominate the overall arrest figures.

The question then arises: If local police policy made such a radical difference to the arrest rates in Cleveland, how can broad arrest patterns be meaningfully analyzed? Here the value of aggregating arrest data across as many cities as possible appears, for such interesting but analytically unimportant idiosyncrasies wash out in the overall rates. Figure 3 shows that between 1907 and 1915 the aggregate patterns of both overall arrests and initiative arrests fluctuated independently of the rates in Cleveland: Although the Cleveland data contributed to the whole, they did not dominate. Thus, changes in the aggregated rates should be looked at as reflective of more than purely local police arrest practices: The graphed values stand for larger social policy shifts and, perhaps, changes in criminal behavior.

Overall crime, as measured by arrests, dropped between 1860 and 1920, largely because arrests for drunkenness and other public disorder offenses fell. As suggested by some of the earlier studies of individual cities or states, crime waves (or arrest waves) occurred in 1861–2, 1865–6, 1870, 1876, 1907, and 1913–17. These peaks in total arrests were not always paralleled by peaks in arrests for homicide, which occurred in 1862, 1865–73 (with 1867 showing the largest deviation for the whole period), 1893, 1898, and 1908.[21] That the two rate peaks do not always parallel one another is not surprising, for although police behavior acted as a major determinant of the overall

rate, homicide arrests represented the level of interpersonal violence much less than they represented policing changes. That there
was any similarity in the peaks of the two rates is a matter pursued
closely later in this chapter, both because the rates represented
causally different phenomena and because the two rates were, for
this whole period, negatively related. That is, most often, when
overall arrests rose, homicide arrests fell. The Pearsonian R of the
two rates is $-.608$ and the coefficient of determination $.37$, indicating that over one-third of the variation of all arrests saw an inverse
movement in homicide arrests. With this statistically and substantially significant negative relationship, we can infer that 1862, the
early 1870s, and 1908 seem to have had real increases in all forms of
criminal behavior.

The temptation to search, ad hoc, for large events to account for
these specific variations or waves should not distract us from the
more significant observation, which must be emphasized, of the
dramatic overall decrease in the total arrest rate through a turbulent
sixty-year period of industrial growth, urbanization, and immigration. This decrease averaged about .5% for each year over the whole
period, yielding over sixty years a total decline of more than 33%.[22]
Although this decline does not automatically indicate a decline in
the rate of non-arrested offenses, it shows the clear decrease in police labeling of offenders through arrest, indicating that from any
measurable perspective, total urban crime decreased from the Civil
War to World War I. This trend runs contrary to commonsense notions about crime and the growth of industrial cities, immigration,
and social conflict. Further exploration of the arrest data will show
in what cases the commonsense perceptions were correct and how
it is that a vision of increasingly violent and crime-ridden nineteenth and early twentieth centuries arose.

Of course, as the portion of Figure 3 graphing the initiative arrest
rate suggests, a very high proportion of the overall arrest rate comes
from offenses that most people today do not consider "real crimes"
– offenses ranging from drunkenness and disorderly behavior to
vagrancy and just being suspicious. What kind of change has occurred in defining real crime – crime where there is a clear victim,
where someone has unfairly been injured or deprived? We cannot
know the actual extent of crime victimization in cities before 1973,
when the federal government began its systematic studies, and we
must always allow the possibility that arrests for offenses with victims may be more a measure of police activity than of actual criminal behavior. If we have a "willing suspension of disbelief" for a

moment, we can examine an estimate of real crime. Figure 3 plots this estimate, the total arrest rate minus the rate for offenses that clearly required police initiative (note that each may be on a different numerical base). Although the graph presents a picture of remarkable stability in this rate with no significant slope, there is a directional change around 1900, becoming much steeper in 1910. (Slope = − .06; sig. = .09). Breaking the rate into two periods, 1860–99 and 1900–20, confirms this slight change; the earlier period has a slight but statistically significant downward slope, the twentieth century reversing to a slight but statistically significant upward slope. (Slope for nineteenth century = − .26; sig. = .003. Slope for twentieth century = .37; sig. = .006.) Interestingly, this change conforms to apparent patterns outside the United States: For instance, a team of researchers headed by Ted Gurr found a similar but more pronounced nineteenth-century decline and twentieth-century rise in London, Stockholm, and Sydney.[23]

Specific annual peaks in the estimated rate of real crime occurred between 1865 and 1876, and 1905 and 1920. Major dips in the rate came in 1863 and 1894. The greatest peak came in 1870. Lesser nineteenth-century peaks came in 1865, 1873, and 1896, whereas the three twentieth-century peaks came in 1905, 1915–16, and 1919–20.

The general trend of homicides, shown in Figure 4, followed a pattern comparable to the trend exhibited by the estimated real crime rate – a nineteenth-century decline and twentieth-century rise – the major difference being the decade-earlier trend reversal for homicide, 1889 as opposed to about 1899 for estimated real crime. (A division of the estimated crime plot into two periods – before 1882, 1883, and after – yields no slope and no significance for the earlier period, a slope of .18 with a significance of .0006 for the latter.) As a measure of real criminal behavior in society – "out there" – the arrests for homicide should exhibit much more reliability than do other arrests for crimes with victims. The confirmation of two trends gives more credence to the interpretation of arrests for estimated real crime. Some of the peaks in homicide arrests conformed to the real crime peaks, notably 1865 and the whole period between 1865 and 1873. Other homicide peaks were close to peaks in real crime, especially the high homicide era 1906–9, but the homicide peaks of 1892–9 ran directly contrary to a period of low arrests for real crime.[24]

At this preliminary point in our discussion we should not venture causal analyses of the decline in all arrests. Nor should we yet try to account for the nineteenth-century decline and twentieth-century rise in the offenses with victims, a dramatic change that the

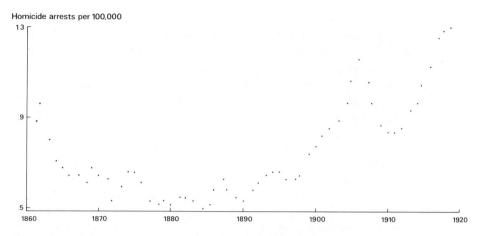

Figure 4. Homicide arrests per 100,000 city population. (Three-year moving averages plotted. Slope of regression line = .001. Significance = .00001.) *Source:* Compiled from annual reports of twenty-three police departments. See Appendix B for list of cities and detail on data and sources.

Gurr study attributed largely to changing police effectiveness. But it is important to maintain our awareness of the presence of the two somewhat contradictory trends in arrests: The declining overall rate delineates a decreasing visibility and activity level of urban police; the shift in the homicide and real crime rate implies a change in the causal linkages among police, offenders, and society. Either urban order actually increased or the demand for order slackened, for, like the overall arrest rate, order arrests (see Figure 3) declined at a steady .5% per year from before the Civil War until after World War I. Although cities may have been becoming more orderly or, conversely, less concerned about public order, it appears they were also becoming more dangerous places to live after the 1880s.

The distracting high points of arrest activity correspond closely with the major social disruptions of the period, wars and depressions. But the interpretive problem, with wars at least, is that they not only created crime waves but also crime troughs – such as 1864, the most dramatic example, when the overall arrest rate fell in one year from 64.4 per 1,000 to 47.9. These crime/arrest waves appearing in the graphs cry out for explanation but, as opposed to the broad trends in the data, they do not lend themselves to statistical analysis, at least without vast amounts of individual and social data that, though collectible, would require the digging of many scholars. Thus, the analysis of crime peaks that follows provides plausible hypotheses rather than the final word.

The crime wave immediately following the Civil War has received some scholarly comment and did not go unnoticed by contemporary observers, particularly prison officials. But the even
greater crime wave of 1862 has gone undiscussed, perhaps because
at the time it seemed small compared to the crime wave in 1855,
perhaps because it was overshadowed by the far greater threats to
political and social order posed by the antidraft urban riots and the
excitement and anxiety of war, or perhaps because it was a part of
the riots – both of the police response and of criminal behavior.[25]
Clearly, the urban arrest peaks of the mid– and post–Civil War
periods must be considered in relationship to one another or, alternatively, perhaps they should be considered as one phenomenon,
with the explanatory burden falling upon the relative lack of arrests
for the final two years of the war. The procedure here will be to
consider the two peaks in the order in which they occurred, returning later to the question of the relative lack of arrests in 1863–4, a
problem that will be partially cleared up in accounting for the two
peaks.

Figure 5 displays the peaks and lows for three broad offense categories during the Civil War period. With a peak in total arrests in
1862 paralleling a larger and longer homicide peak in 1861–3, there
existed the anomaly of a low in estimated crime rates and a concomitant high in initiative arrests. The arrest rate for offenses with victims did not rise until 1865. This suggests that there was a real wave
of interpersonal violence, the police response to which included
massive arrests for public order offenses and relatively few arrests
for crimes with victims, arrests of greater difficulty that require
complaining victims. Then, in 1870, came the second arrest wave
often attributed to the Civil War; with a peak for both total arrests
and estimated real crime arrests, it is the largest in the six decades
under study. (Both greater than 2 standard deviations [s.d.] for residuals. These 2 s.d. peaks remain present in residuals for regressions in Chap. 4, confirming that they were not just caused by the
police.) This peak was paralleled by a moderate peak in homicides.
We must observe, therefore, that the second of the two crime waves
clearly differed in both magnitude and kind from the one occurring
during the war itself.

Scholars have developed five equally appealing explanatory
schemes to account for these two crime waves, several of which
have been asserted to account particularly for the later crime wave.
The first explanation turns to the psychology of individual offenders, showing how war degrades its participants, who are often
unable to behave correctly when they return to normal society.[26]

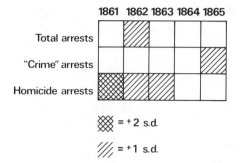

Figure 5. Civil War arrest rate peaks and lows. (Estimated crime may be too low for 1861, 1862.) *Source:* Values from residual plots when arrests regressed against year.

This notion has retained its popularity and commonsense appeal, and was used in the late 1960s to account for the violent behavior of Vietnam veterans. The second explanation finds economic disruption at the root of the crime wave, for the end of the war saw a recession coupled with veterans' difficult reintegration into an economy that had adjusted to their absence.[27] Again, this idea fueled some of the post-Vietnam concern about the high unemployment rates of returning veterans. The third explanation finds community disruption as the cause of the crime wave, the forced geographical and social mobility of the war severing the social ties that presumably make people behave correctly. This explanation depends on the assumption that social norms and community stability make up a fragile lid on an omnipresent powder keg of social disorder. The fourth explanation is more social-psychological, asserting the post–Civil War era to be one of increased anomie, the war having broken up a traditional society.[28] This explanation depends on a somewhat discredited historical view of the Civil War as the sharp divider between a traditional and modern culture. The fifth and final explanation comprehends the crime waves as necessary events in redefining the acceptable boundaries of behavior, first in a war-oriented, then a peace-oriented, society.[29] Although the originator of this interesting idea, Kai Erikson, did not himself apply it to the Civil War era, it is clearly applicable and could form part of the means by which the previous explanatory schemes would have functioned. And although none of these explanations is so logically tight that it excludes the others, and one might feasibly and logically combine them all, my own analysis treads between these five, using elements of each, generally rejecting them individually as causal explanations, opting for simpler and less assumption-bound ideas.

The crime wave of 1862 had been building since the beginning of the war. It represented friction between people trying to loosen previous behavioral norms – mainly single males, many new urbanites, mobilized and freed by the status potential of military service – and the newly created and somewhat insecure police bureaucracies trying both to establish and preserve order in an increasingly uncertain unprecedented situation – a democratic society in a civil war.[30] This increased the clash between those producing the disorderly behavior and urban authorities. Popular resistance to the war and authority also grew in the many well-known riots of 1862 and 1863. There is no direct evidence that the focused war opposition and racism of the riots resulted in many smaller police–civilian skirmishes, although the data certainly imply this. The peak in murders is more puzzling than the other peaks. I have suggested elsewhere that the murder increase represented the conflict between behavior condoned in war (killing) and behavior condemned in society (homicide); this analysis, however, is not altogether satisfactory, for it too easily leans upon the individual motivation and boundary maintenance explanations mentioned above.[31] But the most important reason for the crime peak of 1862 remains the urban bureaucracy's attempt to control one part of a world out of control.

The crime wave of the early 1860s ended suddenly, with the exception of crimes with victims, which rose in 1865. The draft riots of 1863 had triggered the maximum expression of public disorder and its repression by arrests. More important, the army itself, which had been taking men of the crime-prone age group since 1862, had become more effective in recruitment and conscription by 1864, helping to end or at least postpone the disorder until the war's end.[32] As the Civil War sucked up the nation's energy and young men, offenses for crimes with victims began to soar, partially because these were the offenses produced by older, less draft-prone persons. The murder rate behaved most peculiarly, for it fell abruptly after 1863 and rose to a new height briefly in 1870. If we accept the explanation of the earlier and lesser murder peak, that it had been the result of a conflict between war-approved behavior and civilian-disapproved behavior, then the only explanation for the decline in murder arrests is that most homicide producers were at war. The war's end returned them to society and some to an arrest for murder.

The postwar crime wave, which in 1870 reached the greatest peak in total arrests for the whole sixty-year period, does not pose quite the explanatory difficulty of that of 1861–2 (the only overall arrest peak over 1 s.d. when the trend is controlled for). This arrest wave paralleled the most dramatic peak in arrests for offenses with victims, with a concomitant peak in homicide arrests. (Both the estimated crime and homicide rates peaked at over 2 s.d. in 1861, even when the trend is controlled for.) The preservation of military order often leaves individuals incapable of civilian order, and when the end of military order was added to the woes of the socially and economically demoralized returning war veterans, the postwar crime wave seems to have been predictable. If anything, its occurrence in 1870 must be considered a bit delayed. Prison officials, for instance, considered the physically and mentally destructive effects of the war upon veterans as major problems, and some social observers even blamed the tramp wave of 1873 upon war veterans who, they claimed, had learned to enjoy the wandering and economically dependent existence in the army and immediately after the war. Although the increase in tramps in 1873 actually came from the economic disruption of a severe depression, it does become apparent that the postwar crime spree can be attributed to returning veterans.[33]

Writing in the late 1920s, Edith Abbott, a social welfare reformer and historian, described and analyzed the post–Civil War crime wave, the existence and extent of which had been known about since its occurrence. Abbott and earlier observers mistakenly dated the crime wave's peak between 1865 and 1870, but Figures 3 and 4 show the peak to have been 1870, with the exception of homicide, which did show a mild earlier peak. The main reason that people have been mistaken about the timing and intensity of the post–Civil War crime wave is that their sources of information, mainly prison records, have built-in time lags, a real source of measurement disabilities, and were insensitive to the many convicted offenders who were released to the army rather than being imprisoned. (As a consequence of this, the number and proportion of women prisoners increased during the war.) Thus, it is clear that during the Civil War, crime waves would naturally have gone unnoticed by prison wardens, as convicted offenders seldom reached prison, but once the military labor needs had ended, prisons would once again have been affected by the level of arrests.

Abbott cites prison reports from several states to show that a disproportionate number of offenders – an estimated two-thirds to three-fourths of male prisoners – were war veterans, certainly an impressive number when the powerful bargaining position of veterans in pleading for clemency is taken into account. She blames

the degrading effects of military service on the morals and socializa-
tion of military personnel, approvingly quoting a prison report:
" 'The crime cause arises from the demoralization which ever at-
tends on war and armies'."[34]

Although the specific timing of the two crime waves during the
Civil War may be too difficult to explain precisely, their actual occurrence comes as no surprise. The same is true of the lesser crime
wave of the mid 1870s, during a serious depression that caused economic hardship, labor cutbacks, wage reductions, farmer upris-
ings, and a vast geographical movement of people looking for work
– tramps. Much of this disturbance centered around the effects of
the growing railroads, which provided easier long-distance geo-
graphic movement than ever before for the jobless, exacerbated economic fluctuations for the farmers, and created managerial corporate giants sensitive to the power potential in the strengthening
labor movement. The panic of 1872 and following depression
swiftly affected diverse groups through the medium of the railroad,
and arrests soared. As opposed to the crime waves of the war, much
of the wave of the mid 1870s did not have a large component of
police initiative arrests; instead, arrests for offenses with victims,
including to a certain extent murder, climbed most, with two
peaks, 1873 and 1876. (Only 1876 shows a deviation of 1 s.d. when
controlled for trend, less than 1 s.d. after the model in Chap. 4.)
These are grim statistics, for war somehow makes crime more acceptable, if not comprehensible, and the incidence of initiative arrests for public disorder we usually classify as minor. The literate
elite reacted to the obviously serious depression and crime wave
with an angry and quick call for repression. Tramps received most
of the blame for offenses, even though there is no evidence that
they were responsible for the crime wave; of course, the tramps
were victims of the economic disruption just as others were victims
of criminal offenses.[35]

When we consider the modest magnitude of the crime wave of
the mid 1870s, the origins of the public concern about finding a
cause for the events do not become immediately clear, for crimes
with victims (Figure 3) show far smaller peaks for 1873 and 1876
than they do for 1870. And, although it could not be forecast in the
1870s, the next three decades saw arrests remain at a lower level
than expected: The first return to high arrest rates came in the 1870s
for homicide, and not until the first decade of the twentieth century
for other offenses.

In contrast to other arrests, homicides had two moderate troughs in the latter part of the century, one in 1885 and the other in 1897. This latter dip corresponds, of course, to a severe depression, and we should observe that there were also moderate homicide troughs corresponding to the other depression years included in this study. This does not imply any causal relationship, however, for the careful research of Thorsten Sellin on the depression of the 1930s makes clear the lack of any simple economy – homicide relationship.[36] After the homicide peak of the 1875, there was a long decline and then a rise again to the peak of 1908, after which homicides dipped again until the war and the postwar peak of 1917–20. (The 1905 peak disappears when controlled for trend, although it persists in the model of Table 9, Chap. 4, at 1 s.d. The peaks of 1915–20 can be adequately accounted for by this model, however.)

The behavior of the arrests for offenses with victims provides an interesting contrast to the homicide arrest rate. With a peak in 1905, shortly preceding the 1908 homicide peak, the estimated victim crime rate went into abeyance until one decade later, with the peaks of 1915 through 1920 matched only by the activity of the post–Civil War era. This suggests a parallel in causality to the post–Civil War era, both in the early peak, midwar decline as military mobilization bit into the crime-producing age group, then another peak after the soldiers began to return. Although responding to war, the victim crime rate did not always vary with depressions, 1893–7 being the exception, complicating the conclusion of the Sellin study of the Great Depression that there was no direct causal link between depression and crime. (The year 1893 is accounted for by the model in Chap. 4. That is, the peak disappears when changes in police strength, homicide, and lodging rates are considered: This arrest wave had purely system-specific origins.)

On the other hand, the depression of 1905–8 did see a rise in offenses with victims. Although a depression triggered this first crime wave of the twentieth century, the social reaction differed from that in the depression thirty years earlier; public disorder arrests did not rise nearly so much, even though murder again rose to a low peak. This suggests that a subtle but important change had occured both in the producers of the crime and in the police reaction: The police controlled disorder without the magnitude of needless harassment arrests seen previously, and the producers of disorder conducted themselves more circumspectly. The negative aspects of self-control appear in murder rates, for murder is a sign of serious interpersonal conflict, conflict that is not acted out in the larger society but between individuals. Social control mechanisms had apparently become internalized: The result was an increase in interpersonal violence, with a lesser increase than expected in public disorder. This new pattern of handling social tension persisted through the next outburst of crime, attributable to World War I, when public disorder arrests remained lower than almost any point in the post-1885 era.

What happened in this sixty-year period is that the larger social crises most productive of crime waves began to affect the crime-producing population differently, the tensions being internalized to friends and family and away from public disorder. We can predict that if this trend continued, murder and other forms of serious interpersonal violence would reach a natural peak and then begin to decline as crises became even more internalized. Suicide, as an even more internalized form of handling crises, would then replace murder as the response to severe social upheavals.[37] The state of suicide statistics does not allow this prediction to be tested, but Sheldon Hackney's interesting research on the relationship of suicide and homicide suggests that the hypothesis is plausible.[38] Hackney, although not looking for change over time, did find that the suicide/homicide ratio was much greater in the North than in the South, supporting the argument that the internalization of social norms results in an increase in the ratio of suicides to homicides.

Just as criminal behavior that did not lead to arrest cannot be measured in the period under study, neither can we measure police behavior that did not result in some sort of regular reporting. Verbal and physical abuse dealt out by individual officers ("street justice" or police brutality, depending on the perspective of the participants), although an important and feared tool of social control, still goes unmeasured today. But there are two measures that provide proxies for other forms of police harassment: the rate of police initiative arrests that resulted from the offender's appearance or financial status – vagrancy, suspicion, corner lounging – and the dismissal rate, a proxy for trivial arrests, which shows those persons who were arrested and then discharged with no further processing.[39] Unfortunately, dismissals were reported by too few cities to be aggregated before 1875, so the analysis of this rate must cover a period fifteen years shorter than that of the other arrests. We can observe that the nonreporting of dismissals gave the police a harassment tool with no accountability – frivolous arrests with no resulting prosecution.

Arrests for personal condition peaked in the 1870s, remained on a plateau until the turn of the century, and then began a steady decline through 1920. Dismissals, on the other hand, did not peak until the mid 1890s, and then they, too, fell through the early twentieth century. By 1920, both dismissals and arrests for personal condition had fallen below any previous rates.[40] Thus, harassment rates reached high periods during an era of both overall and bureaucratic growth for the police, suggesting that the police were flexing their muscles of intimidation as they moved from one institutionally stable period to another (see Chap. 3). The dismissal rate shows no statistically significant correlations with other arrest rates, whereas the arrest rate for personal condition correlates only with the overall and drunkenness-related arrest rates – a relationship that merely reflects the dependence of these differing arrest rates on police initiative.[41] Evidently, the variation in dismissals and condition arrests resulted from non-criminal-related pressures. This supports the notion that harassment was related to the insecurity of changing status for police forces in the late nineteenth century.

The various arrest data plotted in this chapter demonstrate three trends that should be reemphasized here. First, per capita arrests in major cities declined from 1860 to 1920. Simply considered alone, this information is important, for in these years American cities experienced their most significant growth, immigration, and industrialization. Second, during this era the police developed the strength, organizational forms, and goals that they still maintain. Thus, even if the data were to show stability of arrests, we would express surprise at these results, for the intuitive perspective on all three factors of growth, immigration, and industrialization predicts increases in arrests per capita. That much of the decline in per capita arrests came in those categories most associated with the enforcement of public decorum and morality further contradicts the intuitive perspective. For we might have expected that the police, as formal agents of social control, would have used vigorously all their control techniques to order the cities that they patrolled. Instead, the police produced fewer arrests. Third, the relationship between depression and crime turns out to have been more complex than first appearances might warrant. As opposed to the Great Depression, crime, or more precisely arrests, very often rose during earlier depressions. This suggests that Ted Gurr's observation for Western Europe might well obtain in the United States: Some time in the early twentieth century, the relationship between economic hardship and crime changed, hardship producing more criminal offenses before this period, but producing fewer after the 1920s.[42]

3   *Tramps and children: the decline of police welfare*

> We are confident that the time is not far away when the police
> officer will have the sympathy and regard of not only the indi-
> vidual, but of all those interested in the proper keeping and dis-
> position of the dependent classes. . . .
>
> Col. R. Sylvester, superintendent of police, Washington, D.C.,
> *Proceedings of the Annual Congress of the National Prison Associa-*
> *tion of the United States* (1902)

Overnight lodging in police stations

Other facets of urban police behavior changed along with the
changes in arrest rates, but these other changes formed a more distinct shift in the function of the police in the city. To understand
this shift, it is necessary to focus on a neglected side of nineteenth-
century policing, the social welfare side. In the mid nineteenth century, as now, arrests composed only a small part of daily police
activity. Unfortunately, to accurately quantify and aggregate the
daily impact of police in the nineteenth century and to trace this
over time would be nearly impossible. But the formal, recorded,
and quantifiable side of the non-crime-related police function can
be approached by examining carefully two important welfare services of the police, their provision of overnight lodging for the
homeless and the return home of lost children. These two services
are of interest both in themselves, for what they can show about the
social services of the police, and also in what they can demonstrate
by way of measurable changes. Both these services, but particularly
that of lodging, were part of the repertoire that the police could use
to control the "dangerous class." Ironically, then, the visible decline of police lodging accompanied a less visible shift from class
control to crime control.

Almost from their inception in the middle of the nineteenth century until the beginning of the twentieth, American police departments regularly provided a social service that from our perspective
seems bizarrely out of character – they provided bed and, sometimes, board for homeless poor people, tramps. Year after year

86

these "lodgers," as the police referred to them, swarmed to the police stations in most large cities, where they found accommmoda-
tions ranging in quality from floors in hallways to clean
bunkrooms. Often, especially in the winter or during depression
years, there would be food, usually soup – nothing fancy, but
something. During very bad depression years or harsh winters, the
number of overnight lodgings provided by a police department exceeded all annual arrests. Police attitudes toward lodgers varied
from disgust to sympathy and acquiescence in the role of providing
a place of last resort for the desperately poor. On rare occasions, the
police ventured tentative criticisms of the society that could not
provide better for its members. The attitudes of the lodgers toward
the police, although harder to determine, varied from hostile to
genuinely thankful. But whatever the attitudes, when times were
bad, lodgers appeared at the doors of station houses across the
country, from Duluth to New Orleans and from San Francisco to
New York City.

With the occasional exception of a small town and a generous
officer, the practice of taking in lodgers has disappeared today and
been forgotten. Now the destitute head toward the Salvation Army
headquarters or some city-funded institution. If the police enter
into the process, it is only to give directions, or perhaps suggest an
alternative to a doorway or subway bench. Both the police officer
and the officer's society now envision the roles of the police as stopping crime, preserving order, and controlling traffic. Welfare agencies deal with the noncriminal poor, while police provide a thin
blue line between disorder and order.

An analysis of police lodging practices indicates that there was a
fourth variety of police behavior that political scientist James Q.
Wilson did not delineate in his well-known book *Varieties of Police
Behavior*. In the nineteenth century, the police acted as agents of
class management, a variety of behavior that came under attack
from reformers in the 1890s and that ended around World War I.
The class that the police managed has, linguistically at least, disappeared – the "dangerous class." A descriptive term used throughout the last half of the nineteenth century, the "dangerous class"
appropriately delineated for the larger society the faceless mass of
people who made up the nation's paupers, tramps, and criminals.
Recent research shows that the "dangerous class" had its own hierarchy of five component groups: urban criminals, rural criminals,
rural paupers, urban paupers, and tramps at the very bottom.[1]
From the point of view of the dominant society, such discriminat-

ing description probably would have seemed unnecessary, for the dominant society perceived all persons in the "dangerous class" as threats to the social order. Thus, partly because of this oversimplied idea about the people who threatened society, the police were assigned duties in dealing with the "dangerous class" that were more complex than intended. More than just controlling crime, the police job also included housing of the totally destitute and homeless. The practice of police lodging profoundly affected other police activity, including arrest behavior, in such a manner that to understand either of the two, the police or the homeless urban poor, one must understand the other. Therefore, this chapter focuses on both.

The American economy has required a sizable portion of its labor force to be mobile since the end of the Civil War. Although the nature of the work to be done, the people to do the work, and the labels applied to them have changed considerably, our mobile work force continues to be an oppressed and despised population.[2] Mainly homeless men, some skilled, some unskilled workers, comprised the mobile labor force throughout the nineteenth and early twentieth centuries. Following harvests, railroads, and lumbering operations as the seasons demanded, and wintering in cities during slack periods, these mobile workers were called tramps or hobos, and their population also included the destitute, the incapacitated, and the crazy.[3] Perhaps, as some observers claimed, the nature of the wandering working life produced social misfits. More probably, most of the people perceived as tramps were wandering workers with homes only a part of their life; that is, part of the working-class life course included, for many, a period spent riding the rails and working at temporary jobs.[4] From a non-working-class perspective, tramps would have been perceived as a rough and dangerous crew of twenty- to forty-year-old men forever fixed in their wandering. That it was logically impossible for this group to remain unchanged in age between 1873 and 1893 would not have occurred to non-working-class observers, so it is understandable how behavior that was engaged in by a large part of the working class during a part of their life cycle could have been misperceived as that of a distinct, homeless group of perennial wanderers.

Two other conditions served to further confuse nineteenth-century thinking about tramps. First, in all probability there were at least two distinctly different streams of tramps: one of workers searching for jobs and the other similar to social outcasts making up the skid rows of cities. These quite different social groups, by virtue of their homelessness and poverty, would have appeared in the same food lines, police stations, and sections of town. And from an outsider's point of view, they would have seemed to be one faceless lump of deviant drifters. This confusion of the two kinds of tramps was compounded for, as John Seelye has pointed out, the stereotypical tramp has become a special kind of American anti-hero who helps to define convention, correct behavior, and emphasize the value of hard work.[5] The image of the tramp has discouraged any thinking about the actuality of tramping, and we tend to forget that in the period from the Civil War until World War I unknown thousands spent portions of their lives following work, sleeping on the ground or in police stations and poorhouses.

Police stations offered minimal physical and social amenities to lodgers. Although some station houses had bunkrooms with crude board bunks, more usual were cellars or hallway floors, where the homeless provided their own bedding, most often newspapers. I have never seen any reference to washing facilities, which were common in municipal lodging houses. Some stations provided a night's lodging and nothing more, but many provided a little food – soup, coffee, or bread. Strangely, with the exceptions of Jacob Riis and Walter Wyckoff, most personal narratives about tramping in the late nineteenth or early twentieth centuries make little or no mention of police lodging.[6] That people like Josiah Flynt, for instance, should have been silent on the subject is surprising, for he explored other aspects of tramping lore carefully.[7] Because Flynt went to pains to classify each kind of tramp, from where he slept to what he wore, one needs to speculate about this meaningful omission. Police station house lodging procedures, the very way they hustled lodgers in, allowed them to sleep, and then quickly moved them out early in the morning, almost appear to have been designed to discourage communication between lodgers. Perhaps the lack of fraternization and conversation effectively forestalled the creation of a culture surrounding police lodging; rumors, underground legends, stories, and tall tales could not develop around an institution that essentially disintegrated group consciousness. The homeless did not hang around police stations; they literally "crashed" for a few hours on the floor, then left. Such experience did not make good material for tramp narratives, which tended to dwell on the exotic, nor did it incubate a vocabulary on which writers like Flynt could report. The barren surroundings of the lodging places, their customary three-night limits, and the impossibility of interaction among the lodgers enforced the ancient welfare goal of keeping nonresident undesirables moving – a modern version of "warning out" – and prevented any kind of socially integrative experience to occur through this important form of publicly administered welfare.[8]

The best nineteenth-century description of police lodging from the lodger's point of view may be found in Walter Wyckoff's narrative description of his travels as an unskilled laborer, which includes two different nights he slept in a Chicago police station in the winter of 1891. Wyckoff had spent almost a year working his way from the East Coast as a casual laborer, and not until arriving in Chicago had he experienced the life of the unskilled laborer wintering in an urban area. Up to this point, he had had good luck with warm weather, in finding jobs, and with kind treatment in rural areas. Arriving in Chicago, Wyckoff and an equally penniless friend try to stay out of the cold December rain until past midnight, so they will not have to sleep packed in the crowd with its lice and illnesses, but can use the station hallway. As they huddle in doorways waiting for midnight, a tubercular prostitute gives them a dime, which is enough for two beers and a free lunch. When the time passes midnight, they follow a "score or two" of tramps who have just disembarked from an incoming freight and head toward the station house. Joining the more than 200 lodgers, Wyckoff's friend warns him of lice: " 'If we ain't never had 'em, I guess we'll catch 'em tonight'." Wyckoff adds,

> . . . the words take on a sickening significance as we enter an unventilated atmosphere of foulest pollution, and we see more clearly the frowzy, ragged garments of unclean men, and have glimpses here and there of caking filth on a naked limb . . . . Not a square foot of the dark, concrete floor is visible. The space is packed with men all lying on their right sides with their legs drawn up, and each man's legs pressed close in behind those of the man in front.[9]

Using newspapers for mattresses and wet jackets and boots for pillows, they spend an uncomfortable night in "steaming heat" where most of the men sleep on the bare floor without even coats.

Before allowing them to leave the station, the police ask all the lodgers to check and make sure that nothing has been stolen; then they "file slowly out past the entrance of the kitchen. There stood the cook with an assistant, and he gave to each man as he passed a bowl of steaming coffee and a piece of bread."[10] Although coffee and bread hardly constitute a nourishing breakfast, the lodgers walk out stiff, but at least somewhat rested and dry, provided with some minimal food. Wyckoff's friend lost something in the bargain, however, dignity and the opportunity to get a job, for he finds to his chagrin that at the first really hopeful job interview he has that morning, a louse crawls up his neck and the boss kicks him out. Apparently most of the lodgers held a rather neutral attitude toward the police and the lodging: "Only a few hours before, we had entered the station-house from the streets in eager willingness for any escape from their cold exposure, and now with intensified desire we longed for the outer air at any cost of hardship."[11] The lodgings, clearly, served only to keep the people alive and moving, nothing more; and once revived, the lodgers wanted to escape.

Whereas the accommodations in Chicago amounted to little more than a covered sidewalk and soup kitchen, Boston and New York went one step better, offering the "soft side of a plank."[12] The homeless poor in Boston considered this arrangement as the bottom of the lodging choices, worse than the two cent stale beer dive, where the price of a glass of stale beer also brought sleeping rights. One reformer described Boston's police lodging thus:

> [The men] were huddled together in their damp, reeking clothes, no bed but a hard bench, no food if hungry, turned out at daybreak into the snow of a winter morning . . . this method of caring for the poor tramps was utterly barbarous and heartless, and was imposing upon the police a disagreeable duty, for which no pretense of accommodation was made, either in the way of furnished bedding or . . . food.[13]

Although this description accords with that of the Chicago police given by one who actually had experienced lodging, we should not let the reformer's implied criticism of the police distort the fact that although not luxurious, the police did take care of the destitute. Boston Police Chief Edward H. Savage, in his diarylike account of the Boston police, noted for November 4, 1870: "The Police collected and distributed $1,109.60 among poor persons who were overlooked by others."[14] Thus, in a terse phrase, Savage indicates the position of the police in the social welfare system of Boston – those "who were overlooked by others" came to the police, and though the treatment they received may not have been good, it was something.

Whereas Boston tried to end station house lodging in 1879 by establishing a "Wayfarer's Lodge" that even provided bathing facilities, New York continued the station house lodging practice a good deal longer.[15] However, New York reformers were interested in getting lodgers out of police stations. Theodore Roosevelt, in a report to the Conference of Charities in 1877, described the lodging in New York City station houses:

> These places were filthy in the extreme. The casuals slept on planks, of which there were two tiers. The atmosphere was so foul that it made the policemen, who occupied another part of the building, sick [that is, the off-duty police officers who were required to sleep at the station houses for their reserve duty].[16]

Evidently the crude beds offered did not solve the problem of crowding dirty people into small rooms without ventilation or washing facilities.

Jacob Riis described his experiences in a New York police station lodging room with more drama and pathos than Wyckoff evoked in his description of the Chicago lodging. Riis, a recent immigrant, desperate, penniless, cold, and wet, applied for lodgings in October 1871. Under his coat, he had an equally pathetic and friendless stray dog, but the mean sergeant spied the dog and forced Riis to leave it outside, where it waited. "The lodging-room was jammed with a foul and stewing crowd of tramps. A loud mouthed German was holding forth about the war in Europe, and crowding me on my plank. . . . I smothered my disgust at the place as well as I could, and slept, wearied nearly to death." In the middle of the night, Riis woke up to find his gold locket gone, stolen by one of the "tramp lodgers." Going up to the sergeant to complain, Riis discovered that the sergant too was a German, and he refused to believe that Riis had ever possessed the locket. At this point, Riis lost his temper again (he had started a fight with the German lodger earlier in the evening) and got thrown out of the station. His dog, waiting on the steps, bit the doorman, who promptly bashed its brains out. Riis started throwing paving stones at the station, and finally two police officers marched him to a ferry to New Jersey.[17] A few days later, Riis stayed in an unused cell in Camden, New Jersey, where the police captain gave him breakfast and money to shine his boots and cross the Delaware. This positive experience served as a contrast to the misadventure in the "pig-sty in the New York stationhouse,"[18] which had left him with a firm hatred of both stationhouse lodging and lodgers. Riis's experience is of interest for several reasons. First, it catalyzed his later reform ideology, based on hatred of the tramps and their hosts, the police. Second, it demonstrates the meaning of "indiscriminant" relief, for Riis, a deserving young immigrant, resented being housed with old and smelly tramps, especially Germans. Finally, Riis's attitude toward the po-

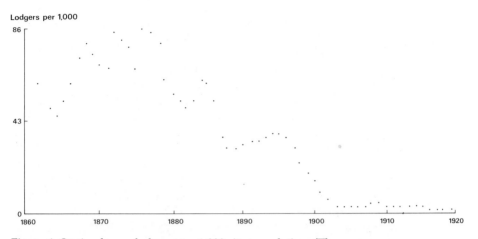

Figure 6. Station house lodgers per 1,000 city population. (Three-year moving averages plotted. Slope of regression line $= -1.53$. Significance $= .00001$.) *Source:* Compiled from annual reports of twenty-three police departments. See Appendix B for lists of cities and detail on data and sources.

lice is important, for it parallels the attitudes of middle-class persons today, who become resentful when stopped for minor traffic infractions, an attitude that implicitly asks the police to differentiate between the "dangerous" and nondangerous classes. For, in Riis's mind, the sergeant had made an error in ignoring Riis's class superiority to the mass of lazy tramps.

A major question to ask about lodging is, how many? Was this a phenomenon that involved relatively few people or many? For if police lodging involved only a few tramps and out-of-work wanderers, it is really little more than a curious way of handling an urban problem. Figure 6 charts the rates per 1,000 persons of lodgers for the twenty-three cities that were ranked as the largest in 1880. The populations of the cities and the annual number of lodgers were combined, the lodgers divided by the population, and the result multiplied by 1,000: The resulting figure is graphed as the number of lodgers per 1,000 population. The peak year of 1869 shows about 89 lodgers per 1,000 annually. In other words, by this measure slightly less than 1 urban person in 10 spent a night in a police station in 1869. This astonishingly high number does not really give a satisfying answer, and some speculation is in order to give it any meaning.

The work of John J. McCook helps to refine these estimates. Early in the 1890s McCook, a professor at Trinity College, made a "census" of tramps by having police officers around the country question tramps.[19] The number of returns for his sample must have seemed enormous at the time, 1,349 "more or less complete autobiographies," but it obviously was only a tiny proportion of tramps. Thus it probably was biased, but it is something concrete to work with. From his census, McCook estimated that 20% of the tramps stayed at police stations, and 10% stayed at poorhouses, the rest using other forms of lodging or sleeping outside. His sample was all males. The difficulty with the figures is, of course, that if police officers did the enumerating, one would expect that a very high proportion of those questioned would have been lodgers, not just 20%. If we use this figure as a multiplier for the 89 per 1,000 rate, we get a stupendous result of nearly 450 persons per 1,000 on the road as tramps. And because we seem to be dealing mainly with males, this raises the rate to 90 in 100 males, clearly impossible. Most of these tramps stayed more than once at police stations, and to make our rates meaningful, we need to know just how long the average tramp spent on the road before making some kind of permanent settlement: How many individuals accounted for the rate of 89 per 1,000? One-half of McCook's respondents claimed to have been on the road only one week, and 80% are covered when the time on the road is lengthened to one month. If we assume that the respondents tended to play down the time that they had been tramping, especially because the questions were being put to them by police officers, one month may be a good median for the annual time on the road. If 20% of this month were spent lodging at police stations, we reduce the rate of 89 per 1,000 to about 15, because each individual on the road accounted for about six nights per year of station house lodging. Again, the rate should be multiplied, for the population "at risk" was largely over twenty years old (McCook found 5% under twenty) and male; if 60% of the population was of tramping age, and 50% was male, then the 15 per 1,000 figure should be raised to 45 per 1,000 of the population at risk. Thus, about 1 adult male in 23 could expect to know the experience of station house lodging. And if we make the assumption that these men had been or would become heads of families with the average size of five, then one family in five would have had a member who had lodged in a police station. Lodging, we begin to suspect, was something experienced or understood by many if not all poor Americans.

McCook, using methods known only to himself, estimated the total population of tramps at 45,845 men. This is about 7.3 per

Table 2. *Annual rates of tramps per 1,000 city population*

Year	Franklin County, Ohio[a]	23 cities[b]	Columbus[c]
1867	.05	67.3	
1868	.49	75.6	
1869	.88	89.5	
1870	2.17	78.0	
1871	2.36	62.8	
1872	2.74	36.4	
1873	3.16	44.4	
1874	11.34	42.3	
1875	2.34	56.3	
1876	4.03	53.1	
1877	1.42	70.4	
1878	3.73	61.1	
1879	2.58	50.3	
1880	2.05	58.3	
1881	.97	51.1	
1882		43.7	
1883		51.3	50.7

[a]From Eric Monkkonen, *The Dangerous Class: Crime and Poverty in Columbus, Ohio, 1860–1885* (Cambridge, Mass.: Harvard University Press, 1975), 120.
[b]Annual rates based on not less than four cities and up to twenty-two for any one year.
[c]From City of Columbus, *Annual Report of the Board of Police Commissioners* (Columbus, 1884), 17.

10,000 total population or 22 per 10,000 population at risk, considerably smaller than my estimate. McCook's estimate is difficult to criticize, for he only says it was "made from the best attainable data." But because he used only information returned from mayors and police chiefs, my surmise is that he was unaware of the annual police report data that provide the basis for my estimation.[20] However, McCook's estimates do stand as a warning to those who try to estimate the size of this large floating population, and suggest that we try one more estimation.

As noted by McCook, many lodgers did not stay at police stations, his returns showing that 10% stayed in poorhouses. Although Columbus, Ohio, was not one of the twenty-three largest cities in 1880, there are data available that allow a comparison of the tramps going through its poorhouse to the number of lodgers at its police station. Between April 1873 and March 1874, 3,175 lodgers were taken by the Columbus police, an annual rate of 50.7 per 1,000 population. The poorhouse, on the other hand, had admittance rates varying from 11.3 per 1,000 in 1874 down to .97 in 1881. Although considerably lower than the police lodging rate, the poorhouse rates are based on the population of the whole county, for which it was responsible, whereas the police lodging rates are based on the city alone. The county population was approximately twice that of the city alone, so we might double the rates for the poorhouse. Nevertheless, the poorhouse rates are a good deal smaller than the rates for police lodging, ranging from 2% to 40% of the one year for which we have the police lodging data. McCook's returns, then, seem to be high in their estimate of two lodgers at the station house for every tramp in the poorhouse. Again, this may be a bias introduced by the enumerators for McCook, police officers whose very presence cautioned tramps against more realistically high estimates of how often they stayed at police stations. Table 2 compares national lodging rates to those for the Franklin County, Ohio, Infirmary and to the one year for which we have data on the Columbus police lodging. The one year from the Columbus police gives very plausible results when compared to the more broadly based rates, whereas the very highest proportion of the poorhouse to police rates, which occurs in 1874, is one to four. This suggests that although tramps told McCook's enumerators that they stayed in police stations about 20% of the time, and in poorhouses about 10%, the ratios may have been more like 10% poorhouse to 40% police station. Thus, this estimation suggests the figure of one male for every five families experiencing a police station lodging should be halved to one male for every ten families.

This complex series of approximations demonstrates the difficulty of estimating the extensiveness of lodging. But whereas accuracy may not be possible, or even necessary, we can estimate that between 10% and 20% of the U.S. population in the late nineteenth century came from families of which one member had experienced the hospitality of a police station.

Even at this minimal level, gradations in quality of service to the poor appeared, racial discrimination apparently keeping blacks out of the pool of mobile workers or out of the police lodging rooms. Relatively little information on the identities of the lodgers has survived, except for that of a fragmentary nature. For instance, the original list of tramps staying overnight in the Third Precinct Station House in Washington, D.C., in the early 1890s has been preserved, and this list has racial designations. Although black people accounted for almost a third (31.2%) of the population of Washington in 1890, only 14.2% of the tramps asking for police shelter were black.[21] To the west, an even smaller proportion of black tramps used the Columbus poorhouse from 1860 to 1885; 1.6% of the tramps were black, compared to 4.1% of the city's population, again showing that police discrimination against blacks exemplified a larger pattern of racial discrimination in public assistance.[22]

Further confirmation of racial bias in nineteenth-century police service comes from the survey of fourteen cities conducted by J.J. McCook during the depression of 1893, which found a similar pattern of black underrepresentation in police station house lodgings: Only 1% of the total lodgers were black, with no easily comparable population statistic.[23] The only population of the homeless poor that had an overrepresentation of blacks was in Chicago in the first three years of the twentieth century, where in a detailed survey of 1,000 homeless men, 4.2% were black, higher than the 1.8% to 2.0% of the city's population that was black. But this case does not so much indicate a different situation or change over a decade, as that a large number of poor and homeless blacks were unable to demand assistance from the most commonly used tax-supported sources, poorhouses and the police. The men in the Chicago sample all represented the most destitute and dissolute wanderers, having entered the survey sample by being referred to the Chicago Bureau of Charities. Alice Solenberger, author of the Chicago report, noted that different types of people applied for aid at different places, and commented that "able-bodied workmen will be most numerous among those who seek shelter at the municipal lodging house."[24] In other words, only when people seeking aid at the least discriminatory agency are examined do we find a fair representation of poor blacks.

The two decades between the depressions of 1873 and 1893 saw attempts by early progressive reformers to end police station lodging, but it did not end nor was there an improvement in the quality of lodging. In Chicago, the need for lodging was so acute that the lodgers who could not fit on the "stone corridors" of the police stations were put into the city hall, with the usual newspaper mattresses. The rules at city hall were more lax than at the station houses, and there was a constant threat of fire because of smoking.[25] Apparently Walter Wyckoff had sought police lodging before this practice was introduced, for he makes no mention of it. The Boston Wayfarers' Lodge, created to end station house lodging, closed its doors early in the evening, and lodgers continued to go to the police station. When the police were ordered to admit no more lodgers, and the Wayfarers' Lodge stayed open until 2:30 A.M., the police of nearby towns ended up accommodating the excess lodgers.

In New York City, the police closed their station house lodgings only after a long struggle culminating in 1896, and the homeless were sent to the municipal lodging house, where conditions were reportedly worse than at the police station.[26] This is difficult to believe, for since mid century lodging in New York had been grim. James F. Richardson discusses lodging in New York City police stations mainly in terms of the danger that the lodgers created for the police – not danger from violence, but from disease. One can only imagine the danger to which the lodgers themselves were exposed. The infamous Tombs, located near the Five Points slum, in the 1850s "had the highest number of arrests, the highest number of absentees, and the most requests for lodgings. Captain Matthew Brennan reported that sewage constantly seeped in and that no one could possibly stay there in wet weather." The police surgeon reported, " 'More miserable, unhealthy, and horrible dungeons cannot well be conceived of'."[27] Richardson suggests that the presence of diseased lodgers accounted for the high incidence of illness and tuberculosis among police officers. By the late 1860s, police surgeons were asking to have lodgers removed from the stations, not for reform or social concern, but " 'to protect the health of the police force'."[28] And by the 1890s the concern for the well-being of police officers who had to be near the lodgers had spread to the lodgers themselves. Jacob Riis, who had slept in station house lodgings, claimed that " 'never was parody upon Christian charity more corrupting to human mind and soul than the frightful abomination of the police lodging-house, sole provision made by the municipality for its homeless wanderers'."[29] Not until Theodore Roosevelt became a police commissioner were his and Riis' long-standing complaints about station house lodgings finally heeded.

If it was true that the police officers were infected by contagious diseases carried into the station houses by lodgers, we can surmise the threat was much greater for nondiseased lodgers. Strangely, Wyckoff, who was usually a perceptive and accurate observer, did not mention disease other than lice. Of course, he spent time in a Chicago station house, but no evidence shows it was any cleaner than those of New York. In John McCook's tramp "census," he did ask his contributors the extent of diseases "of special loathsomeness, both known to be contagious" among the tramps, and he found 10% had the disease associated with physical uncleanness and 5% had the disease associated with moral uncleanness.[30] Leah Feder suggests that these diseases were tuberculosis and syphilis respectively, but it is not clear if the total proportion of diseased tramps came to 10% or 15%.[31] My suspicion is that 10% is the correct figure; that is, 5% of the tramps had both syphilis and tuberculosis, and 5% had only tuberculosis. Nine percent of the tramps entering the Columbus poorhouse had some form of noted physical ailment, ranging from "froze feet" to syphilis; thus that 10% of the tramp sample was found to have "loathsome" diseases by less experienced observers seems not unreasonably high.[32] Although the disease rate of 10% must not have been comforting to the lodgers, it should be used to temper the allegations of the danger posed to police officers from lodgers, and indicates that not every lodger carried the germs of death. Rather, we should interpret the nineteenth-century observers' perceptions of disease metaphorically as perceptions of filth, which clearly was a dominant feature of police boarding.

Gaining insight into the life of station house lodgers is difficult because first-hand accounts of the police lodging practices of the nineteenth century, even when including reformers' descriptions, remain rather slender. Only Walter Wyckoff's has the concrete detail and immediacy that indicate his interest in having a story to tell rather than an ax to grind. A better, and far more numerous, set of primary sources comes from the annual reports published by most police departments. Although one might expect a consistent propolice, antitramp bias in such sources, they in fact contained expressions of an extensive range of attitudes, from revulsion at the sight of the jobless and homeless to more sympathy than shown by reformers or ex-tramps. The insight and sensitivity shown by some nineteenth-century police chiefs should destroy some of our contemporary prejudices about the early police.

As an example of a slightly negative kind of police attitude, we may examine the "Report of the Police Department" of Cincinnati covering the year 1876. The police superintendent first notes that "75,331 indigent persons without homes" had been sheltered and lodged. He goes on to say he wished to avoid discussing the broader implications of tramping, for it "has become a social problem that I leave to others to discuss and solve. That they are a burden and nuisance to the police, is clear, and that they consume much of the charity that should go to our own worthy poor is also true. Work," he continues as he warms to the subject, "they will not, and rarely can they be convicted of vagrancy or sent to the work-house. Even if this were possible, it would be doubtful policy, as our prisons and houses of correction would soon be taxed beyond their limit to care for them. One thing seems certain from past experience, they will continue a charge until something can be done to make them work, and thus render their stay here less inviting."[33] Clearly, this superintendent felt that tramps were homeless because of their own laziness; on the other hand, their care, burden that it was, automatically fell upon the police. In a sense, he is saying that he wishes tramps were not there, but his social analysis of their meaning goes no farther. His thinking is similar to that of the character in Harold Pinter's play *The Caretaker* – tramps are "work-shy." More than that, the superintendent is pleading for help, for "others" to straighten out the social mess that left almost 200 tramps per night at police stations in Cincinnati.

The police surgeon in Providence, Rhode Island, in his report to the chief for 1891, expressed a more vigorously negative and hostile attitude toward lodgers, although he seemed more concerned about the dirt and odors tramps brought into the Central Police Station. Pointing out that the building, not originally intended for use as a police station, had been also a courthouse and lodging house for thirty years, he indicates that it was simply handling more people than its sewage system could accommodate. During 1891, 3,000 tramps were given lodging, but the surgeon does not explain whether or not these were individuals housed for several nights, or if there were 3,000 lodgings in all. The surgeon continued:

> The tramps' army, as a rule, are filthy, vermin infested, and possess physical and moral conditions favorable to contracting and transporting contagious diseases. Tramps should not, therefore, be lodged in police stations. If the great and growing army of tramps must, as a social evil, be provided with food and shelter at the city's expense, then, in my opinion, barracks should be built as the tramps' quarter, to be under police control, and daily fumigated.[34]

This version of the surgeon's perception of police lodging is interesting because he implies that the reason for lodging was to keep a group of people who were by their very nature a "social evil" under police surveillance – "police control." Thus, whereas the Cincinnati superintendent, somewhat like Chief Savage of Boston, seemed to see the police as the bureaucracy that dealt with a chaotic problem in society, the Providence police surgeon saw the police as agents of social control over the "dangerous class," a part of which was the "growing army" of tramps.

The surgeon's report to the chief contrasts markedly with that made by Providence's Chief Child for 1889, a report expressing far more sensitivity and understanding of tramps. "There is no doubt that a large amount of sneak thieving is done by them [tramps], but I think that in the main many of the reports are exaggerated. The class that seeks lodgings at the station house is composed mainly of roving operatives and coasting seamen, whom the rigors of winter have placed in destitute circumstances."[35] Within this small police department, then, at least two somewhat conflicting attitudes toward the lodgers found formal recording, with the chief of police having the much more sympathetic stance and the police surgeon the more hostile and critical one. Extrapolating from these conflicting attitudes, we might conclude that the uniformed, professional police officer knew more about the lodgers and had a more accurate perception of their difficult life than did the professional medical person, presumably representing the views of the enlightened reformer.

Even more interesting, though less original and more guarded than the occasional paragraph or two in the typical chief's annual report, is the long letter on poor relief written by the major and superintendent of the Washington, D.C., police, William McDye. In his letter and the reply to it from the executive committee of the citizens' relief fund, both of which McDye included in his annual report, he describes the work of the police in relief efforts for the winter of 1883–4. He gives a careful accounting of the money raised at a public meeting, called at his urging by the Citizens' Executive Committee for Relief of the Poor. Although his description of the food, clothing, and coal distributed by police officers has inherent interest, more important for this analysis is the manner in which the police initiated the relief efforts. McDye explained how one black family in eight and one white family in thirty received assistance. He continued:

> This is a large percentage of our population to be dependent upon charity. And we are liable every year to have an experience similar to that of the passing one. Cold weather exposes poverty. At the beginning of the severe weather the poor thronged the Police Stations, and were to be seen going from door to door appealing for food and fuel to keep starvation away and temper the wintry blasts. . . . The labor devolving upon the Police Department in the aid given to the Committee in its efforts to relieve the poor, was performed cheerfully by the Department's subordinates, to whom belongs whatever credit may be due for successful work.[36]

McDye continued to suggest that a poor person self-help organization be created, similar to one in Geneva, Switzerland, apparently having forgotten about the difficulties of doing so in a transient population. His specific solutions should not hold our attention, however, but rather the urgent necessity he felt in proposing any solution. In a sense, his solutions to the problems of destitution remove the poor from the aegis of police responsibility, but very clearly the Washington police felt the original responsibility to take initiative. This perception of the police role in public welfare must also have been felt by the poor who "thronged" the police stations, demonstrating the special relationship between police and the poor in the nineteenth and early twentieth centuries, a relationship that had elements of conflict in police arrest practices but also elements of help and cooperation that, on occasion, extended beyond returning lost children to their parents.

One can argue that the police welfare practices functioned to keep the "dangerous class" away from the "more favored classes," as McDye called them, just as police arrest practices were designed to preserve the order demanded by the "more favored classes." From this point of view, the Washington police call for a public meeting to solicit aid for the poor contained no contradictions, as it was a necesary part of the preservation of the boundary between order and disorder, the poor and the nonpoor. But this argument does not eliminate the fact that the police were the ones who felt the initial responsibility to the poor, and were also the agency to which the poor appealed. For whatever functional reasons, the police did care for destitute people. "Poor persons who were overlooked by others," in Boston's Chief Savage's appropriate phrase, were not overlooked by the police.

There is an implied hypothesis in the relationship I have described here. If the police did act out of a genuine concern for the welfare of the poor, then police administration of welfare should have affected police behavior toward the poor. This hypothesis can be tested if we make several assumptions about the means of measuring police behavior. Ideally, negative police behavior toward poor people should be measured through incidents of police brutality in dealing with the poor, and police welfare should be measured through a combination of the amount of aid administered, the number of police officers who actually were involved in giving assistance, and the number and kind of poor people aided. Needless to say, such ideal measures are not available, even today. However, it is possible to build on the arrest data established in Chapter 2 with two additional variables that will show some broad patterns of police behavior toward the poor. The two additional variables are the total number of police personnel and the total annual number of lodgers, each adjusted per capita.

The total number of arrests made annually by a police department measures a complex of things, not just police interaction with poor people. But when the composition of an annual arrest rate is considered, it appears to be a good substitute measure. Most arrests in the nineteenth century were for misdeameanors, with very few for what we would consider "serious" crimes, that is, crimes with suffering victims, crimes involving a property loss, a loss of dignity, or physical harm. Further, most arrests occurred as the result of police initiative, or, in other words, there was no complainant pressing the police to action. Rather, the individual police officer observed an offense, made a decision whether or not to take the initiative, and then made an arrest. Most of these offenses were included in the various public drunkenness charges and other catchall categories such as vagrancy, "corner lounging," or being a "suspicious person." For example, 62.5% of all arrests in eighteen of the largest cities in 1880 came under the categories of drunkenness, drunk and disorderly, suspicion, vagrancy, or corner lounging. In the same year, on the other hand, for sixteen cities only .097% of all arrests were for all degrees of homicide, manslaughter and murder. These figures should not be taken to represent the relative proportions of kinds of bad behavior in the community, but they demonstrate the lower boundary estimates of the percentage of arrests that resulted from an officer making a decision to arrest without the backup of a complainant.

It can be assumed that in the nineteenth century, as today, the majority of people arrested for all offenses were relatively poor, or people with only a modicum of wealth, status, or prestige; the reasons for this have not altered – age structure, public time at risk, police bias and, perhaps, proclivity towards offending.[37] This is not to say that those arrested were the same people as those who applied for lodging, nor does it mean that those who were arrested were of exactly the same status as the lodgers. Probably those arrested for drunkenness and vagrancy were almost as poor as those who applied for lodging, but it does cost money to get drunk. And when a two cent glass of stale beer will also buy a night's lodging, as it did in Boston, we must assume that those arrested for violations involving drunkenness may have been slightly better off at the moment of their arrest than those who applied for lodging.

Lodgers, at the least, watched their expenditures more carefully. If the arrest data were disaggregated so as to separate misdemeanors from felonies, then the assumptions would be different, for some evidence shows that persons who were arrested for felonies had, as a group, somewhat higher status than did the destitute.[38] To refine and clarify the status assumption, then let us assume that whereas the majority of those persons who were arrested by the police were of the same class as those who applied for lodgings – the "dangerous class" – they held a somewhat higher status within the "dangerous class." Thus, overall arrest rates may stand as a measure of police behavior toward the "dangerous class," at least part of which included the poor.[39]

The total number of police department personnel per capita provides the basis of the measure of police strength rather than the number of on-the-street officers for several reasons. In theory, for a small department the ratio of on-the-street officers to all personnel is large, for there is not enough nonpatrol work to justify the additional staff. In effect, then, the patrol officers also do more nonpatrol work to compensate for the lack of nonpatrol personnel. In a large department, the ratio of on-the-street officers to all personnel is smaller because there is greater specialization, the nonpatrol personnel giving the on-the-street officer greater power through technical help and more time to patrol. There is also an additional reason to use total police personnel as a measure of police strength. For the major U.S. cities, there was great variety in the organization and titles of police departments. Some departments had roundsmen, who were actually high-ranking patrol officers. In others, roundsmen were the equivalent of sergeants, while sergeants were the equivalent of lieutenants. And in others, sergeants did patrol duty. As a result, there is no reliable way of comparing and aggregating on-the-street officers from city to city.

Police departments reported annual lodging statistics with almost the same regularity as they did arrest statistics. Of course, we should conceive the figure as the annual number of overnight lodgings given by the police, not individual lodgers, because we have no way to control for repetitive lodgers, "revolvers" as they were called in New York City.[40]

The hypothesis that the taking in of lodgers affected police arrest behavior can be tested with both simple correlations and partial correlations of the relevant variables: These correlations are displayed in Table 3. The results make apparent that the taking in of lodgers powerfully influenced police arrest behavior, but the direc-

Table 3. *Lodging influence on police arrest behavior*

	Total arrests	Police	Lagged police	Lod-gers	Lagged lodgers
Total arrests		−.45	−.46	.79	.75
Initiative arrests	.80	−.30 (.009)	−.41	.69	.60
Police strength	−.45			−.73	
Partial correlations					
Total arrests with police controlling lodgers	.32 (.007)				
Total arrests with lagged police controlling lagged lodgers	.19 (.079)				
Initiative arrests with police controlling lodgers	.409				
Initiative arrests with lagged police controlling lagged lodgers	.04[b]				

Unless noted in parentheses, R is significant at greater than .001. All varia-bles in population-based rates.
[b]Not significant.

tion is problematic. An increase in police strength alone correlated with a decrease in overall arrests, but by controlling for lodging this relationship reverses. Moreover, as shown by the high positive cor-relation between order arrests and lodging, the performance of wel-fare functions did not increase police tolerance of public disorderly behavior, but decreased tolerance. The more homeless poor the po-lice accommodated, the more they also took the initiative in making public order arrests. Was this a case of familiarity breeding con-tempt? Or did the awareness of the multitude of poor, sober, des-perate lodgers increase police frustration and despair in dealing with those people who could afford to drink? To put it another way, did the police officers distinguish, as did reformers, between the deserving and nondeserving poor?

This statistical relationship between police lodging and police behavior demonstrates what was, in fact, the broad social function of pre–World War I urban police, the management of the "dangerous class." Their managerial tools included both supportive techniques–

food, lodging, and, in some cases, assistance in job hunting – as well as destructive techniques – beatings, contempt, and arrests for offenses ranging from drunkenness to the most vague offense of all, that of being a suspicious person.[41] The hostility of welfare reformers toward the police came partly from the competition that police lodging gave the reform schemes of this rising new profession. And, late in the nineteenth century, the management and control of the "dangerous class" became a multi-agency chore, the police dealing only with criminal behavior, professional social welfare workers handling other forms of disreputable behavior such as tramping.

Social welfare reformers did not like the practice of lodging the homeless in police stations. Their writings never quite clearly express whether this was because the lodging and lodgers were dirty and uncomfortable, because the police were indiscriminate in who they aided, or because there was no effort to uplift the lodgers and thereby end the evil of tramping. As a result of this ambiguous hostility, writings on the subject sound either antipolice or antitramp, but almost never humanitarian. That reformers concerned about the welfare of the poor should attack a practice so clearly beneficial to the working poor makes sense only when we remember that the same era saw intensifying criticism of the cross-class practice of taking boarders in private homes. A sensible practice for easing people through family cycle transitions, through unemployment crises, and for allowing women to contribute to the family income, boarding conflicted with the growing strength of Victorian decorum, and had to slowly yield to the pressure of reformers.[42] Lodging, like boarding, represented a flexible and inexpensive way of meeting social and economic needs; its demise would create social welfare problems that continue to plague modern urban society.

In one sense, the fight against police lodging was part of a larger battle led by Josephine Lowell, among others, against the giving of outdoor relief, a form of aid that she felt merely perpetuated poverty. Although the giving of lodging or soup was not literally outdoor aid, it worked to the same ends because no demands were made upon those aided. The giving of lodgings without some sort of work in return encouraged laziness and degraded the applicants even further. Lowell voiced the same criticism of municipal lodging as she did of any kind of relief assistance that did not attempt to reform and demand work. Discussing relief of the unemployed during the winter of 1893–4, she wrote,

It was no kindness to feed and lodge him [the tramp], and to do no more. Such a life is degrading, and either more or less should have been done. If the man could have been held and trained and influenced for good, and put in the way of decent self-support, by all means it should have been done. . . . But to offer free meals and lodgings . . . was an injury to every individual man. . . .[43]

Probably the most dramatic fight against police lodging practices occurred in New York City, where it took the likes of Theodore Roosevelt and Jacob Riis, together with a host of reformers, to force the police to end the practice. Roosevelt had been against the practice since at least 1877, whereas Riis had harbored a grudge against the police since his cruel treatment late in 1870. Riis's vindictiveness was, he claims, the beginning of his reform work, but he waited twenty-six years before he tasted the "sweetness of revenge." Riis described how he and Roosevelt in 1896

. . . together drove in the last nail in the coffin of the bad old days, by persuading the Charter Revision Commission to remove from the organic law of the city the clause giving to the police the care of vagrants, which was the cause of it all. . . . It was never the proper business of the police to dispense charity. They have their hands full with repressing crime. It is the mixing of the two that confuses standards and makes trouble without end for those who receive the "charity" and even more for those who dispense it.[44]

Riis took Roosevelt on a 2 A.M. visit to the same station where he had been mistreated years before. The lodging room remained unchanged, and Riis told Roosevelt the story of his dog. Roosevelt responded: "'I will smash them to-morrow'." Within a week, on February 15, 1896, the chief of police closed forever the lodging rooms. "The battle was won. The murder of my dog was avenged. . . ."[45]

A year later, Edward T. Devine, in an article on the means of eliminating the "Shiftless and Floating City Population," analyzed the evils of police lodging in a more rational and less personal manner than Riis. "Vagrants crowded to the city in vast numbers, especially in the early autumn. If unable to pay for a cheap lodging they were entertained in a free police station lodging house. . . . Under such favorable conditions, the number of the floating and the shiftless steadily grew, and became increasingly dangerous."[46] In other words, the first step in eliminating the "dangerous class" was to end indiscriminate relief, epitomized by police lodging. Devine insisted, contrary to many reformers, that the city was a good place for the shiftless vagrants for, once police lodging had been ended, there they could be forced into controlled situations and reformed. "The whole of the repressive and remedial work can be done more efficiently and with better opportunities to watch the results than in the country."[47]

Concurrent with the closing of police lodging rooms in New York City, the Raines Law ended free lunches given out in bars, which had been the sustenance for many of the homeless. The result was that "the tramp was literally left out in the cold, cursing reform and its fruits," as Riis happily reported.[48] If the attitude of the reformers seems cruel to us, it also did to many people at the time. One of the "Yellow Newspapers" printed a cartoon showing a shivering man standing in the snow, labeled "deserving but out of work." He looks at a sign beside a thermometer standing at zero, which proclaims: "Police Station Lodging for Unfortunate Wayfarers. Closed. By order of T. Roosevelt." Riis dismissed such criticism as the misguided thinking of a "few tender-hearted and soft-headed citizens."[49]

The end of police lodging foretold the end of an era when poor people, tramps, ethnic minorities, and criminals were all conceived as being a part of the "dangerous class." The function of policing also changed, the earlier emphasis on management of the "dangerous class" turning to the repression of crime and the management of a new form of urban disorder – automobile traffic. From the point of view of the homeless poor this change was bad, for they were forced to beg, save enough for commercial lodging houses, or go to municipal lodging houses with their work tests, which usually involved some form of meaningless make-work such as piling and unpiling wood.[50] This change also meant an end to police familiarity with the difficulties of the life of the poor, although police arrest behavior did not get more vigorous but actually decreased. In a sense, even though police departments are numerically large today, their importance in the life of the city has changed, and they are no longer charged with the management of urban problems ranging from stray dogs and open sewers to the homeless poor. The nineteenth-century urban police, charged with the job of making order out of chaos, which they did quite well, provided unemployment relief and repressed disorder at the same time. And in their efforts to provide welfare, the nineteenth-century police provide a model for today, when more and more the concepts of community police and service policing are demanded. The model is not quite so benign as community and service police advocates wish, and it may be that contemporary reform demands conceal a desire to return to police management of the "dangerous class," when increases in police aid to the poor paralleled increases in arrests for disorderly behavior or for being a suspicious person or vagrant.

The police care of lost children

> Go up to the kind policeman,
> And simply say,
> I've lost my way,
> Please tell me what to do.
>
> Song for children in the late 1940s – a fuzzy recollection

In 1895, an article with detailed illustrations on "The Lost Children of New York" appeared in *Harper's Weekly*. The best description of lost children and the police in the nineteenth century, the article also contains the predictable amusing and sorrowful anecdotes. The opening anecdote is important, however, for it makes the point that a street vendor selling rabbits knows immediately what to do with a small lost child –get the police. The author emphasizes three other points: First, few people think about the problem of lost children; second, a "quietly ordered" "system" run by the police handles the problem; and third, all kinds of city dwellers use this police service, a point emphasized by a graphic portrait of waiting parents showing a humble, poor mother, an anxious, wealthy father, a bewildered police officer (apparently a bit of humor – even the children of the police get lost), and an exhausted laborer. The author expresses surprise at the small number of black children, at the inexplicable decline in the lost children handled by the police, and at the older children who get lost – children in from the country shopping with their parents and would-be runaways. He also asserts that "Jews and foreigners" on the East Side deliberately take advantage of this police service to obtain both free child care and food for their children while they work. This observation clearly represented the police point of view, which had been driving the number of lost children handled by them downward, even earlier than 1895. Thus within this one article the main dynamics of the parent–police interaction appear.[51]

There are three major, dissimilar reasons to discuss lost children in a book on the development and behavior of police. First, like lodging, the return of lost children was an important police service.

Second, unlike lodging, it was a service of low visibility that the uniformed police, with their hierarchical organization, could uniquely provide. Third, from a methodological perspective, the annual counts of lost children returned to their parents provide us with the one indicator of police activity that was not open to easy manipulation; that is, the count conformed to the actual number of lost children returned by the police. Most other statistics generated by the police were probably subjected to manipulation at one time or another, and it is for this reason that most of the arrest analysis in this book focuses on the aggregated data of several police departments – the individual manipulations are randomly distributed. But there was simply no reason for the count of lost children to be manipulated: The paucity of contemporary literature on the subject suggests no one really cared particularly about this service, except the parents of lost children. Most other police statistics represented either controversial conflict-laden actions that could have had negative consequences for the police, or actions that the police might have chosen to exaggerate or conceal. And even the external factors affecting the numbers of lost children returned, that is, those factors that increased or decreased the propensity of children to get lost, were factors that produced seasonal variation; did not affect annual data; or were long-term developments, such as the declining number of children per family, the increasing proportion of women working outside the home, or changing public schools, none of which affected the important short-term variation in rates.

Thus, whereas the return of lost children and the annual statistic it produced might seem innocuous and irrelevant, it is just the kind of information that gives insight into the ordinary interaction betwen the police and a public with which they otherwise had little formal contact. The statistic of lost children returned home gains its value to the historian precisely because it is the measure of a common, accidental activity. Given the data available, it may be the only systematic way to gain an entré into the everyday world of police and public in the nineteenth-century city. Thus, as the finding and returning of a lost child was, in itself, hardly an event breeding class conflict or ethnic hostility, the data created by this fairly value-neutral police activity can serve as an indicator of citizen demands on the police. However, we must not erroneously think that because finding and returning a lost child is in itself value neutral, the finding of lost children was an activity for which the police were loved. Nor should we assume this police service affected all strata of society equally. But the service was value neutral in that most parents did not want their children lost, and the reuniting of lost children with parents was an activity that did not represent the enforcement of what would otherwise have been perceived as class-biased and alien laws. Almost every other service provided by the nineteenth-century police unquestionably operated with class and ethnic biases. For instance, city health ordinances almost always discriminated against the activities of the poor – for example, the proscription on keeping pigs because of their excretia deprived people of a free source of meat, while the wealthy kept their manure-producing horses in town. One can argue that station house lodging, although a service to the poor, kept the homeless army of workers ready to serve the fluctuating needs of industry. But in every society lost children need to be returned home.

In a small community, parents would not have to make demands upon the police for help in finding lost children; presumably, children would never really be lost unless physically away from the community. But in a large and impersonal community, where most children are not known to other members of society, a child may quite easily wander a short distance from home and become lost. Once a child had become lost, the parents had the choice of finding the child themselves, getting help from neighbors and other family members, or asking for some larger institution with better information sources to help in the search. The critical question is – When did parents start asking the police for help? That is, in the prepolice era, especially when a child became lost in the daytime when there was no regular patrol system, parents had no city officials to call upon for help; in the evening, presumably they could ask the watch to be on the alert for the child. At best, a single individual would wander about the city, child in one hand, bell in the other, trying to find the parents; at worst, a newspaper ad would have to suffice. But with no regular patrolling officers or central information system, there would have been little point in asking the irregularly available constable and watch for assistance. When a uniformed police force began to patrol the city regularly, how long did it take before people developed the perception that the police had both the ability and obligation to help in finding a lost child? The rise of this notion is important for more than the recovery of lost children, for it indexes the creation of the modern urban notion that freedom from crime and disorder is a right, not just a privilege of the privileged.

The police reported the annual number of lost children with imperfect but fairly high regularity. Occasionally a department gave as separate figures the number of children reported lost and the number found – numbers that diverged with alarming regularity, some years more found than lost, other years more lost than found. Other departments kept track of lost children found on a monthly basis. And in at least one city, Pittsburgh, the department kept a list of all children found, specifying the child's name, "nativity," age, and the relationship of the person who picked up the child at the station house.

By describing the people who turned to the police for non-crime-related assistance, a suggestive picture of who felt a right to make a demand on the police can be drawn. Through the examination of people's behavior in non-crime-related situations, as in the case of finding lost children, we can avoid the study of overtly hostile interactions and come as close as possible to value-free voluntary police–citizen relations. Of course, one must make clear that the persons who made these demands were, in a larger sense, the victims of social and economic injustice. That is, for some people to depend on the police for aid more than others was and is an aspect of an essentially inequitable society, and the study of people who used the police should never turn into a paean to the generosity of society. Rather, it can be a way of understanding society's mechanism for responding to its self-created evils. We should consider the people making everyday, non-crime-related demands on the police as a sample of ordinary people who began in the nineteenth century to feel they had a right to simple personal safety and security in their daily lives.

Different kinds of parents made different demands on the police. As the evidence is rather fragmentary on this subject, we cannot specify the nature and extent of these differences with precision. Nor can we separate which portion of these differences came from police discrimination, from varying child-rearing practices, or from parental perceptions. Table 4 makes clear that over a period lasting from the Civil War through the early twentieth century black people received less help from the police than whites in finding lost children. One suspects that this continuing underrepresentation resulted from two related causes: police hostility and general neglect of blacks, and black parents' compensatory accommodation to their position as a small and discriminated-against minority in a large city through careful child protection. The clear implication that the most oppressed and one of the smallest minority groups in New York City had less contact with the police than their proportion of the population warranted should not be too startling. We know, for instance, that in mid-nineteenth-century Columbus, Ohio, blacks

Table 4. *Percentage of lost children who were black compared to percentage of total population that was black, New York, 1864–1900*

Year	Percentage of lost children black	Percentage of total population black
1864	.43	1.52[a]
1890	.74[b]	1.46
1900	.72[c]	1.76

[a] All persons of color.
[b] Includes all years 1885–94.
[c] Includes 1895–1901, 1905.
Source: Lost children from *Annual Reports* of the New York City police department, 1864, 1890, 1900 (New York, 1865, 1891, 1901); city population from Tenth U.S. Census, *Social Statistics of Cities*, Pt.1 (Washington, D.C.: GPO, 1887), Thirteenth U.S. Census, *Population*, V. III (Washington, D.C.: GPO, 1913).

were underrepresented both in criminal court proceedings as well as in the poorhouse.[52] We might make a more ominous and equally plausible interpretation of the small number of black children returned by the police: The police simply refused to help black parents, who had to find their lost children as though living in the prepoliced era.

The experiences of other ethnic groups help clarify some of the reasons why so few black children appear to have become lost. Table 5 shows the ethnicity of a sample of lost children in New York for 1864, when Irish children outnumbered by far all other ethnic and racial minorities. Re-percentaging this distribution without the Irish makes the underrepresentational pattern even more interesting. The Germans were the most underrepresented, followed by other immigrant groups, the native born, and finally blacks, who had proportionately more lost children than the other nativity groups, excepting the Irish. Although this restricted evidence is too slim to base any substantive interpretation on, it does suggest that demands upon the police were made by, in descending order, the Irish, the blacks, the native born, and the Germans. This also indicates that, on occasion, other ethnic groups utilized police services even less than blacks, an exception that should not obscure the more persisting invariance of black underrepresentation across many cities and over a long period of time.

If we look at lost children in Pittsburgh for the last decade of the nineteenth century, an interesting comparison to New York emerges. Both cities had a similar underrepresentation of black

Table 6. Ethnicity of lost children, New York, 1864[a]

Ethnicity	Lost children (%)	Total population (1870) (%)
Native-born	12.5	56
Irish	83.4	21
German	2.3	16
Other foreign-born	1.5	7
Black	.4	1.5

[a]These percentages are based on 3,492 lost children out of a total of 10,040. It is unclear in the New York Police's annual report (see source below), but apparently these were the children who were not picked up at the local station houses but taken to the main station. It is possible that there were ethnic and racial differences between those picked up at local station houses and those taken to the main station, but there is no evidence to suggest directions to the bias. Further, it is unclear if the classification by place of birth refers to parents or children – based on the more accurate classification scheme of the Pittsburgh police, my guess is that place of birth here refers to parents, justifying the classification of the child's ethnicity.
Source: New York Police Commissioners, Annual Report, 1864 (New York, 1865).

children – in Pittsburgh, the mean black population of the decade of the 1890s was 4.4%, yet only 1.6% of the lost children were black. The same mechanism at work in discriminating against blacks functioned in Pittsburgh as New York. However, unlike New York, the Pittsburgh native-born whites, rather than the Irish, dominated the lost children lists. As Table 6 shows, even while the city changed from native-born predominance to an immigrant majority, the native-born lost children always exceeded the foreign-born by about 20%. Unlike the tabulations of the lost children in New York, these figures cannot be compared with the total population of the city, ethnic group by ethnic group, for the police recorded "nativity" by an unusual mixture of birthplace and religious identification – for example, Polish, German, and "Hebrew." The ethnic differences between the two cities make one question the criteria used by police for recording ethnicity – it appears that, with the exception of Jewish children, the Pittsburgh police actually recorded the child's place of birth. On the other hand, the New York police apparently recorded the ethnicity of the child's parents, thereby inflating the relative native-born/foreign-born ethnicity ratio of lost children in New York as compared to Pittsburgh. The Irish do not account for over a tiny fraction of lost children (1.3%) in Pittsburgh,

Table 6. *Percentage of native-born (all races) lost children compared to percentage of native-born population (linear estimate), Pittsburgh, 1890–9*

Year	Lost children	Population
1890	96.5	69.3
1891	80.8	66.0
1892	82.3	62.7
1893	73.1	59.4
1894	77.1	56.1
1895	71.9	52.8
1896	65.5	49.4
1897	67.1	46.1
1898	—	—
1899	61.7	39.5

Source: Pittsburgh Department of Public Safety, *Annual Reports,* 1890–9 (Pittsburgh, 1890–9).

partially reflecting their relative decline in immigration as compared to East Europeans in the booming steel town. And one can only wonder how many of the children whose nativity was recorded as native-born were second-generation Irish.

The data for Pittsburgh tell us more about racial than ethnic use of the police. They also show an interesting and subtle change in the way the police were used. Part of the police records of lost children for the 1890s and for 1909 noted who picked up the children at the station house. Presented in Table 7, this information demonstrates an interesting trend. In the two decades between 1890 and 1909, the retrieval of lost children took on a more serious and formal aspect as the proportion of siblings, neighbors, and friends picking up lost children declined from a small but statistically significant proportion of 27% to 18%. Some of this change came from the changing ethnicity of the children: Native-born white parents tended to have siblings or neighbors pick up their lost child more than did the growing proportion of recent Polish immigrants. For a newcomer to the United States, a lost child in the hands of the police evidently had more serious ramifications than it did for the native-born. In addition to the changing ethnicity of the lost children, the drop in the proportion of siblings and neighbors picking up the children reflects a police–citizen relationship growing in formality. By making the parents pick up lost children, the police were assured that their station houses did not become drop-in centers for lost children, their friends, and siblings. Had such a rela-

Table 7. Percentage of persons picking up lost children at police station, Pittsburgh, 1890–9

Child's "nativity"	Parents	Kin	Siblings	Neighbors	Total	Number (N)
Native (white)	71.7	6.0	14.4	7.8	100	1,158
Native (black)	75.9	3.4	3.4	17.2	100	29
Polish	79.2	3.4	10.7	6.7	100	149
Hebrew	67.9	8.3	16.5	.9	100	109
German	73.3	6.0	16.4	4.3	100	116
Finnish	100.0	10.0	30.0	35.0	100	7,000
Total	72.5	6.0	14.5	7.2		1,643

In 1890, 80 parents and kin and 31 siblings and neighbors picked up lost children at the police station; in 1909, 261 parents and kin and 58 siblings and neighbors picked up lost children. $Chi^2 = 4.73$, sig. = .05.
Source: Compiled from Pittsburgh Department of Public Safety, *Annual Reports*, 1890–1909 (Pittsburgh, 1890–9, 1909).

tionship been encouraged, the falling lost child rate might have instead soared, enmeshing the police more deeply in helping families cope with urban society. More and more, the authorities of families became the appropriate persons to deal with the authorities of society.

The return of lost children to their homes may be value neutral, but unfortunately the statistics of the annual rate at which they were returned do not become immediately transparent by virtue of their neutrality. The statistics do not reflect the true number of children who got lost – this is clear simply because the numbers varied so greatly from city to city. For example, Richmond, Virginia, almost always reported a tiny number of lost children, fewer than the number of dead infants found, whereas Pittsburgh, then only a slightly larger city, often reported ten times as many lost children as Richmond for the same year. In 1894, only 17 lost children were found by the police in Richmond, 152 in Pittsburgh. Perhaps children were more easily confused in Pittsburgh, but one hopes not to this degree.

Nor do the statistics merely reflect the vagaries of police reporting practices. The visual impression of the series' remarkable consistency and intercity similarity (Figure 7) is confirmed by a calculation of the slope of the rate over time, where out of the twenty-one cities with enough data to plot, thirteen had negative slopes, four had positive slopes, and the remainder had no clear trends. (See Appen-

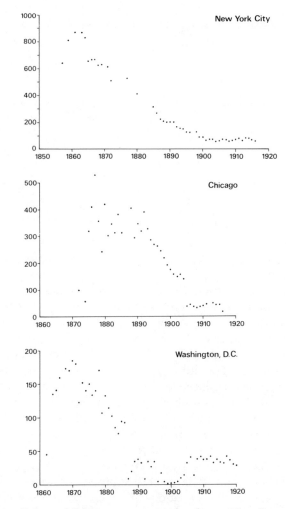

Figure 7. Lost children return rates for three cities. *Source:* Compiled from annual reports of New York, Chicago, and Washington, D.C., police departments. See Appendix B for detail on sources.

dix D for complete data.) One might argue that although consistent, the police statistics still only reflect their somewhat regular data-gathering activities. However, for the cities that give numbers of lost children by month, a clear seasonal pattern exists, more children being returned in the warmer months, fewer in the cold months (see Figure 8). For example, only 41 children were found in December 1874 in Brooklyn, whereas 382 had been found the pre-

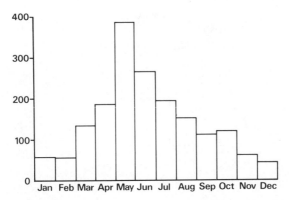

Figure 8. Seasonal variation in lost children, Brooklyn, 1874. *Source: Annual Report* of police (Brooklyn, 1874).

vious May. This seasonal variation presumably indicates more than seasonality in police activity.

Where the comparative intercity statistics bear greatest resemblance to reality is in their rate of change for each city rather than in absolute numbers or in levels. At the simplest level, this rate of change is determined by changing demands made by parents for assistance in finding their lost children and by changing police response to these demands. For although it is reasonable to argue that the actual number of lost children varied seasonally, it makes little sense to argue that the actual numbers of lost children changed over time. Essentially, two conditions determine the number of children at risk to get lost: First, the children must have been outside their homes; second, they must have been under inadequate supervision. The determinants of the first condition are related to the weather, to the socioeconomic status of the family, and to its ability to afford a dwelling suitable for indoor or contained outdoor play. Supervision of outdoor play is determined by family size, neighborhood supervisorial practices, and whether or not the primary care-giver works or is at home and free to watch the children outdoors. No doubt the degree and intensity of outdoor supervision was also determined by ethnicity, some ethnic groups protecting their children more than others.[53] But the awareness of what determined whether or not a small child was liable to get lost does not really enable us to make meaningful predictions about the change in rates of getting lost; nor does it suggest any feasible controls to make the rates relative to children at risk. It is more reasonable to argue that across the cities under study and over the sixty years being examined, the rate at which children actually became lost remained relatively stable. To argue otherwise, one would have to demonstrate that child supervision practices, housing, and outdoor play space had changed dramatically, a notion that is interesting but doubtful. Thus, this analysis of the changing rates of lost children returned home assumes that children got lost at a fairly constant annual rate between 1860 and 1920 and, therefore, fluctuations in the rates reflect broad changes in police practices and changing demands made by parents upon police.

Ideally, one would like to examine the effects that the introduction of the uniformed police had upon the rates of lost children being found and returned home, but this cannot be done because before the creation of the uniformed police lost children were handled by informal means. And whether handled by the constable, the watch, or "the old man,"they produced no regular statistics. Part of the set of reforms introduced by police formalization included an annual report with statistics – informal policing required only informal accounting, but uniforms required uniform reports. What we do have to examine, then, are data produced concurrent with an institutional change, and we can only surmise what came before. The data, in effect, are like the ripples produced by a stone thrown into a pond; the earlier wave action can only be estimated. Fortunately, in the case of the introduction of the uniformed police, there seems to have been a lag in their general social effect, so that the general response to their availability came during years rather than days or weeks.

Two independent pressures, one from the police and the other from parents, affected the changing rate of lost children returned home. Parents determined the basic reporting rates, because only through their requests were lost children searched for and found children returned home. Moreover, two independent but similar things could make them turn to the police: First and most obvious, children actually had to be lost completely enough so that they apparently could not be returned without police help. Second, parents had to perceive their own right to make a demand on the police for help. Assuming that the number of children lost varied by season and weather, but not by year, this leaves parents' perceptions as the major determinant on the demand side of the rate of lost children returned by the police. In fact, as we shall discover, as soon as people began to perceive the central communications, regular patrol, and visibility of the new uniformed police, they began quickly to escalate all their demands for assistance. Parents of lost children participated most visibly and vigorously in this changing demand pattern, availing themselves of this sensible new way of finding lost children.

Police behavior determined the supply side of the lost children rates. Because we can characterize the scope of the police function as narrowing during the last quarter of the nineteenth century and the first quarter of the twentieth, we could expect that the return of lost children would be a non-crime-related job that the police would try to shed, along with taking in overnight lodgers, shooting mad dogs, and rounding up stray cattle. And although the police did not and have not shed this duty, we can see how their tendency to play down this service corresponded to the narrowing range of their duties; it is a duty they retain only because they are the one centralized bureaucracy to be on twenty-four-hour availability and to actively patrol the public spaces of the city. Therefore, we can predict that as the police intake of lodgers began its decline between the mid 1890s and World War I, the police would be trying to curtail their assistance in finding and returning lost children during the same era.

Given these two groups – parents and police – determining variation in the rate of lost children returned by the police, we can predict variation in the relative pressures of these elements and can estimate the shape of the resultant curve. This curve should be that of a "lazy question mark," a question mark laid over to the left. We can expect that the sharply rising slope $A - B$ of Figure 9 will define the local rate of change in the perception of the police function and the concomitant right to be helped by the police, that the falling slope $B - C$ will represent a police deescalation of service in helping with lost children, and that the relatively horizontal line $C - D$ will represent an equilibrium condition between citizen demands and police supply. We cannot predict in advance the levels at which each of the two major direction changes will occur, that is, points B and C in Figure 9, nor can we predict the steepness of the two slopes, $A - B$ and $B - C$. We can imagine that this hypothetical curve represents the interaction of our two predicted curves of parents' demands and police responsiveness, the first, $P_1 P_2$, representing the quick rise in demands once the new function of police is perceived, and the other, $R_1 R_2$, representing the growing and then narrowing range of police services.

The exact shape of this curve should have varied in each city, depending on somewhat idiosyncratic local conditions and upon the time at which the uniformed police were introduced. All else

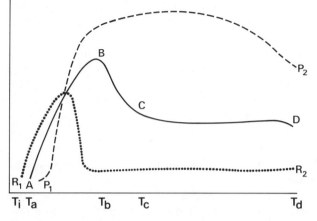

Figure 9. Hypothetical curve of annual rates of lost children returned by police. T_i = introduction of regularized, uniformed police; T_a = earliest demands for help with lost children; T_b = police begin to resist demands for assistance; T_c = minimal tolerable level of police assistance; T_d = equilibrium between public demands and police assistance; P_1, P_2 = public's perception of appropriate level of police service; R_1, R_2 = range of services police are willing to provide.

being equal, cities with early policing should have had less steep slopes and more variation in the line of equilibrium than cities where the uniformed police were introduced later. And at some point in the late nineteenth and early twentieth centuries, the line A – B should have all but disappeared as urban dwellers migrated from places where the perceptual change signified by this curve had been completed. We might expect that for some of the newer Western cities, settled and built by people with previous experience with uniformed police, there would be no curve, just a fluctuating line of equilibrium, adjusting preconceived notions on both the part of the citizens and the police.

Before examining the actual empirical distributions of rates, it is important to note that the data for numbers of lost children do have some rather frustratingly difficult gaps: As might be expected, the crucial first part of the curve representing the growth of citizen demands for assistance was more often the time period when police were not recording the lost children returned. In a sense, for many departments the recording of such data took place only when the work had become a large or perhaps too onerous part of police work. This means that the most theoretically interesting part of the data, that representing changing perceptions by citizens of their rights to make demands on police, are just the data most often missing. Because the information is missing, we cannot say with assurance whether the missing portion has the expected distribution, or one that runs contrary to expectations. Figure 7 presents the scatterplots for three cities that confirm the predicted curve shape, and Appendix D has tables showing the slopes of the rates for all cities and tables of the rates for the first fifteen years of each city's series.

The data suggest that the introduction of uniformed police triggered a sharp rise in the demand for help in finding lost children in, at the minimum, the six cities of New York, Chicago, St. Louis, Washington, D.C., Detroit, and Pittsburgh. This sharp uptake lasted only a decade or so until negative pressures from the police forced the number of demands down, or at least the number of demands that required centralized, recorded, tabulated police action. This curve is very regular and clear. Probably most of the cities that did not exhibit similar curves, such as Brooklyn and Boston, deviated because of gaps in their early data. Or, for instance, the reported data for Philadelphia, sporadically beginning in 1880, twenty-five years after the uniforming of the police, simply come too late to show what was most likely a curve similar to that of New York or Washington. For the two cities with clearly unexpected patterns that cannot be blamed on missing data – Newark and Milwaukee – the contradiction lies not in the first or second parts of the curve but in the last part, which should have been a horizontal equilibrium line. No doubt there were substantive local reasons why this adjustment process proved so unstable in Newark and Milwaukee, but they would require a local analysis, no doubt worth pursuing on its own but irrelevant to the main point here. In fact, even in these two deviant cases there was an initial period of quick growth in the lost child rates, followed by a decline.

Despite the exceptions to the basic pattern and the cities for which there is too little information to make any firm judgments, the basic shape of the lost child curve, a curve produced at the intersection of public demand and police response, holds for cities as different as Boston and New Orleans, as big as New York or as small as New Haven, Connecticut, as industrial as Buffalo or as service based as Washington, D.C. The major differences come in the timing of the pattern and in the differing levels of service. New York City saw a maximum lost children rate of 794 per 10,000 persons, Richmond a maximum of 200. The New York rate stabilized after 1895 at about 55, whereas Richmond stabilized at the incredibly low level of about 10, comparable to Washington's 19. All cities stabilized at a rate so much lower than the maximum that we must conclude several factors were at work: The police probably reported only those cases that involved a long stay for the child in the station house; parents' demands must have diminished somewhat, reflecting their dampened perception of the police as public servants; and private agencies took on some of these services.

The relative levels of services in the cities reflect both regional and economic differences. Although patterns were the same, the intensity varied greatly. Northern cities had the greatest range of differences in their peak services, from 105 to 794 per 10,000; Southern cities the lowest level of service but with some intercity variety, the range of maximums from 65 to 200; while the West and Midwest showed a consistent and moderately high level of maximum service, the range from 341 to 530. These differences both within and between regions help characterize some of the regional and developmental differences in cities. The Northern industrial cities, which provided the earliest uniformed police, also had the highest demands for help with lost children – New York and Boston, for instance; cities with slightly later growth showed a more moderate peak, for instance Buffalo at 217; whereas cities that developed comparatively late in the nineteenth century, like Pittsburgh, showed a low peak, 105. Throughout the major cities, as the century waned, public demands lessened with declining police response, reflecting the cumulative experience of the national city system. Southern cities never provided a level of service to match other cities – the mean for New Orleans was 40, for Richmond 44 – so that one wonders what happened to all the lost children in these cities. And Western and Midwestern cities show maximums well above those of the South, but with far more homogeneity and less experimentation than the variegated Northeast, reflecting the West's use of the police experiences in the East.

Because each city went through its rising-then-falling lost child rates at different times, national/intercity equilibrium was not achieved at any one point in the nineteenth century. This makes a cross-sectional analysis relatively unsatisfactory, as differences in timing between cities and within regions may easily obscure important similarities. Keeping this fragility in mind, we can still learn something from a cross-sectional snapshot of the United States in 1880, when the volume of the census devoted to the "Defective, Dependent, and Delinquent Classes" reported answers to queries about police in cities of more than 5,000 inhabitants. One hundred and twenty-five cities, ranging in size from New York

City with over a million people to Creston, Iowa, with only 5,081, reported both the numbers of lost children and the annual costs of their police for 1880. Using city size, cost of the police per capita, and region in a multiple regression analysis, almost 27% of the variation from city to city in the rate of lost children can be explained. The cost of the police is the most powerful predictor, the power increasing when the regression controls the Southern region and then population size (see Table 8). This confirms the notion that, except for the South, better-funded police provided at least moderately better service and that large cities had a few more lost children per capita than did correspondingly smaller cities. For examples of how this regional difference affected even the smaller cities, we can compare Wilmington, North Carolina, with a population of 17,350, to Waterbury, Connecticut, with a population of 17,806. The Wilmington police reported six lost children compared to ten in Waterbury; yet the Wilmington police had a much higher annual budget of $15,098 compared to Waterbury's $9,000. While the Southern police were costly and concerned with preserving public order, they did not help families whose children experienced one of the most frightening effects of cities – the loss of both physical and social bearings and identity.[54]

We might be skeptical today of the notion that the return of lost children by the newly uniformed police of nineteenth-century cities had any special meaning, or that the increase in parents' demand for this service reflected any perceptual changes. Although there is little literature on the subject, an editorial did appear in the *New York Daily Times* in 1857, soon after the newly uniformed Metropolitan Police began to help regularly and systematically to return lost children.[55] The editorial, an example of that genre still beloved of urban dailies, examines in some depth a situation that while not in itself important reflects the quality of city life. The tongue-in-cheek title of the article, "Five Thousand Children Lost," sets its tone. The author quickly reassures the presumably alarmed reader that the children have all been found and "returned to their crying friends." "None will so much marvel," the author continues, "at the numbers lost and found as they who remembered [sic] the solemn procession of old when a single child was lost – the old man ringing the bell and crying at intervals, 'Anybody lost a baby'." It is unclear if the "old man" refers to a member of the watch, but the importance of this passage is in its marveling at the large numbers of lost children the police can process and its reference to preuniformed police times when the lost child was taken about the streets in an unsystematic search for its parents. The author continues to describe the

Table 8. *Lost children regression for 1880*

$$L = -.161 + .802C + .748R_3 + .14S - .429R_1$$
$$\quad\quad (.996) \quad (.279) \quad\quad (.358) \quad\quad (.081) \quad (.248)$$

Step	F to enter	Sig.	R^2 change
C	25.6	.0001	.172
R_3	8.8	.004	.056
S	3.1	.082	.019
R_4	3.0	.086	.018
R_5	.15	.701	.001
R_6	.04	.847	.000

$R^2 = .265$; $\overline{R}^2 = .241$; $F = 10.84$; sig. $= .0001$. Standard deviation $= 1.13$, standard error is in parentheses. Key: L, lost children rate per 1,000 population; S, city population in one hundred thousands; C, annual cost of police per 1,000 population in dollars; R_1, Northeast coastal region; R_2, Northeast inland region; R_3, Southeast region; R_4, Midwest region; R_5, Plains region; R_6, Western region, with regional variables being dummies.
Source: Tenth U.S. Census, *Report on Defective, Dependent, and Delinquent Classes* (Washington, D.C.: GPO, 1888).

wonders of the efficient new system, with the imagined dialogue of a mother reporting her child's disappearance to an unbelievably matter-of-fact, objective, and formal police officer at the station house – "Will Madam please describe her child?"

One might doubt the speed that the author claims for the new system; "the whereabouts of the absent little one is often learned in two or three minutes." More interesting is the author's assertion, "The facilities which the Police and Police Telegraph afford, for the discovery of lost children, is now pretty generally known, so that when a child is missing some one repairs to the nearest Stationhouse immediately." This observation conforms with the rising statistics of lost children returned for New York City, a rise that turned abruptly downward six years after the article appeared. That the *Times* patronizingly took note of this evidently unexpected police service four years after New York's police had been regularly uniformed indicates a lag in the essentially middle- and upper-class media's awareness of an important change and supports the inference that the apparent rise in the number of children lost and found came from the demands of ordinary parents.[56]

Forty years later, when Jacob Riis wrote a story about a lost three-year-old child who mysteriously reappeared after two years, he made clear it was the norm for the parents to go to the nearest police station house.[57] In the story, pathos and charm come from the parents' two-year vigil on the steps of the station house. The Riis story shows that from his and the police's perspectives, children in poor neighborhoods like Mulberry Bend seemed to be lost more often. He claims that the "Police Commissioners thought seriously of having the children tagged with name and street number, to save them trotting back and forth between police station and headquarters." The story Riis relates represents a "chip" of the human "maelstrom" of the area, the lost child one of a "host of thousands" who drifted "from the tenement and back." Riis's attitude and treatment of the lost child problems shows how far urban society had come in forty years – from the *Times* editorialist's astonishment at the large numbers of lost children and "marvel" at the efficiency of the police in returning them, to Riis's world-weary and mildly amused acceptance of this police activity as commonplace. So systematized had the finding of lost children become that in New York the Society for the Prevention of Cruelty to Children had as one of its regular duties the dealing with the "surplus" of lost children – those children who went unclaimed and who, in the late 1850s, had been sent to the poorhouse. Ironically, Riis's comments about the police and lost children came at a time in New York when the police role had dropped to an all-time low (see Figure 7). In the story, he speaks of his "twenty years' acquaintance with the police office," apparently unaware it was a period in which the lost children were being returned at only one fourth of the former rate. Yet by the mid 1890s the perception of this police function had become so firmly fixed that the changing reality of police activities, which had begun a reorientation toward crime control and away from non-crime-related activities, did not affect even a perceptive observer like Riis.

The police's deemphasis on the return of lost children also proceeded because they cooperated with and aided private groups. Starting as early as the mid 1870s in New York City, urban reform activists had begun to seek out and help suffering children. The New York Society for the Prevention of Cruelty to Children (NYSPCC hereafter), founded in 1874, concerned itself with the various forms of child abuse in nineteenth-century cities, ranging from parental physical abuse to prostitution, overwork, and exploitation in various circus and theatrical entertainments. As opposed to all other agencies taking care of children, this society did not wait passively for a child to be brought to its attention. Rather like the uniformed police in contrast to the constable and watch they replaced, the society aggressively sought out cases of child mistreatment.[58] In the 1870s and 1880s, societies similar to the NYSPCC spread quickly among the major urban centers of the United States.[59] Unlike their European counterparts, American societies had the willing cooperation of the police, who were just as anxious to get out of the child care business as the societies were to get into it.

Societies modeled on the NYSPCC helped to privatize the public welfare service provided by the police. In 1887, the president of the NYSPCC emphasized this contrast in European and American police. In the United States, he said, "the Law and Humanity go hand in hand . . . . And instead of the local police . . . being antagonistic to the efforts of the Society so working for the public good, as too often occurs in European countries, they are assisted in their official duties, strengthened in their efforts. . . ."[60] A typical police–NYSPCC interaction involved the police discovering child abuse or neglect, or in some cases a child offender, after which the police asked the society to intervene and take the case. Often the society placed children in foster or orphan homes and actively aided in the criminal prosecution of parents.[61] Concurrent with these forms of police–private cooperation, the police began more and more to use the society's assistance in dealing with lost children. In 1877, the society helped return only twenty-five lost children to their parents; twenty years later, the figure had leapt ten times to 2,810 lost children returned. Clearly, this private agency accounted for a substantial portion of the decline in the number of lost children returned by the police in New York.[62]

We saw earlier in this chapter how an outcome similar to the privatization of police welfare services for lost children also occurred with tramps, the high rate of overnight lodgers declining in the 1890s. Although different arguments were presented to rid police of lodgers and different public agencies intervened, the result paralleled the decline of the high rates of lost children returned. Between the 1890s and the end of World War I, the important public service functions that police departments had practiced disappeared or were substantially diminished, and police systems presenting viable alternatives to the subsequent system disappeared. Cops were now to be crime fighters.

This cooperation with private reform groups allowed the police to alter their focus from general public service and to begin to concentrate on crime control. But as the police began to divest themselves of the job of ordering a disorderly city, the demands they had triggered continued. City dwellers began to expect lives free from the most outrageous aspects of disorder and danger. The agencies that had provided these services became privatized, damaging long-term prospects for the provision of reasonably safe and orderly urban settings, but this did not reverse the expectations of city dwellers. The introduction of the uniformed police, although not solving any problems, had created the feeling that problems should be solved, that city life should not have to be devastatingly anonymous and dangerous. That police did not remain service oriented may have been a missed opportunity to help order American cities; that separate private agencies competed with the police in supplying social services may well have destroyed a potentially useful means of helping ordinary people resist the disorganizing effects of industrialized urban places.

A perceptual revolution already had occurred by the time the police got out of the welfare business around the turn of the century. This activity had grown because public demands had grown, demands reflecting a changed perception of the rights of urbanites of all classes to be free from the troubles of crime and disorder. The physical, visual, and symbolic presence of the police themselves had triggered this change. Apparently, the police response had been sufficient to encourage the escalation of the demands, as well as demonstrate the feasibility and responsibility of the government's providing a more orderly urban existence for ordinary people. And the privatization of the welfare services that followed, although peculiarly American, did not reverse the perceptual shift. By the early twentieth century, Americans felt they had every right to a life where lost children would be returned home and crime be prevented.

4   *A narrowing of function*

> There is in every large city, a dangerous class of idle, vicious persons, eager to band themselves together, for purposes subversive to public peace, and good government . . .
>
> *Report of the General Superintendent of Police,* Chicago (1876)
> [beginning of Haymarket Affair report]

Police and crime

In Chapter 2, we examined the extreme variations in the arrest rate trends relative to larger social and economic events. In this chapter, the rates will be examined more narrowly and precisely from the perspective of the direct producers of the arrest rates, the police. Following methodological techniques implied by the modified labeling perspective described in the Introduction, the explicit causal world here will be restricted to measurable variations in the police and to immediate forces predicted to affect police behavior. The measure of police behavior is, of course, variation in arrests. Variation in police behavior, arrests, which cannot be explained with the severely simple models specified here, will be subjected, in the next section, to a more speculative analysis of external forces that affected long trends. In a sense, up to this point we have been looking at arrest rates in their larger social context while ignoring the concrete conditions of their production. What we want to see now is how much can be explained by policing alone: What remains, we can more confidently attribute to other social causes.

Not only is there a theoretical reason to exclude broad social forces from this part of the study, but there is an equally forceful methodological reason. I have not accounted for levels of employment, prices of food, industrial or urban growth, population density, racial or demographic factors, or the myriad other social factors often used to try to explain criminal behavior. Two factors lead to this omission. First, adequate annual data for the twenty-three cities included in this study are not easily obtainable; possibly they can never be created. Second, the place to begin a close and precise

129

statistical analysis of arrest rates is with those who produced them, the police. The arrest event is a two-part interaction, requiring an offender who exhibits some form of behavior that makes him or her identifiable as a potentially arrestable person, and a police officer willing to make the decision and effort to arrest the offender. As relatively few criminal offenses today are cleared by arrest, with the exception of murder, the arrest rate is largely determined by police action. Only when the arrest rate approaches the number of offenses actually occurring can we safely forget about the police role in measuring the arrest process. This does not mean that the analysis of crime is impossible without controlling for police behavior, but if an analysis of arrest rates does not account for police behavior, then it must adopt the perspective that crime is that behavior the dominant society cares about repressing and is not necessarily reflective of all bad behavior.

This section limits itself to a statistical explanatory model that includes only the dependent variables to be explained, various arrest rates, and one other measure of police behavior, lodging rates. Homicide rates and rates measuring variations in the structure and strength of the police are used as independent variables. Specifically, the independent variables to be examined here are the number of police officers per 1,000 persons and the homicide arrests per 10,000. By using various correlation statistics, we can work from measuring somewhat oversimplified and deceptively significant relationships to the more complex structure underlying the police relationship to arrests.

A Pearsonian correlation of police strength and arrests produces what appears to be important information confirming the notion that an increase in policing represses crime. About 38% of the initiative arrests and 22% of all arrests can be accounted for by the police strength the previous year. As police strength increased, arrests the following year decreased. However, only about 2% of the arrests for crimes with victims can be accounted for in this way, suggesting that police could successfully repress public disorder but not crimes with victims.

These apparently clear relationships must be seriously questioned for three reasons. First, why should increased policing have produced fewer arrests? What were they doing? As pointed out by historian Eugene Watts, the increase in police strength accompanied a decrease in working hours; thus the trend toward more police obscures the opposite trend toward fewer person-hours on patrol. Second, the long-term trends may statistically dominate critical short-term changes. That is, although important to the overall analysis of this book, the sixty-year trends may very likely be due to structural shifts that the models have not specified. And our analysis, at this point, must be precise in capturing police–arrest relations on the lowest common level. For these two reasons, it makes sense to base the statistical analysis on annual differences rather than annual rates: That is, the variation to be examined will be the rate change from the previous year. (Arrest difference = arrest_t − arrest_{t-1}.) A final reason to reject the simple negative relationship between police strength and total crime is that the model, even if true, does not tell us enough either about variations in police strength or arrests.

Given the perspective of policing developed in this book, and given the limited universe of variables relating to police and arrests, we can create a model of the police–crime relationship that may be estimated using the time series data on the twenty-three cities. The dependent variables will each be a part of police arrest behavior or lodging rates. Total arrests, as a variable, lumps all arrests together with no analytic distinction. In so doing, we make explicit the assumption that a part of the police job is to label offenders, that offense distinctions are of less importance than the basic criminal label. By stepping back a little from this grossly leveling assumption, we can create two slightly disaggregated arrest rates to work with as dependent variables: the rate for all initiative arrests, which is clearly dependent on police aggressiveness; and the rate for all other arrests, an estimate of the rate for offenses with victims, which I have called "crime" arrests. In short, the model relates policing to the annual variation in the three rates graphed in Figure 3. Lodging will enter as the fourth dependent variable, a variable indicating police service production.[1]

Two independent variables will be considered simultaneously, by use of multiple regression, a statistical method that estimates the relative contribution of each independent or predictor variable in a model as well as estimating the overall predictive power of the model.[2] The model asserts that variations in police strength and the homicide arrest rate determined arrest rates. In this step, exogenous variables have been excluded, as the first task in explaining arrests should come at the most basic level possible: the police and direct influences upon them. Therefore, police strength per capita continues to be incorporated as the major independent variable. By using annual differences to remove the effects of the trend toward more police per capita, the issue of the changing trend in the ratio of officer hours on the street to officers employed is avoided. Station house lodgers per capita is considered in a second model to provide a measure of the class-control activities of the police – here, one of their positive, welfare contributions – the carrot to the stick of arrests. As it is clear from the variation in lodger rates in the nineteenth century that these rates also function as an indicator of unemployment, the lodger variable is partially determined by a variable outside the equation, one for which no annual data are available. Homicide rates per capita, the one arrest variable that can be assumed to reasonably accurately reflect the changing incidence of one kind of criminal behavior, captures whatever pressures the incidence of crimes of violence had on the police. If anything, the police should have been sensitive to murder waves.

Diagrammatically, the models appear as follows:

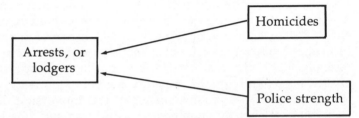

The model's overall ability to explain the variation in total arrests for all cities from 1860 to 1920 is of only marginal statistical or substantive significance, leaving most of the variation unaccounted for. (See Appendix C for the correlation matrices and regression tables.) Only one of the two predictor variables, police strength, has a statistically significant, positive, coefficient. The homicide variable's coefficient has such low statistical confidence that even the attribution of a sign is risky. We can only observe at this broad level that the police variable has a positive sign, whereas the homicide variable has no clear contribution. In other words, an increase in police strength produced more arrests. These results compare interestingly with the simple correlations for each pair of variables, which turn out to mask an important relationship. Arrest rates correlate with homicide rates, with $R = .66$ (sig. $= .001$); arrest rates correlate with police strength, with $r = -.45$ (sig. $= .001$). This negative correlation describes the trends of police strengths and arrest rates, which are negative, but when the correlation based on first differences is examined it is positive ($R = .31$; sig. $= .007$). Thus, both the regression coefficient and the correlation of the first differences show that, in the short run, more police did produce more arrests, even as the long-run trends were the opposite.

Before coming to any subtle conclusions about these various paths of interaction centered on the police, the measures must be pried apart, first by using as a dependent variable only those arrests clearly up to the initiative of police officers, and then by examining the "crime" arrest rates – in a sense, victim-initiated arrests. (These dependent variables and equations parallel to the ones for total arrests are detailed in Appendix C.) For initiative arrests, the model has high predictive power, an $\bar{R}^2$ of .43 implying that the two independent variables in the model account for about 40% of the variation in the initiative arrests. Further, annual differences in the strength of the police account for most of this variation: As with total arrests, the relationship is positive, but for initiative arrests the rate is more than twice as sensitive to variations in police strength. Homicide, on the other hand, contributes even less to the initiative arrest pattern than it did to the total arrest pattern. Arrests for the estimated rate of crimes with victims show up some subtle differences from the total and initiative arrest models. With somewhat less, but still statistically significant, explanatory power, $\bar{R}^2 =$ .24, the homicide variable has even less contribution and police strength accounts for most of the variation. However, as implied by the smaller $\bar{R}^2$, the actual sensitivity of the annual differences in the arrest rate to annual differences in the strength of the police is considerably less than that of total or initiative arrests.

Having reached the limits of an analysis that so far has ignored deliberately local differences between cities in favor of the overall behavior in the national urban network and has assumed a constant set of relationships over almost two-thirds of a century of great change, the same analytical approach must turn to more finely tuned sets of data that still retain the advantages of aggregation. The following section begins by considering separately the two time periods previously identified as having essentially different trends, 1860–90 and 1890–1920. After completing the two-period analysis and exhausting the analytic utility of lumping all cities together, the third section disaggregates all the cities into two groups that showed different behavioral directions. This section will ask whether there were emergent typological distinctions in urban police behavior.[3]

Old world, new world

The recent analysis of changing arrest and policing patterns in three different Western cities – London, Stockholm, and Sydney – by political scientist Ted Gurr and his colleagues points to a changed relationship between policing and crime in the nineteenth and twentieth centuries.[4] For each city, Gurr and his associates found that in the earlier period policing served to repress crime, but by the twentieth century this pattern had reversed, with the police no longer able to suppress or control the crime rate. Of course, a bold assertion like this always has behind it the untestable counterfactual hypothesis – that the police could still repress crime, but that new forces in the production of crime made this ability either unimportant or invisible. Perhaps the ability of the police had remained constant, and only their removal could demonstrate their relationship to criminal offenses. Although this may have been true, Gurr's assertion of an important and deep change should alert us to the likelihood that in the sixty-year period here under study we have combined two different sets of causal relationships, each of which obscures the other. Further, the shift in the direction of the trends for homicides and estimated crimes with victims, which occurred around 1890 (see Figure 4), reinforces the notion that some sort of structural shift in the relationship of policing to offenses may also have occurred. For these reasons, then, this section explores the same models of policing and arrests as did the previous section, this time using the two time periods 1860–90 and 1891–1920, as separate sets of data (where $N = 31$ and $N = 30$). This section, like the previous one, will only use analyses based on annual differences of the various arrest rates. The table in Appendix C shows the model estimates for total arrests for both periods, for arrests that required police initiative, and for the estimated "crime" rates, offenses with victims.

Dramatic differences emerge from the division of the time series into the two periods. Whereas the previous equations had only accounted for about 7% of the variation in total arrests, the periodized data produce dichotomous results. For the period before 1890 the model has no statistical significance, but for the post-1891 period its $\overline{R}^2$ rises to .18. This shift came about as a consequence of a strengthened ability of the police to produce arrests and as a moderate rise in the significance of murder to pressure the police to make arrests. For initiative arrests, the periodization proves to be even more discriminating, the earlier period moving to the surprisingly high $\overline{R}^2$ of .54, the equation for the later period losing all significance. Again, police strength determined most of this relationship – more police produced more initiative arrests in the early period, whereas their strength showed no relationship to initiative arrests in the period after 1890. This statistical change over the two periods dramatizes clearly the changed function of the police: In the early period, changes in police strength positively determined changes in the rate of arrests for offenses against public order, but this relationship disappeared after 1890. For the annual changes in the rate of lodgers, results similar to those of the initiative arrests appear, with an equation of only marginal statistical significance for the early period dropping to nonsignificance for the later period, and police strength showing a positive relationship for the first period. For the rate of the estimated crimes with victims, the division into periods has discriminating power similar to that of the initiative arrests, with an $\overline{R}^2$ of .25 for the earlier period and a nonsignificant relationship for the post-1891 period. For these "crime" arrests, the police strength variable continues to contribute the positive explanatory power, and homicide arrests have a nonsignificant contribution.

It is possible to expand the range of variables in this model a bit to include one seemingly important exogenous variable, that of real wages for unskilled urban workers. This additional variable indexes the general economic well-being of the working poor in the major U.S. cities: Unfortunately, one cannot get good annual data on urban unemployment of the working poor, an exogenous variable presumably as important as real wages. Nor can the unskilled real wage index be disaggregated by individual city to explore regional and city-specific differences. Nevertheless, the crude impact of conditions outside the strength of the police on arrests and lodging should be demonstrated by the inclusion of this variable (see Appendix C for the regression results). In three out of the twelve relevant regressions, the unskilled real wage variable contributed to the equation and to the equation's somewhat improved predictive power (adjusted R^2). Only one of the three improved equations relates to crime, that dealing with initiative arrests from 1891 to 1920, where the adjusted R^2 moved from nothing to .13 – not spectacularly large, but interesting. In this equation, real wages show an inverse relationship to initiative arrests: That is, when wages went down, arrests for drunkenness, disorderly conduct, vagrancy, and the like, went up. Although this relationship seems intuitive and predictable, it is important to note that the relationship did not obtain during the earlier period of class control. The suggestion is that although the police had begun to move away from the class control model, they were still not averse to making public order arrests during economically difficult times. Moreover, as the other two equations affected by the wages variable make clear, economically difficult times for the working poor no longer prompted the positive side of class control. From 1860 to 1890, when wages fell the number of lodgers rose, but in the later period, 1891–1920, there was no relationship. Thus, the inclusion of this interesting exogenous variable shows how the changed focus of the police affected their punitive and supportive means of dealing with the "dangerous class," the punitive continuing and the supportive disappearing.

All these results emphasize the decline of the control of the "dangerous class" and public order more than they delineate the rise of crime control. The coefficients of determination ($\bar{R}^2$) indicate the decreased overall effectiveness caused by the police focus on crimes with victims alone, but they also point out the relative ineffectiveness of the nineteenth-century police in dealing with crimes with victims. This change did not emerge simultaneously in every U.S. city, however. As the next section shows, three major cities, each a representative of the new urban policing model, led the way.

Two city types

Just as the breakdown into two periods of long-term trends in the police arrest behavior helped clarify the meaning of the whole period, a similar decomposition of cities into two types can also help explain the larger patterns. Individual plots of the arrest rates for each of the twenty-three cities in this study showed what appear to be two distinctly different urban patterns from 1860 to 1920. On the basis of this visual evidence, with impressions reinforced by the measure of the slopes of arrests for each city, two new sets of aggregated data were created, using the same technique and rules as for the unified set of data. As with the splitting up of the original long period into two shorter periods, this methodological step represents a loosening of the original rigorous and restrictively defined universe of urban arrests to include all attainable information for the cities above 50,000 persons in 1880.

The two city types are best characterized by the trend differences that appeared at the turn of the century, when for the first group of cities – New York (including Brooklyn), Chicago, and Washington, D.C. – the overall decline in total arrests abated only slightly, but for all the other cities the downward trend began to reverse and show an increase. These intercity differences paralleled one another for all four kinds of arrests, but did not appear in police or lodger trends, which remained similar across all cities. Essentially, then, the analysis separates a small group of three (or four, before Brooklyn became a part of New York City) cities with strong declines in rates for total arrests, for arrests requiring police initiative – public order arrests – for arrests for offenses with victims, and with steady rates for murder. All the other major cities showed very slight declines in total arrests and initiative arrests, coupled with overall increases in murder arrests and arrests for crimes with victims. Crudely put, there were a small group of rather important large cities where things were getting better, and a large group of mostly smaller cities where things were getting worse. In this section, we will refer to the former as Group I (dominated by New York City), and the latter as Group II (with the largest cities being Philadelphia and Boston). Our analysis of these two city types will determine if New York, Washington, and Chicago, as the lively centers of commercial, governmental, and industrial growth in the post–Civil War era, developed criminal justice systems different from those of the rest of the urban United States.

Whether looking at the two city groups over the whole period or dividing them into the two periods that have been established as critical, similar contrasts emerge. To simplify, two differences appear: First, the model shows somewhat more utility for the first group of cities (eight vs. four significant regressions). Second, the model works best for arrests for crimes with victims in the first group and best for all arrests and initiative arrests in the second group. In a sense, we have divided the cities into two behavioral groups. For the first group – New York, Washington, and Chicago – overall arrest rates declined from before the Civil War until after World War I, and criminal arrest rates figured prominently as a focus of police behavior. For the second group, on the other hand, rising overall arrest trends, especially after 1890, concealed the lack of criminal arrest importance but showed an emphasis by the police on public order offenses – crimes without victims.

Changes in the police strength coefficients of the multiple regression estimates and in the simple Pearsonian correlations confirm statistically the shift in police functions that occurred between the 1860–90 era and the 1890–1920 era. For "crime" arrests in Group I cities, the coefficient dramatically shifts from negative for the early period to positive for the later period, whereas the simple correlation moves from nonsignificance to .30, significant at .057. At the same time, the coefficient for police strength in the initiative arrest equation drops from positive to nonsignificance, indicating a parallel decrease in emphasis on public order arrests. For the Group II cities, the multiple regression estimates are nonsignificant, forestalling an examination of coefficients. However, for this second group of cities, a shift in the Pearsonian correlation parallel to that of the Group I cities does occur, R moving from nonsignificance to .34, significant at.048.

This indicates that the analysis in the section titled "Old world, new world" above, which described the shift in police function from control of the "dangerous class" to crime control, must be qualified, for this change in policing occurred most overtly in the cities of New York (including Brooklyn), Chicago, and Washington, D.C. These three important and different cities led the others because New York dominated the urban hierarchy both in size and innovation, Chicago dominated as the fastest-growing industrial and commercial center in the late nineteenth and early twentieth centuries, and Washington had begun to dominate as the center of federal policy, a kind of national city.

A slice in time

The analyses of the three previous sections of this chapter have been enmeshed in the dynamics of the major cities of the United States as they developed in the critical interwar era of industrial and urban growth from 1860 to 1920. The data excluded cities with fewer than 50,000 persons in 1880 – small cities that soon grew into major urban places like Los Angeles (11,183 in 1880) or Dallas (10,358 in 1880), as well as cities that remained relatively small, like Keokuk, Iowa (12,117 in 1880), or Winona, Minnesota (10,208 in 1880). These kinds of cities will be included in this part of the chapter, a cross-sectional analysis, focused on three points in time – 1880, 1890, and 1903 – where each city makes up one case, regardless of size. This means that the arrest, police, homicide, and lodging rates and their relationships enter the analysis with the same weight, whether the city was large or small. The data in each regression have been ordered by size of city so that systematic bias further introduced by size could be checked for in the Durbin-Watson statistic.[5]

The interesting and surprisingly thorough census volumes dealing with the *Social Statistics of Cities* for 1880, 1890, and 1903, when combined with information from appendixes to the 1880 and 1890 census volumes dealing with institutionalized people, make this cross-sectional analysis possible.[6] For the 1880 and 1890 census, the Bureau of the Census sent forms to every city over 10,000 asking for complex sets of information, including data on police and arrests.

The 1903 enumeration declined in scope from the earlier surveys and did not ask for information on the "miscellaneous" activities of the police, including lodging. A surprising number of city officials took the time to reply as best they could to these decadal surveys. Although city officials in the nineteenth century were amazingly attentive to the production of annual city reports, the completion of census questionnaires must have been an onerous burden, involving queries to other part-time city officials and digging through annual report data, compiled and published for a different, closer constituency.

The analysis of cross-sectional data allows the further relaxation of the prior assumptions that limited the analysis to an examination of police behavior accounting for only a very narrow range of socially relevant variables. Because the cross section is a different kind of analysis, one that does not capture change over time, its results are not directly comparable to the earlier time series analysis. Further, because social indicators of other sorts could be gathered for the cross section whereas they could not be gathered for the time series, this part of the analysis can account for differences in the social and economic structures of the cities, and for more subtle differences in police departments. The variable list in Table 9 has essentially four different kinds of indicators in the model: (1) the policing variables, expanded to include a measure of bureaucratization by the proportion of middle-level police managers (B), a measure of the police intensity by number of stations (S), and the number of officers per square mile (D). (2) As an indicator of industrial structure, a variable showing the proportion of the work force engaged in manufacturing is included (I). (3) As social indicators, the percent foreign born has been included (F), and, for 1890, the age structure could be crudely accounted for with a variable giving the proportion of the population between twenty and forty years old (A). (4) Finally, the four major regions of the United States were accounted for with dummy variables. The comparability for each of the three different years examined is bedeviled by missing variables from decade to decade and by missing data, which forces different cities to be included in each cross section. Thus, when the results are interpreted variable by variable, the outcome is more frustrating than revealing, except in the broadest terms.

And in the broadest terms, the results conform with the theme of changing police behavior that has run throughout this book. On this level, we can simply examine the $\overline{R}^2$. Here, we find a minimal relationship between the independent variables and the arrest rates

Table 9. Cross-sectional regressions on arrests and lodgers, United States, 1880, 1890, 1903

Variables[a]	1880		1890		1903	
	Arrests	Lodgers	Arrests	Lodgers	Cities over 100,000	Cities under 100,000
Constant	56.4	−3,129	5.3	45.9	—	—
P	9.28 (10.2)	−589.5 (1,562.7)	−2.93 (7.1)	7.7 (10.7)	14.6 (7.5)	16.3 (10.1)
C	—[b]	1.72 (2.39)	.000001 (ns)	−.00001 (.00001)	*	*
B	*[c]	*	−.011 (.010)	.03 (.01)	*	*
D	.068 (.36)	40.2 (60.6)	*	*	*	*
S	*	*	—	.42 (.50)		
H	−.244 (1.0)	112.9 (150.4)	—	−.28 (.51)	.26 (.68)	1.89 (.29)
I	−.052 (−.044)	−18.8 (6.6)	−.023 (.025)	—	*	*
A	*	*	.112 (.054)	−.10 (.07)	*	*
F		38.1 (9.4)	.007 (.018)	.04 (.02)		
R	N (F = 1.2) MW (F = .01)	S (F = 1.1) MW (F = .04)	MW (F = 26) W (F = 7)	NE (F = 0.02) S (F = .41)	W	S, W
$\bar{R}^2$	.063	.348	.496	.112	.20	.54
N of cases	37	37	72	72	35	92
F	1.41	3.47	9.74	1.99		
D-W	1.953	1.949	1.897	2.145	2.17	1.94

Standard error is in parentheses. This set of regressions uses the city as the case, so each place counts as one, regardless of size: This directly contrasts with the other regressions in this chapter, where the rates are for several places aggregated together, with the larger places tending to dominate the outcome. The variables used here are in rates per 1,000, with the exception of the four regional dummy variables, whose inclusion is noted where significant. For 1903, no lodging data were available. The cities have been ordered by size so that the *D–W* statistic reflects spatial autocorrelation. The two size groupings used correct for hetroscedasticity, caused by the diseconomies of scale of larger cities. See Kenneth Fox, *Better City Government: Innovation in American Urban Politics, 1850–1937* (Philadelphia: Temple University Press, 1977), for a discussion of this diseconomy.

[a]*P*, police per 1,000; *C*, cost for police per 1,000; *b*, number of middle-level police bureaucrats (sergeants to captains) per total police personnel; *S*, number of police stations; *D*, number of police officers per square mile; *H*, rate of homicide arrests per 100,000; *I*, rate of persons working in manufacturing per 1,000; *A*, proportion of the city population between the ages of 20 and 40; *F*, rate of foreign-born per 1,000; *R* includes four regional dummies – *NE* for the Northeast, *W* for the West, *S* for the Southeast, and *MW* for the Midwest.

[b]Indicates *F* too low to enter.

[c]Variable data not available.

Sources: 1880, *Defective, Dependent, and Delinquent Classes* (10th U.S. Census); 1890, *Crime, Pauperism, and Benevolence* (11th U.S. Census); 1903, *Statistics of Cities* (Census Bulletin #20).

for 1880. But for the lodging rate in 1880 the story is quite different, with a substantial $\bar{R}^2$ of .35, which can be read as the model accounting for over a third of the variation in lodging. By 1890, this relationship had reversed, with the $\bar{R}^2$ for arrest rates leaping to .5 and the $\bar{R}^2$ for lodging falling to .11. This change could have been predicted by the overall shift in policing from class control to crime control. Were the data available for the period after the depression of 1893, say for 1895 or 1900, we would expect the change to be even more dramatic, for in the early 1890s the police were still very much in the business of taking care of overnight lodgers.

Although caution must be urged, some observations can be made about the other social and economic indicator variables in the model in Table 9. For lodgers, the percentage of the city population that was foreign born had an important, positive effect. Not too surprisingly, the greater the number of immigrants in a city, the greater the number of station house lodgers. Presumably, this relationship reflected the position of immigrants in the work force – easily displaced by unemployment and forced to move without families in search of work. Equally important, immigrants did not figure in the production of arrests when entered into this relatively complex model. The proportion of a city's work force in manufacturing also had an interesting, negative relationship to the lodging rate in 1880 that had disappeared by 1890. This relationship is ambiguous, and needs much more research, for it raises several questions – did heavily manufacturing cities have police with fewer social services? Did they have more stable employment than other cities? Did the unemployed in these cities seek other forms of temporary housing? Or did commercial and service-oriented cities soak up those displaced from agricultural and industrial work? Of less surprise than this indicator, the variable controlling for age in the 1890s model shows what we can infer to have been true throughout the whole period with policing on the modern model – age structure affected those at risk for arrest. Youthful populations, when controlling for other factors, produced a more arrest-prone (and perhaps more crime-prone) population.

The additional variables relating to the structure of policing prove to be either predictable or nonsignificant. When density can be controlled for, as in the 1880 data, it shows what we might expect, that the more police per square mile, the more arrests per capita they produced. On the other hand, this variable, expectedly, showed no relationship to the rate of lodgers. The variable that ac-

curately brings in the proportion of middle management police officers for 1890 shows no meaningful relationship to total arrest rates
and a positive relationship to lodgers, suggesting that lodging continued as an important feature of the more sophisticated police departments.

Finally, regional variables figured importantly in the 1890 arrest
model, the Midwest and West showing significantly higher arrest
rates than the Northeast and South. If the data could be more finely
tuned, and if we could produce a cross section through time, then
we could predict a more complex set of locational factors to be operating. The disaggregation of the time series into a two-city typology
suggests that within the urban network of the larger cities there
were cities that innovated and produced institutional and bureaucratic patterns that smaller, less important cities imitated. Independent of the communication effects within the urban network, we
can speculate that region also operated as an influence on the behavior of urban bureaucracies. The proper typology of city behavior
would therefore account both for region and urban network position simultaneously, something that needs to be examined through
a less complex lens than that of police and crime.

One final difference in the cross section and the time series appears in the analysis for 1903. The time series tends to reflect the
behavior of the police in the larger places, where the crime-control
focus of policing emerged earlier and the class-control function diminished more rapidly. The cross section provides some interesting contrasts for the smaller cities in 1903. The homicide arrests
contributed positively to the equation: Homicide had contributed
in a statistically significant, positive degree only to the pre-1890
time series. This suggests that homicides did produce pressure on
the police, but only when the police had a broadly active community role. Ironically, in the larger places and when their focus had
shifted to crime control, the police responded far less sensitively to
the pressures of interpersonal violence.

Bureaucrats

Having reached the apparent limits of the predictive power of simple rates of police strength, the next most logical variable to analyze
is the structure of the police force. Did police departments grow
more top-heavy in their bureaucratic structures as they aged, expanded, and became essential parts of city governments? Did the

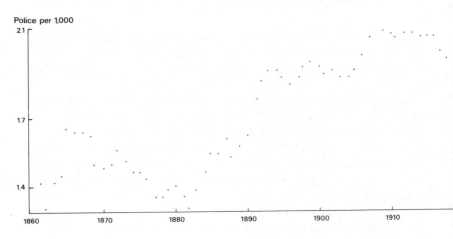

Figure 10. Total police personnel per 1,000 city population. (Three-year moving averages plotted. Slope of regression line = .012. Significance = .00001.) *Source:* Compiled from annual reports of twenty-three police departments. See Appendix B for list of cities and detail on data and sources.

proportionate size of bureaucracies affect the arrest behavior of officers on patrol positively or negatively? Can the equations be sharpened by controlling for structural changes in the police?

By the end of the period under study, urban police forces had attained a kind of bureaucratic maturity; they had approached the strength at which they would remain for the next fifty years. Figure 10 graphs the growth of police strength in officers per 1,000 population, with values ranging from a low in 1863 of 1.32, to a high of 2.07 in 1908, which compares to a current national median of 1.7 and a big city median of 2.3. The graph suggests two periods of police development and change – 1860–95 and 1903–20 – with a transitional era between. The first period, up to about 1890, must be interpreted as a time of stability and entrenchment, during which uniformed urban police became permanent parts of city government. The transitional period, from the late 1890s until the turn of the century, was an era of expansion of police forces as they rapidly increased their per capita strength past all earlier levels.[7] The third period saw a slight decrease in the turn of the century peak and stabilization at modern levels. Thus, the graphs reflect the initial period of introduction of the uniformed urban police – a period of bureaucratic establishment and stabilization – followed by a growth spurt after the entrenched police systems had become a con-

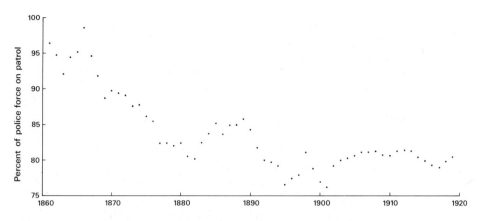

Figure 11. Percentage of police force on patrol. (Three-year moving averages plotted.) *Source:* Compiled from annual reports of twenty-three police departments. See Appendix B for list of cities and detail on data and sources.

venient institution for the dominant society to turn to for social control, ending up in the twentieth century firmly established and restabilized.

The changing proportion of nonpatrol to patrol officers demonstrates the bureaucratic growth of police departments and confirms this interpretation (Figure 11). In the mid 1870s, a decade before police strength increased, the proportion of nonpatrol to patrol officers began to rise, this enlarged bureaucracy paving the way for overall police growth. The increase of nonpatrol proportions ceased in the late 1890s, quickly followed by a stabilization of the overall growth rate: Larger bureaucracies made possible larger and stronger police departments. This rise of police strength resulted from the increased proportion of police bureaucrats who had the time, positions, and power with the city governments to press for more officers per capita. A Pearsonian correlation of the proportion of nonpatrol officers (an indicator of bureaucratization) to the overall strength of the force, a simple measure of growth and bureaucratization, gives an R^2 of .16. The causal effect of bureaucratic growth on overall departmental growth may be caught by lagging the nonpatrol officer variable; a three-year lag gives an R^2 of .24, and a five-year lag raises this figure a bit to .27. In other words, an overall increase in police strength predictably followed an increase in bureaucratization, a response strongest at three and five years.

Interestingly, this growth pattern occurred mainly in the pre-1890 era, with the highest R^2 of .31 appearing with a two-year lag. Lagged correlations in the post-1890 era produced no statistically significant relationship between bureaucratic and overall growth. We can conclude that it was no accident or natural phenomenon causing the increase in police strength, but growing internal specialization and bureaucratization.[8]

How did bureaucratization affect police arrest behavior? Theoretically, a more specialized and bureaucratized police force should be more efficient in its criminal arrest behavior than an old-fashioned force with a high proportion of its members on patrol. On the other hand, the rise in the three-platoon patrol and eight-hour day worked against this trend.[9] But we should be able to refine one of our original predictive equations by controlling for the bureaucratic structure of the police.

One can hypothesize that the strength of nonpatrol forces would be related to arrests for those offenses with victims (called "crime" arrests for simplicity), tentatively confirmed by a slight, positive, partial correlation. In fact, the partial correlation gives a stronger explanation of crime arrests than any simple correlation. This simple correlation between crime arrests and nonpatrol force is nonsignificant ($R^2 = .040$), but the partial controlling for homicide arrests improves the R^2 to .080. Although not particularly large, this does suggest that bureaucratic growth did have some effect on arrests for crimes with victims.[10] As with the relationship of police strength to bureaucratization, seen above, most of this relationship holds only for the pre-1890 period, when $R^2 = .176$, as opposed to the post-1890 era, when $R^2 = .011$. (All these partials are based on first differences.) One interesting aspect of these relationships is that the sign for the R is in each case negative. This has two alternative and mutually exclusive implications. We can either speculate that the new police bureaucrats more successfully increased the strength of the institution than they produced more arrests (cleared more crimes by arrest), or, alternatively, that the new bureaucrats successfully repressed crimes with victims, each incremental increase producing fewer arrests, presumably because of fewer crimes. Of course, because we have no measures of crimes known to the police for the era covered in this book, we cannot resolve this argument, and must leave it with the knowledge that however ambiguous the consequences for the control of crime, the bureaucratization of the police did affect both their strength and behavior.

Summary

This analysis of arrest trends and the police-caused variations in the trends lends additional support to the theme running throughout the previous chapters – that the focus of police attention shifted from control of the "dangerous class" in the nineteenth century to an attempt by the early twentieth century to control criminal behavior only. Although the exactitude of the date falsely implies precision, we can say that this shift occurred for critically important cities by about 1890.[11] This change in the role of the police in controlling urban behavior came concurrently with a new kind of police bureaucracy that had a level of nonpatrolling officers higher than ever before. The bureaucratic change represented, in some cases, the final removal of police decision- and policy-making activities from the specific local demands of ordinary citizens, a change and hardening observable both in the rates at which the police returned (or no longer returned) lost children and the decline in the overnight lodgings that they provided for the homeless.

These changes both in the role of policing and in the structure and behavior of the police bureaucracy came about through external demands upon the police by urban government, through social reformers' demands for the poor as their own clients and, to a lesser extent, through the "natural" growth of the police bureaucracy. Of these three causal factors, only one, the reformers' usurping of the poor and beset-upon, part of the "dangerous class," as their own clients, could not have been predicted. The other two, rising public demands for service and bureaucratic growth, came as predictable if unanticipated consequences of the creation of uniformed patrolling officers. The particular intersection of these three sets of demands and expectations in the last decades of the nineteenth century produced the model of policing that became the twentieth-century norm. That contradictory police roles and abilities, and resulting excesses, have persisted should come as no surprise, considering the confused origins and abilities of the modern urban police. Today's popular image of the police, even when focused on crime control, portrays them as helpers of the victims of crimes; although inaccurate, this image does have historical roots and should be considered a goal from the past and for the future.

Conclusion

Two periods of urban change

By 1920, the policing of American cities had gone through two periods of innovation, the first from approximately 1850 to 1885, the second in the 1890s. Each period shaped a new model of social control for cities; however, the precise way each model worked and to whose benefit it functioned could neither have been clearly perceived nor precisely intended at the time. Even today the existence and nature of these two innovational periods remain obscured by misfocused arguments over the social causations of criminal behavior, by analyses of social control agencies that assume all important consequences were intended and had simple antecedents, and by confusion over the behavioral outcomes of the progressive reforms of police. An analysis and understanding of criminal justice systems, not accounting for individual propensity to commit criminal offenses, does show how social institutions control and divert this behavior. To assume that social control by its very nature is reprehensible gives no insight into the controlled behavior, the social control institution, nor the society that houses the institution. And to examine police reform outside a precisely defined description of both its structural location in society and its behavioral effects does little to promote our understanding of social institutions. The implicit perspective of these three issues – the "cause" of criminal behavior, the assumption that all social control is oppressive, and the examination of reform without prior understanding of structure – have tended to raise wrong questions and inappropriate methods. Although these three earlier focuses have helped us to understand certain aspects of the emergence of the modern police, and have clarified the conflicts centering on police institutions, they have not adequately described what were in fact the two critical transformations.

The speed and pacing of each transformation varied significantly, partly because of the differences in the transformations and partly because of the changes in the urban structure of the United States. The change from constable and watch to uniformed police took a

148

long time, approximately two decades, within each of the first cities that made the change, but by the mid 1880s cities could mandate the change to occur literally overnight. Thus within cities the change took a diminishing amount of time as it became less innovational. Not only did the process of the first change vary within cities, but it varied across space and time, moving through the city system at a relatively predictable rate, with smaller and more isolated places lagging behind their more populous neighbors. The change symbolized by the uniforming of the police, in its earlier and slower phases, represented a process internally drawing together cities that were, individually, spreading out and losing sociopolitical cohesiveness. The ward-based constable–watch system, first supplemented by separate day and night police forces, often did not disappear until the day and night police were unified and the constable and watch could be finally terminated. The new police, although often continuing ward- or precinct-based locational power, had a centralized hierarchical command structure, which would provide one of the few centralizing ties in nineteenth-century cities. The importance of the hierarchy came, not from the central exercise of power downward, but from the flow of information upward, to one place. The very organizational shape of the new police helped them provide informational order to otherwise fragmented cities.

As a consequence of this first transformation within each city, cities became more alike. Already tied together by an increasingly important urban economic network, the more efficient internal communications provided by the police also accelerated intercity communication. Police departments grew closer to one another through simpler and quicker communication links and through the growth of national organizations, emergent bureaucracies, and new professions. As a result, the second transformation of policing came about almost simultaneously over a decade, partly because it signaled a change in social control relationships, only one aspect of which required the creation of new bureaucracies. For example, the creation of municipal lodging houses for tramps augmented the new focus, but the new focus did not solely depend on this new alternative to station house lodgings.

This second transformation changed the behavior of the uniformed police, whereas the first had created them. Because the second transformation was largely behavioral and not bureaucratically visible, it has gone undiscussed and unanalyzed: Rather, historians have focused on one of the subsequent flurries of political activity that followed the second transformation, the progressive reform of police corruption and recruitment procedures. The progressives made the police more rational, while attempting to remove them from the corrupt control of urban political machines and their working-class constituencies.[1] But this set of reforms simply made visible the severing of the police from the special relationships with their "dangerous class" constituents, which had already occurred. And with the formal severing of the police from the control of the "dangerous class" came a changed definition and dissolution of the concept and term themselves. Each component group of the "dangerous class" – the poor, the criminal, the ill, the homeless – gained a more specific group label and specialized agencies came into existence to serve the needs of each. By 1915, when the *New Republic* editorialized about unemployment, it could claim that what it called the "dangerous class" was recruited from the ranks of the unemployed, equating "dangerous class" with the notion of a revolutionary class. Clearly the editorialist was unaware that fifty years earlier the definition of "dangerous class" had incorporated under its umbrella the unemployed as one of many other social subgroups within the class.[2] What had at one time been a broadly applicable class label had become by 1915 an archaic and misused term applied to a specific group of potential revolutionaries.

Police forces and urban order

The introduction of uniformed police to U.S. cities in the mid nineteenth century changed the means and nature of urban social control. The uniforms symbolized both the organizational hierarchy of the police as well as the authority backing them up, blatantly signaling the intentions of this formalized social control organization. Presumably, the public perceived the new police differently from the previous, traditionally organized, city police, yet with the exception of behavioral indicators such as lost children returned to parents, there is surprisingly little information on the image of the early uniformed police.[3]

We must not confuse people's perceptions that they had a right not to be victims of crimes or that a legitimate demand might be made upon the police to help find a lost child with their images of the police. In the nineteenth century, as today, people with property and prestige to protect had a more positive, if condescending, attitude toward the police than did poor people, who had hostile attitudes toward the police. But the holding of a hostile attitude toward the police does not preclude the same person from perceiving the right to have a life free of crime and disorder or from perceiving that the police exist as agents to make an abstract right actual. Therefore, group or class or ethnic attitudes toward the police, although interesting, have little theoretical importance for the analysis of the rise of the uniformed urban police. On the other hand, the changed perception of the duties and obligations of the police guided policymakers both within the police and in city government.

Ostensibly created to prevent crime, the uniformed police quickly inherited the burden of urban disorder and industrial poverty. If the development of the uniformed urban police confirms any historical law, it is the not always comforting principle that human actions often have unintended consequences. For whether one argues that the intentions of those who introduced the uniformed police into the Anglo-American world were to bureaucratize class control, control riots, or prevent crime, the idea of freeing the lives of poor and ordinary people from crime and disorder was most clearly not a purpose of the new police. The idea that people have a right to be free of crime in their daily lives and that the government has an obligation to provide this security was new to nineteenth-century America: It came as an unexpected consequence of the intervention of the uniformed urban police into the public aspects of the lives of ordinary people. Our hazy notion of community crime control in the pre-uniformed police era is for the most part a romanticization of a practice that meant that victims had a right to prosecute offenders, but they had to bear the burden and cost of prosecution.[4] The practical result was that one learned to retaliate when possible and to "suffer and be still" when necessary. As a corollary to the unexpected benefits that the class-control efforts of the uniformed police conferred on ordinary and poor people came the free overnight lodging the police gave to homeless migrants. Thus, another unintended consequence of the introduction of uniformed policing was that the poor turned to the police for emergency aid with the expectation of at least minimal assistance.

Few observers attached much importance to the first transformation of the police or to the new kind of urban world where people wearing uniforms enforced public order. In the case of lost children, where the effects of the change were most visible, the greatest reaction seems to have been simply in the large number of parents flooding the station houses looking for their children. The second transformation of the police seems to have elicited no thoughtful contemporary reaction other than some criticism of the closing of station house lodging. But the diminished amount of noncriminal police services, their high levels of bureaucratization, and high per capita strength escaped even contemporary observers. Legal historian Lawrence Friedman recently pointed out how the "functions of the criminal justice system . . . have been more and more handed over to the police." We can see this as an outcome entirely predictable from the early twentieth century onward, the corollary of the late nineteenth-century divestment of the various welfare services from the police.[5]

Both these transformations came about in a context of urban growth and development, where they played a leading but almost invisible role. The transformation signaled by the uniform marked the transition from a relatively relaxed, traditional form of city government to a rule-bound, less personalistic form of city bureaucracy necessary in a numerically large society peopled by transients. This transformation of the structure of city government, traced by Michael Frisch in a book aptly titled *Town into City*, marked the end to ancient methods of community-based social control – the constable and the watch – and the origins of the modern city's administrative bureaucracy.[6] The second transformation came at the beginning of a remarkable and creative era of urban activity, the Progressive Era, which saw the formalization and fragmentation of the running of the metropolis as we know it.

Historian Samuel Hays has shown how decentralization of services and politics paralleled urban growth in the late nineteenth century, and has emphasized the particularistic and divisive role of the ward in city development from 1850 until 1900. Around the turn of the century, new integrating forces began to reunite the city at the expense of neighborhoods and local needs: This new integration of the city based itself on elites from particular groups and locales and followed the administration patterns of emerging corporate enterprises.[7] In many ways, the development of the police preceded this larger urban development, for it had already provided the unifying groundwork of urban order that made the larger integrative changes appear feasible. From their early days, the uniformed police tied the city together in a way no other formal or informal administrative branch of government could. In fact, Seymour Mandelbaum has shown how New York's Boss Tweed and Tammany Hall machine could flourish precisely because of the absence of any communications alternative in the city in the 1870s.[8] With the exception, that is, of the police. By virtue of the uniform alone, the police daily tied together an incredible multilingual, class-fragmented city. That they should have been in demand for returning lost children or delivering the votes that allowed urban political machines to fend off rural state machines simply reflects their unique position on the city's streets.[9] Thus, the fragmenting, "centrifugal," forces, both spatial and social, of the American city in the post-1850 era, delineated by Hays, could have only worked within the context of the modicum of order and stability provided by the police, centralized and uniformed, along with the fire departments, both formed far earlier than most of the city's services.[10]

In a similar manner, the second transformation came about in a context of urban change, but this transformation, rather than having the police play the flexible role of urban integrator and order producer, actually narrowed and functionally fragmented policing in the city. This transformation could only have come about as a part of the general spatial reintegration and centralization of increasingly specialized city services and administration. Hays specified the examples of "recreation, planning, health and welfare," to which we would add the police, especially in their narrowed role, a role trimmed partly to create just those services enumerated by Hays.[11] He also brought forth evidence to show how the newly integrated city administrations fostered the reentry of urban elites into city governance in the early twentieth century. Both within and outside police departments, the efforts of progressives to professionalize the police confirm this general pattern sketched by Hays. The police professionalization movement had the multiple aims of ending police corruption, stopping their fledgling unionization attempts, and eliminating what had become the painfully apparent working-class nature of police values and attitudes.[12] In twentieth-century cities, where professionals, experts, and managers administered services, the working-class attitudes and behaviors of police officers became increasingly anomalous – the police officers themselves had to be "upgraded" – even the word has status-hierarchic implications. The general success of reformers in removing the police from the corrupt political process through election and civil service reform was not matched on the personnel level. The police remained steadfastly working class and resistant to upgrading, partly because of their job culture, which was almost a half-century old by 1900. In fact, in the 1980s this culture still keeps advanced positions limited to former rank and file officers, thus insuring a police administration responsive to rank and file demands.[13] This rank and file resistance to upgrading achieved its limited success because the police still maintained some of their centralized communications in the city, although they had lost their vital monopoly of the nineteenth century.

The consequences of these two transformations influenced the relationship of the police to their services – the decline in lost children returned home, the almost vanished housing of tramps, the changed arrest behavior that included the decline in police-initiated order arrests, and the not very effective but important focus after the 1890s on arrests for crimes with victims. The police substantially withdrew from interacting with children and their parents, although, of course, they still intervene to a limited extent. By 1908, when a Saint Louis social reformer wrote to advocate the building of neighborhood centers, he could accurately claim, "The only American institution with which [the immigrant] is brought in contact is the police-station, where he is summoned for the violation of some ordinance . . . it is not surprising that he is suspicious of American institutions, that government to him means punishment rather than protection."[14] This reformer's perception of the purely negative police–immigrant interaction reflected the narrowed police role in the community. The police had almost totally abandoned the care of the homeless: The mass supply of bunk rooms and breakfasts by the police had become a service almost exclusively tied to the nineteenth century. And the decline in arrests for public order offenses, both per capita as well as per officer, indicated a decline in active involvement of police with people's behavior in public.[15] The decriminalization of public drunkenness in the 1970s simply finalized a trend that had begun over a century earlier, almost with the creation of the uniformed police.

The brief period in almost every city that saw an increase in lost children returned by the police shows how, for a while, all the people of the city quickly realized the potential usefulness of the police in dealing with urban anonymity and disorder. Yet this had its ironic aspects. In a broad and simplified model summarizing 500 years of Anglo-American development, we can say that the growing state, to protect itself and the economic base of society through the criminal law, created the uniformed police as the most effective means of administering the law. It is possible that the police did successfully protect the state and the economic structure it represented. But their physical presence and organizational structure had the unintended consequence of giving ordinary people a realistic notion that they had a right to a life free from the distresses of urban industrial life as well as from the annoyances of crime and public disorder. As the police were not capable of readily attaining this end, especially but not only in an inherently unjust capitalist society, their ultimate "failure" really reflected an inadequacy of the social and economic structure. The state, in protecting itself through the criminal law and the police, had made apparent its prime contradiction, both its and its economic substructure's inability to provide a context for safe and meaningful lives for all. And, ironically, the state's initial efforts at self-defense created demands from ordinary people for more and better policing to accomplish an end that the state could not deliver, thus leading to new discontent on the part of ordinary people. This discontent manifests itself, both today as well as in the past, in hostility toward the police and concurrent demands on the police for more protection and repression of crime.

Like the diminished return rates of lost children to their parents, station house lodging attenuated in the last decade of the nineteenth century. Although lost children attracted little attention or controversy, lodgers did, and the transfer of the responsibility for their care from the police to separately administered municipal lodging houses came in the wake of criticism of the police as not being the proper persons to take care of tramps, partly because the police were too lax morally. Tramps needed cleaning up. They also needed some sort of forced labor to pay for their housing. From the perspective of reformers, lodging in police stations amounted to an indiscriminate charity. This charity promoted poverty. It did not inculcate the values of hard work and forethought that many reformers still expected to end poverty.[16] The transfer of this welfare responsibility away from the police meant that police departments, strongly entrenched and highly bureaucraticized by the 1890s, had their duties formally narrowed to correspond with the behavioral narrowing of their activities that had already begun. Crime control, not class control, became the new police role in the early twentieth-century urban administration.

As the police became less active in the problems of everyday urban life, they also became less active in arresting people. As shown in Figure 3, both the overall arrest rate as well as the rate for public order arrests fell to about half of their Civil War levels by the end of World War I. For both sets of arrests, the greatest decline came before the 1890s, but while overall arrests tended to level off and homicide arrests climbed after the turn of the century, order arrests continued to fall until 1920. This divergence suggests that while the police continued their disengagement from everyday life, thus arresting fewer people in cases without complaining victims, the post-1890 rise in homicide and slight rise in crimes with victims indexed a rise in the actual offense rate, a rate over which the police had little control. The premier social control agency of American cities in the last part of the nineteenth century was the police, and their role became substantially narrowed and redefined by 1920, even though numerically they stayed quite strong.

Crime control and intercity relationships

The first transformation of policing, although it occurred in individual cities across the United States, created police departments the mirror image of one another. Yet the departments were financially and administratively quite separate. This separateness belied growing national identity and intercommunication, especially among administrators and chiefs. The founding in 1893 of the National Chiefs of Police Union, which quickly became the International Association of Chiefs of Police, formalized the national intercommunication of police administrators. This represented a final convergence, for premature efforts at national organization had begun as early as the summer of 1871, when the chief of the St. Louis police went on a national tour to promote a police convention for the fall in St. Louis.[17] The next national meeting and organizational efforts did not come for more than two decades, although police chiefs continued to get together annually at the meetings of the National Prison Association. By the last part of the 1890s, a "central bureau of criminal identification," supported by the subscriptions of individual police departments, had been formed. Although efforts to create a federally funded bureau failed several times during the first decade of the twentieth century, for all practical purposes national coordination of the unified police had been accomplished.[18] And, significantly, the substantive reasons for creating a national coordinating scheme focused on crime control, to the exclusion of the myriad other duties with which the uniformed police had begun life earlier in the nineteenth century. As Colonel Sylvester, Superintendent of the Washington, D.C., police commented at the National Prison Association meeting in 1902, "The interchange of ideas which is had through the annual convocations of the chiefs of police of this and foreign countries is doing much to eradicate old time prejudice and practices. . . ."[19]

The new, post-1890s model of policing would march to the tune of crime control conceived on national, deliberately nonlocal terms, ultimately paving the way for the Federal Bureau of Investigation.[20]

Colonel Sylvester approvingly cited a House Judiciary Committee report that neatly summarized the new way of thinking: "The police business in the United States has largely become a man hunt in which all parties participate; and when the game is taken in any one quarter, all others join in rejoicing. . . ."[21] Thus, although the second transformation of the uniformed police into crime fighters did not create a total national organization, a national identity and intercommunication network did come about with the completion of the first transformation of the police into uniformed quasi-military social control agents.[22] In a sense, the S-shaped curve of uniform adoptions (Figure 1) traces the course of the first transformation and ends with the beginning second transformation.

The nineteenth-century uniformed police performed a vitally necessary and humane function on city streets. But they did not serve to implement justice because of the specific class focus of police activities. As argued at the end of Chapter 1, the class focus of the pre-1890 police constituted an occasion where the persons suffering unjust treatment were of a specific group, the one situation in a partially just society that is unjust. That this focus of the police had its humane and ameliorative aspects, although important, is not relevant to the justice problem. If the police had dropped their class-control focus but retained their broadly humane range of services, they would have entered the twentieth century with potential for both humanitarian service and just crime control. But they did not.

The modern crime-control version of policing that developed out of the nineteenth-century police, although less humane and less concerned with the well-being of all people, ultimately had in it the potential for shaping a police that could help implement justice, even in a partially just society. For as the police became less focused on class control, they became more concerned, by definition, with crime control. The well-documented tales of late nineteenth- and early twentieth-century police corruption, complicity in vice operations, and extortion of confessions through torture, the "third degree," although hardly showing the police as humane or even effective, does not change this evaluation. The police focus on criminal offenders, rather than on the whole "dangerous class," meant that the victims of police injustice would be more random and less targeted groups than before. That this happened accounts for the growing issue of police malfeasance with urban reformers, as early as 1894 with the Lexow committee in New York, and more pronounced in the first two decades of the twentieth century.[23] For

with their focus diverted away from the "dangerous class," the police more often mistreated members of other classes, and the previous clearly defined and secure pool of potential arrestees became
more vague and diffuse for the police.

Further, the police no longer could offer the positive means of
class control, particularly lodging. People who would have been at
risk to be labeled as members of the "dangerous class" twenty-five
years earlier interacted with the police only negatively by the early
twentieth century. Thus the growth of the black urban population
in the post-class-control era meant that black people never experienced the benefits of police lodging as had many of the earlier urban migrants. This also meant that the police bureaucracies only
dealt with black people through coercive means and that the relationship between post-1890s urban migrants and the police, although theoretically more just than for earlier migrants, would be
only in conflict-produced situations. That is, although the police
shifted from less just class control to more just crime control, their
range of options for dealing with people narrowed considerably.
And urban migrants who lived in the most densely populated sections of the city, who had the lowest incomes, and who spent more
time in places subject to police patrol mainly had contact with the
police when subject to arrest. Certainly, previous urban migrants
had experienced arrests. But with the arrests they also knew the
police as providers of shelter, as helpers in finding lost kids, and
occasionally as sources of jobs – in other words, as sources of help
in the varied crises produced by the late nineteenth-century city.
As a result, urban reformers' criticism of police corruption and malfeasance added to the increasing police distance and isolation from
the "dangerous class." And police officers became an isolated subculture, while the police role, on the surface, appeared to continue
as class control.

Even from the first half of the nineteenth century, one element of
the crime-control focus of the police had posed a potential threat to
civil liberties and to the police implementation of justice: the notion
of crime prevention. When the prevailing assumption had been
that the "dangerous class" produced crime, the prevention ideology focused on the repression and control of the "dangerous class."
Class containment accomplished crime prevention. Without a class
on which to focus crime-prevention tactics, the whole ideology provided motivation for subverting any person or group perceived as
potential offenders. As a component of police duties since the intro-

duction of the uniform, the prevention mission grew in importance in the twentieth century, and, with a goal irreconcilable with Anglo-American notions of civil liberty, the police were cast into the position of subverting civil liberty.[24] For to ask the police to act to prevent crime assumes that the police can identify potential offenders and on the basis of this identification act in such a way as to prevent a criminal offense. Of course, such prevented action cannot be empirically examined, and unprevented action can be defined as the result of poor prevention means. The prevention goal, which had accorded so well with class control, would be destined to keep the police involved in criminal activity themselves in efforts to prevent crime.

It is important to conceive the developmental changes of the police in each city as a part of a much broader pattern, cities responding and adapting to national social and economic changes. No longer will municipal studies be able to begin with locally isolated and developmentally unique phenomena before moving to larger patterns. For although case studies have critical importance to historical analysis, certain kinds of problems, including much of the analysis of urban government and police behavior in particular, must begin with a solid understanding of the national baseline of change and development. The best example of this kind of approach can be found in the work of historian Kenneth Fox, who in a recent study of urban government stresses the importance of an era of national innovation between 1894, when the National Municipal League was founded, and 1913, when the Bureau of the Census developed new functional accounting schemes.[25] During this period, a cadre of city innovators fashioned a model of city government designed to respond adequately to the various crises introduced in the late nineteenth century by industrial and population growth. Prior to this era, Fox emphasizes, ward-based and fragmented city governments' inabilities to deal with problems ranged from street cleaning to finance. Although the two transformations of policing described in this book parallel Fox's periods, in important ways they predated by one step some of the larger shifts in urban governance. First, although the uniformed police may have had ward-based personnel recruitment, they still had uniquely centralized formal power structures and, more important, communication networks. Because the police organizational structure cast its net over the whole city, an unintended consequence of the adoption of the semi-military model of communication meant that the police ended up with access to and coordinating power over the city's daily operations not achieved until the twentieth century by other parts of the city government.

Ironically, of course, the uniformed police were themselves an urban innovation, an innovation that actually lost its scope of power at the expense of the broader wave of urban innovation commencing in the 1890s. For the early 1890s saw many changes in the structure of urban government and reform, not just in policing. J. J. McCook, the tramp reformer, publicly changed his position from one of blaming the tramps themselves for their indigence to that of blaming unemployment – the depression of 1893 simply forced this new perception on him. As historian Paul Boyer notes, across the country the depression "called into question the two ideological pillars of the charity organization movement."[26] Another historian, Melvin Holli, emphasizes that, for municipal reform, the depression of 1893 was a "watershed . . . [which] shook the cities with a special ferocity."[27] Neither these historians nor I claim that it was the depression itself that made the change, but rather that it was a precipitant of many urban changes that had been brewing for decades. Although one of the efforts of the national urban innovators in the 1894–1913 era was to develop comparable city accounting systems, individual city police forces had had comparable, if not superior, record-keeping schemes from the moment of their creation. Thus, being ahead of their times in important ways, the police made possible the modicum of urban stability and order within which their other innovations could occur, and they also suffered a narrowing of their scope of activities as a result of these innovations.

From their inception over a century earlier, the urban police have been agents of class control and social control in general. But changes in their targets of control, their means of accomplishing control, and the ends to which control worked reflected the increased complexity of urban government. As the police changed from an agency controlling a class of people through both positive and coercive means to an agency controlling a specific class of behavior, they played an integral role in the general transition of city government in the post-1890s era to a "functional" model of organization, where agencies and their responsibilities focused on like tasks defined by the overall set of activities of the city government. For the city as a whole and the police specifically, the new focus obliterated class- and neighborhood-oriented city services, imitating the emerging managerial models of corporations. Although efficient from the government's point of view, this organizational mode increased feelings of urban estrangement and anonymity. The new governmental structure allowed cities to operate smoothly within the national network of cities and increased the viability of the city itself as a part of the national production apparatus. And although the prevention mission of the post-1890s police contained an implicit threat to civil liberties, the police focus on crime control also had the as yet unrealized potential for a fair, consistent, and perhaps just form of social control.

Appendix A *Police uniform adoption dates*

The list in Table A.1 shows the date when a city uniformed its police department and the rank size of the city (relative to all cities with information) in the next census year after adoption. It may not be apparent, but this list is the result of a good deal of time-consuming effort, particularly on the part of well over 100 librarians and archivists. Those cities for which I have cited no date belong to the frustratingly large category with missing information. I presume that the information is randomly missing and that complete information would fill out the plotted curves more adequately. Although the dates for a few cities were easy to determine, most required the energy of many people: For the cities where I have not reported any dates, I have been assisted by both librarians and historical societies in attempting to determine the precise moment at which the police were uniformed. If the missing information has a nonrandom structure, two possible kinds of bias could be introduced. Most likely could be the situation that places without noted dates were late adopters, the adoption of uniforms being commonplace and nonnoteworthy by the time of the late adoption. This could change the shape of the diffusion curve from an S to a U, the late adopters coming as a burst in the 1880s and 1890s. Similarly, a delay in adoption by the missing cities would change the shape of the rank/date distribution, probably flattening the slope but not changing the order of the rank and adoption relationship. However, it is more likely that additional data would produce a more pronounced S curve, particularly if the missing cities were clustered with the bulk of other adopters. In all cases, the diffusion curves also represent comunication lags, influenced both by urban rank and by space as well: By not factoring out space in the rank order dispersion, a bias away from a neat linear relationship has been introduced. I conclude that although it is possible biases introduced by missing information would contradict my interpretation, it is far more likely that missing data have obscured the relationships. Discussing early and late adopters will clarify this problem.

The most deviant cities in the uniforming and modernizing process deserve some comment. Two cities were noticably early adopters – Albany, New York and Savannah, Georgia. Given Albany's proximity to New York City, the high degree of state interference in New York City's police, and Albany's status as the state capital, it would not be surprising if the legislature had mandated a uniformed police force for Albany shortly after New York City. This in fact it did, but a search of the newspaper does not confirm that the police actually appeared in uniforms in 1854. Thus it cannot be confidently asserted that Albany actually uniformed its police in 1854. Savannah, on the other hand, clearly did uniform its police in 1854. Although small in size, the port city of Savannah had the urban functions of a much larger place, serving as the metropolis for a large and commercially valuable agricultural hinterland. In other words, its population rank belies its urban importance. Moreover, its police were clearly used as a means of slave control, their size and organization more akin to a militia or military occupation forces than those of any other city. Charleston, South Carolina, uniformed its police in 1856 for reasons identical to Savannah's. Like Savannah, Charleston was the entrepôt for a rich agricultural hinterland and had high-order urban functions for its size. Also like Savannah, the Charleston police served as a militia for slave control. Jersey City, New Jersey, the fourth early adopter, could in certain ways be considered almost a suburb of New York City. Moreover, like Albany, it is not perfectly clear if its propensity to innovate was matched by actual uniform adoption, as the main evidence for Jersey City is statutory.

Five cities that adopted uniforms late also merit attention. New Orleans, ranked 5th largest city in the United States in 1860 with regional importance equal to Savannah's, apparently did not uniform its police until forced by Reconstruction. There is some evidence that uniformed patrols policed the city earlier, but I have not been able to confirm this. Also, the city's unusual political divisions and racial and ethnic diversity kept it with a government unique in its lack of centralization. Both Milwaukee and Buffalo were also late in adopting uniforms, but this was partly because they had both recently entered higher ranks in the urban size hierarchy. As recently as 1840, Buffalo had been only the 15th largest city, whereas in 1860 Milwaukee was only 21st. Both cities lagged their rank position when they uniformed because they had grown quickly in the early period of police modernization. Erie, Pennsylvania, also had only recently moved to its rank in cities: In 1900, it ranked 41st, but in 1891, one year before its uniform, it had been 73d. And Terre Haute, Indiana, ranked 58th three years after the adoption of its uniformed police, had ranked only 104th in 1890.

One can see that the scheme of ranking cities by size at the time of innovation is only a crude proxy for growth, spatial location, information access, and rank itself. Some of the cities that deviated did so because the rank measure was not adequate. Other places deviated for other reasons, particularly those where slave control was an overwhelming concern of the city elite. But the point to be kept in mind is that the underlying propensity of a city to innovate and change the structure of its policing came from its location in the urban hierarchy, throughout which information diffused along relatively predictable lines and with relatively predictable speed.

Table A.1. *Police uniform adoption dates*

Rank	Date	City	Source
45	1879	Auburn, N.Y.	Henry M. Allen, *A Chronicle of Auburn from 1793 to 1955* (Auburn, N.Y.: n.p., 1955), 48.
11	1854	Albany, N.Y.	Codman Hilsop, *Albany: Dutch, English, and American* (Albany, N.Y.: Argus Press, 1936), 305 (lacks independent confirmation).
53	1874	Atlanta	Eugene J. Watts, "The Police in Atlanta, 1890–1905," *Journal of Southern History* (May 1973), 166.
50	1869	Augusta, Ga.	Charles C. Jones, Jr., *Memorial History of Augusta, Georgia* (Syracuse, N.Y.: D. Mason, 1890), 187.
03	1857	Baltimore	de Francias Folsom, *Our Police: A History of the Baltimore Police from the First Watchman to the Latest Appointee* (Baltimore: J. D. Ehlers, 1888), 24.
04	1859	Boston	Roger Lane, *Policing the City: Boston, 1822–1885* (Cambridge, Mass.: Harvard University Press, 1967), 104.
44	1862	Bridgeport, Conn.	*History of the Police Department of Bridgeport, Connecticut* (Bridgeport, Conn.: Relief Book Publishing, 1892), 35.
09	1866	Buffalo	William H. Dolan (comp.), *Our Police and Our City: The Official History of the Buffalo Police Department* (Buffalo: Bensler and Wesley, 1893), 92.

Table A.1. *Police uniform adoption dates*

Rank	Date	City	Source
26	1868	Cambridge, Mass.	*Cambridge Chronicle Semi-Centennial Souvenir Issue* (Cambridge, Mass.: Cambridge Chronicle, 1896), 96.
41	1868	Camden, N.J.	Charles S. Boyer, *The Span of a Century: A Chronological History of the City of Camden* (Camden, N.J.: Centennial University Committee, 1928), 41.
20	1856	Charleston, S.C.	Michael S. Hindus, "Prison and Plantation: Criminal Justice in Nineteenth Century Massachusetts and South Carolina," Ph.D. dissertation (Berkeley: University of California, Berkeley, 1975), 62.
08	1858	Chicago	George E. Ketcham, "Municipal Police Reform: A Comparative Study of Law Enforcement in Cincinnati, Chicago, New Orleans, New York and St. Louis, 1844–1877," Ph.D. dissertation (Columbia: University of Missouri, 1967), 223.
06	1859	Cincinnati	Ketcham, 223.
19	1866	Cleveland	William G. Rose, *Cleveland: The Making of a City* (Cleveland: World, 1950), 334.
38	1868	Columbus	Jack G. Shough, *History of the Police Department; Columbus, Ohio, 1821–1945* (Columbus, n.p., n.d.), 21.
54	1873	Denver	Eugene F. Rider, "The Denver Police Department: An Administrative, Organizational, and Operational History, 1858–1905," Ph.D. dissertation (Denver: University of Denver, 1971), 115.
57	1876	Des Moines, Ia.	Charles Corcoran, "Des Moines Police Mark One Hundredth Anniversary," *Des Moines Tribune* (July 3, 1976), 5.
17	1865	Detroit	John C. Schneider, "Detroit and the Problem of Disorder: The Riot of 1863" *Michigan History* (Spring 1974), 23.
43	1873	Dubuque, Ia.	Dubuque *Daily Herald*. (Feb. 6, 1873), no p.
48	1891	Erie, Pa.	*Nelson's Biographical Dictionary* (Erie, Pa.: S. B. Nelson, 1896), 414.
52	1871	Grand Rapids, Mich.	Albert Baxter, *History of the City of Grand Rapids* (New York; Munsell, 1891), 179.
37	1862	Indianapolis	*Common Council Proceedings*, vol. 7, (manuscript), 353. I am indebted to

Table A.1. *Police uniform adoption dates (cont.)*

Rank	Date	City	Source
			James W. Williams for his detailed analysis of the process of uniforming and modernizing the Indianapolis police. 1862 is a bit early to conform with my argument about uniforms and the diffusion of innovations, and Williams says uniforms may not have been worn even by 1869, a more predictable date. Private letter, July 22, 1977.
23	1856	Jersey City, N.J.	*Jersey City Ordinances, 1843–1866* (Jersey City, N.J.: n.p., n.d.), 85.
59	1874	Kansas City, Mo.	Theodore S. Case, *History of Kansas City, Missouri* (Syracuse, N.Y.: Mason, 1888), 213.
36	1878	Lynn, Mass.	Frederick A. Watson, *Some Annals of Nahant, Massachusetts* (Boston: Old Corner Book Store, 1928), 297.
33	1859	Manchester, N.H.	*Ordinances of City of Manchester with a Compilation of the General Laws Relating to the Government of Cities and Special Acts Relating to City of Manchester, Acts of June, 1858,* Sec. 15 (Manchester, N.H., 1888).
29	1866	Memphis	Ken Rose, "History," in *Memphis Police Department, 1827–1975,* Frank and Gennie Myers, eds. (Marceline, Mo.: Walsworth, 1975), 40.
18	1874	Milwaukee	Bayrd Still, *Milwaukee: The History of a City* (Madison: State Historical Society of Wisconsin, 1948), 232.
56	1874	Minneapolis	Alix J. Muller, *History of the Police and Fire Departments of the Twin Cities* (Minneapolis: Minneapolis, St. Paul, American Land and Title Registration Association, 1900), 41.
10	1860	Newark, N.J.	*History of the Police Department, Newark* (Newark, N.J.: Relief Book Publishing, 1893).
34	1876	New Bedford, Mass.	"Development of the Police Department of the City of New Bedford," *Sunday Standard* (New Bedford, Mass., Feb. 5, 1911), 24.
21	1861	New Haven, Conn.	J. Birney Tuttle, *Guardians of the Peace and Property of New Haven* (New Haven, Conn.: Evans, Gardner, 1889), 23.

Table A.1. *Police uniform adoption dates*

Rank	Date	City	Source
05	1866	New Orleans	Henry J. Leovy, *The Laws and General Ordinances of the City of New Orleans* (New Orleans: Bloomfield and Steel, 1866), 367.
49	1866	Newport, R.I.	*Newport Mercury* (Aug. 18, 1866), 1.
01	1853	New York	James F. Richardson, *The New York Police: Colonial Times to 1901* (New York: Oxford University Press, 1970), 64.
47	1866	Norfolk, Va.	*Norfolk Journal* (Dec. 22, 1866), 3.
58	1868	Omaha, Neb.	Arthur C. Wakeley, ed., *Omaha: The Gate City and Douglas County, Nebraska* (Chicago: St. Clarke, 1917), 118.
35	1871	Paterson, N.J.	*History of the Fire and Police Departments of Paterson, N.J.* (Paterson, N.J.: Relief Association Publishing, 1893), 113.
40	1870	Peoria, Ill.	James M. Rice, *Peoria City and County, Illinois* (Chicago: S.J. Clarke, 1912), 340.
02	1856	Philadelphia	Howard O. Sprogle, *The Philadelphia Police: Past and Present* (Philadelphia, 1887; New York: AMS, 1974), 105.
30	1874	Pittsburgh	Christine Altenburger, "The Pittsburgh Bureau of Police: Some Historical Highlights, *Western Pennsylvania Historical Magazine* (Jan. 1966), 27.
44	1865	Richmond, Va.	*Richmond Whig* (Dec. 12, 1865).
28	1865	Reading, Pa.	"History of Reading Police Department," *Fourteenth Annual Convention, Fraternal Order of the Police* (Reading, Pa., Aug. 11–14, 1930), 17–21.
32	1861	Rochester, N.Y.	*Union Advertiser* (May 20, 1861), 204.
32	1865	Salem, Mass.	*Special Rules and Regulations for the Government of the Salem Police* (Salem, Mass., 1865), 21.
31	1854	Savannah, Ga.	Richard H. Haunton, "Law and Order in Savannah, 1850–1860," *Georgia Historical Quarterly* (Spring 1972), 15.
07	1861	St. Louis	Ketcham, 223.
46	1872	St. Paul	Muller, 53.
13	1857	San Francisco	Roger W. Lotchin, *San Francisco, 1846–1856: From Hamlet to City* (New York: Oxford University Press, 1974).
55	1872	Springfield, Ill.	*Illinois State Journal* (Oct. 21, 1956), no p.
24	1869	Syracuse, N.Y.	New York, *Laws of the State of New York* (Albany, 1870), Chap. 17, Act of Feb. 15, 1869.

Table A.1. *Police uniform adoption dates (cont.)*

Rank	Date	City	Source
51	1897	Terre Haute, Ind.	*Tribune Star* (Oct. 18, 1970).
42	1867	Toledo, O.	Marge Main, "Pantalooned Police Once Patrolled City," *Toledo Times* (Sept. 24, 1943), no. p.
39	1874	Trenton, N.J.	*Charter and Ordinances of the City of Trenton, New Jersey* (Trenton, N.J.: Waar, Day and Naar, 1875), 132.
30	1859	Utica, N.Y.	Utica *Morning Herald* (Oct. 26, 1859), 2.
12	1858	Washington, D.C.	Kenneth G. Alfers, "The Washington Police: A History 1880–1886," Ph.D. dissertation (Washington, D.C.: George Washington University, 1975), 48.
27	1864	Worcester, Mass.	Charles B. Pratt, *Report of City Marshall* (Worcester, Mass.: n.p., 1864), 162.

Appendix B *Arrest data sources*

Table B.1 shows the cities included in the data base for the arrest series. The years listed after each city indicate those years for which at least the total arrests were found. Notice that the Brooklyn data end in 1896, after which these arrests were reported with the New York City police. All the actual values for the variables gathered for each city – total arrests, initiative arrests, discharged cases, total and patrol officers, homicide arrests, lodgers, and population estimates – are available for anyone's use from the Criminal Justice Archive and Information Network (CJAIN), P.O. Box 1248, Ann Arbor, Mich. 48106.

Table B.1. *Arrest data sources*

City (by rank size)	Years with at least total arrests
New York	1860–1920
Philadelphia	1860, 1862–7, 1869–70, 1872–5, 1877–85, 1887–1920
Brooklyn	1860–9, 1871–96
Chicago	1867–70, 1872–1920
Boston	1860–1920
St. Louis	1861, 1864, 1866–1919
Baltimore	1864, 1867–73, 1875–1920
Cincinnati	1862–4, 1867–1916
San Francisco	1862–1905, 1907–17
New Orleans	1880, 1887, 1891–8, 1900–15
Cleveland	1872–1910, 1912–15
Buffalo	1872–87, 1889–90, 1897–1902, 1904–8, 1910–20
Washington, D.C.	1862–1920
Newark, N.J.	1870–87, 1889–1920
Louisville, Ky.	1870–1, 1873, 1875–1915
Detroit	1862–3, 1865–1918
Milwaukee	1868–70, 1873–5, 1880, 1883–1920
Providence, R.I.	1863–4, 1870–1908, 1911–12, 1914–15
Rochester, N.Y.	1877, 1887, 1902–18
Pittsburgh	1887–97, 1899, 1908–1915
Richmond, Va.	1872–1920
New Haven, Conn.	1870–1920
Lowell, Mass.	1870, 1876–1901, 1903–20

Appendix C *Multiple regression tables and correlation matrices*

The following tables report the results of the regressions that form much of the basis for Chapter 4. All the variables were used in the first difference form, and all were adjusted by population and so were in the form of rates. Note that the relatively low value of the adjusted R^2 values partly results from the use of first-difference values, rather than using absolute values and correcting for trend with another variable. Note also that these results tend to be used for hypothesis testing rather than for careful coefficient estimation. Thus, the interpretive weight falls on the signs of coefficients. This more conservative approach seems reasonable given the possibility of unknown biases in the data.

Table C.1. *Total arrests as dependent variable (based on first differences)*

Period	C	Police (SEE)[a]	Homicide (SEE)	$\bar{R}^2$ (F)	D-W
All cities					
1860–1920	−57.5	12.47 (6.13)	.202 (.27)	.071 (3.27)	2.31
1860–90	−66.5	10.64 (2.11)	.31 (.24)	.019 (1.29)	2.40
1891–1920	−51.1	21.14 (7.96)	.09 (.05)	.175 (4.08)	1.66
Group I cities					
1860–1920	−.84	−16.32 (3.48)	.20 (.59)	.034 (1.99)	2.77
1860–90	−1.30	−24.98 (3.43)	.21 (.29)	.059 (1.84)	2.74
1891–1920	−.35	21.52 (13.31)	−.04 (.03)	.281 (6.66)	1.76
Group II cities					
1860–1920	−.84	19.25 (4.33)	1.35 (7.25)	.250 (10.82)	2.86
1860–90	−.80	11.92 (.98)	2.14 (8.06)	.350 (8.78)	2.84
1891–1920	−.76	28.48 (2.39)	.30 (.21)	.038 (1.58)	2.32

[a]SEE = standard error.

Table C.2. *Initiative arrests as dependent variable (based on first differences)*

Period	C	Police (SEE)	Homicide (SEE)	$\bar{R}^2$ (F)	D-W
All cities					
1860–1920	− 133.8	32.14 (10.11)	4.61 (34.42)	.430 (23.22)	3.05
1860–90	− 79.0	30.43 (4.83)	6.26 (27.96)	.543 (18.21)	3.23
1891–1920			Not significant		
Group I cities					
1860–1920	− .47	11.18 (2.52)	− .49 (5.28)	.090 (3.81)	3.04
1860–90	− .26	13.33 (1.90)	− .63 (4.93)	.149 (3.36)	3.12
1891–1920	− 1.23	0 (0)	.87 (3.99)	.090 (3.99)	3.22
Group II cities					
1860–1920	− .52	− 3.34 (.10)	− .90 (2.39)	.030 (1.88)	2.37
1860–90	− .83	3.01 (.04)	− 2.30 (6.21)	.177 (4.12)	2.64
1891–1920	− .92	18.05 (1.65)	1.03 (4.50)	.172 (4.01)	2.24

Table C.3. *"Crime" arrests as dependent variable (based on first differences)*

Period	C	Police (SEE)	Homicide (SEE)	$\bar{R}^2$ (F)	D-W
All cities					
1860–1920	− 5.13	3.02 (1.03)	1.02 (19.50)	.244 (10.51)	2.36
1860–90	− 22.80	2.28 (.29)	1.20 (10.94)	.254 (5.95)	2.44
1891–1920	21.4	3.92 (.69)	.61 (5.35)	.106 (2.72)	1.79
Group I cities					
1860–1920	− .19	− 9.96 (1.28)	.63 (5.70)	.078 (3.42)	2.75
1860–90	− .67	− 16.74 (1.85)	.78 (4.74)	.142 (3.24)	2.78
1891–1920	.87	21.15 (3.30)	− .91 (3.55)	.133 (3.23)	2.78
Group II cities					
1860–1920			Not significant		
1860–90			Not significant		
1891–1920	− .37	19.73 (3.09)	.12 (.09)	.054 (1.83)	2.01

Table C.4. *Lodgers as dependent variable (based on first differences)*

Period	C	Police (SEE)	Homicide (SEE)	$\bar{R}^2$ (F)	D-W
All cities					
1860–1920	− 207.98	50.20 (7.02)	1.73 (1.39)	.103 (4.37)	2.35
1860–90	− 243.2	58.61 (4.03)	2.39 (.92)	.109 (2.77)	2.36
1891–1920	− 77.4	− 11.77 (1.22)	− .88 (2.15)	.025 (1.38)	1.39
Group I cities					
1860–1920	− 1.06	37.42 (5.74)	.40 (.71)	.074 (3.28)	3.03
1860–90	.22	47.90 (3.69)	.48 (.44)	.075 (2.09)	3.09
1891–1920			Not significant		
Group II cities					
1860–1920	− 1.98	35.67 (2.60)	.86 (.51)	.054 (2.70)	1.76
1860–90	− 2.94	34.12 (.90)	1.53 (.46)	.033 (1.50)	1.49
1891–1920			Not significant		

Table C.5. *Correlation matrices (based on first differences)*

	I	C	H	P	L
All cities, 1860–1920					
T	.36	.54	.08	.31	.21
	(.003)	(.001)	(.272)	(.007)	(.050)
I		.69	.59	.34	.59
		(.001)	(.001)	(.004)	(.001)
C			.51	.14	.55
			(.001)	(.145)	(.001)
H				.05	.16
				(.357)	(.109)
P					.33
					(.005)
All cities, 1860–90					
T	.35	.54	.13	.28	.23
	(.030)	(.001)	(.253)	(.066)	(.107)
I		.76	.71	.36	.61
		(.001)	(.001)	(.024)	(.001)
C			.55	.16	.60
			(.001)	(.205)	(.001)
H				.13	.22
				(.248)	(.127)
P					.38
					(.020)
All cities, 1891–1920					
T	.55	.51	− .08	.48	.08
	(.001)	(.002)	(.347)	(.004)	(.344)

Table C.5. *Correlation matrices (based on first differences)*

	I	C	H	P	L
I		.23 (.110)	.15 (.208)	.15 (.208)	.09 (.320)
C			.38 (.019)	.05 (.394)	.07 (.351)
H				−.24 (.105)	−.23 (.114)
P					−.14 (.226)

Group I cities, 1860–1920

	I	C	H	P	L
T	−.08 (.274)	.24 (.030)	.09 (.242)	−.19 (.068)	−.30 (.011)
I		−.87 (.001)	−.28 (.015)	.19 (.073)	−.30 (.011)
C			.30 (.011)	−.03 (.412)	.45 (.001)
H				.02 (.428)	.12 (.195)
P					.33 (.005)

Group I cities, 1860–90

	I	C	H	P	L
T	−.10 (.305)	.22 (.116)	.09 (.318)	−.28 (.064)	−.30 (.053)
I		−.88 (.001)	−.39 (.020)	.24 (.112)	−.33 (.043)
C			.38 (.022)	−.09 (.316)	.49 (.003)
H				.02 (.464)	.13 (.256)
P					.38 (.021)

Group I cities, 1891–1920

	I	C	H	P	L
T	.09 (.315)	.47 (.004)	.01 (.483)	.57 (.001)	−.24 (.099)
I		−.83 (.001)	.35 (.028)	.03 (.443)	−.18 (.173)
C			−.31 (.049)	.30 (.057)	.02 (.452)
H				.06 (.378)	−.04 (.414)
P					−.21 (.135)

Group II cities, 1860–1920

	I	C	H	P	L
T	−.07 (.320)	.06 (.338)	.47 (.001)	.43 (.001)	.33 (.009)

Table C.5. *Correlation matrices (based on first differences) (cont.)*

	I	C	H	P	L
I		.34	−.25	−.15	−.31
		(.008)	(.041)	(.120)	(.012)
C			−.08	.05	−.03
			(.291)	(.342)	(.405)
H				.47	.21
				(.001)	(.058)
P					.28
					(.020)
Group II cities, 1860–90					
T	−.30	−.13	.61	.46	.40
	(.066)	(.252)	(.001)	(.006)	(.015)
I		.41	−.48	−.24	−.34
		(.014)	(.005)	(.114)	(.036)
C			−.19	−.03	−.07
			(.152)	(.431)	(.399)
H				.56	.26
				(.001)	(.087)
P					.29
					(.069)
Group II cities, 1891–1920					
T	.77	.50	.16	.31	−.09
	(.001)	(.001)	(.229)	(.060)	(.301)
I		.17	.43	.32	−.11
		(.198)	(.015)	(.057)	(.299)
C			.14	.34	.20
			(.245)	(.048)	(.156)
H				.25	−.01
				(.110)	(.488)
P					.19
					(.164)

Key: *T*, total arrest; *I*, initiative arrests; *C*, "crime" arrests; *H*, homicides; *P*, police; *L*, lodgers. Significance is given in parentheses.

Table C.6. *Regressions with additional variable of unskilled real urban wages (first differences on all variables)*

	C	Police (SEE)	Homicide (SEE)	Wages (SEE)	$\bar{R}^2$ (F)	D-W
Total arrests						
1860–1920	−56.6	12.47 (5.04)	.065 (.39)	−.63 (2.95)	.055 (2.16)	2.31
1860–90			Not significant			
1891–1920	−45.0	19.86 (8.70)	.101 (.427)	−3.18 (10.42)	.146 (2.66)	1.68
Initiative arrests						
1860–1920	−128.3	31.8 (10.17)	4.61 (.79)	−4.00 (5.89)	.424 (15.5)	3.03
1860–90	−75.1	30.37 (14.06)	6.26 (1.20)	−3.24 (7.56)	.528 (11.8)	3.21
1891–1920[a]	−26.9	−1.29 (11.01)	.64 (.54)	−30.3 (13.18)	.130 (2.45)	2.64
Crime arrests						
1860–1920	−7.3	3.16 (2.99)	1.02 (.23)	1.61 (1.73)	.242 (7.28)	2.39
1860–90	−24.4	2.31 (4.27)	1.20 (.36)	1.58 (2.30)	.239 (4.04)	2.49
1891–1920	11.9	5.91 (5.44)	.61 (.27)	4.92 (6.51)	.091 (1.97)	1.74
Lodgers						
1860–1920[a]	−23.8	52.02 (18.44)	1.70 (1.43)	22.1 (10.68)	.151 (4.51)	2.36
1860–90[a]	−265.5	59.0 (28.67)	2.41 (2.45)	21.8 (15.42)	.141 (2.58)	2.34
1891–1920			Not significant			

[a]Wage variable contributes to the equation and also shows improved $\bar{R}^2$ over equation without wage variable.

Source: Unskilled urban real wages index from Jeffrey G. Williamson, "The Relative Costs of American Men, Skills, and Machines: A Long View" (Institute for Research on Poverty Discussion Paper 289–75, University of Wisconsin, July 1975), Table 11, p. 41. I wish to thank Professor Williamson for allowing me to use this important series. I also wish to thank Colin Loftin for alerting me to the need to use wages and employment data of the working poor rather than data for all workers.

Table D.2. *Annual rates of lost children per 1,000 city population, (for earliest fifteen years of data series) (cont.)*

Wash-ington	Newark	Detroit	Mil-wawkee	Provi-idence	Rochester
1.7	1.8	4.2	1.0	2.8	2.0
1.7	1.9	3.2	1.0	2.2	—
1.9	1.8	3.0	—	2.3	—
1.7	1.9	3.0	—	1.9	—
1.2	1.6	3.2	—	2.0	—
1.5	1.4	2.8	—	1.9	—
1.4	1.6	1.8	—	—	—
1.5	1.2	1.9	—	1.2	—
(1876) 1.3	(1884) 1.9	(1882) 1.9	(1882) —	(1886) —	(1885) —

Pittsburgh	Richmond	New Haven	Lowell
(1898) .6	(1873) 2.0	(1862) .8	(1877) 1.2
.8	1.6	1.0	.9
.6	.8	—	.8
.7	.5	.2	.9
.6	.4	.8	.7
.7	.3	—	1.0
.8	.2	1.8	1.2
1.0	.2	.8	1.3
—	.5	.6	.6
.9	.7	1.3	.6
—	.8	1.5	—
.1	1.0	1.9	—
.1	.9	1.9	1.0
.3	.8	1.8	1.1
(1894) .1	(1887) .6	(1876) 2.3	(1891) 1.1

Table D.3. *Rank order correlations (Spearman's rho) of lost children by region, 1880*

Region	Number of cases	Children by costs	Children by city size
Northeast coast	39	.608	.515
Other	86	—	.265 (.007)
Northeast inland	27	—	.256 (.099)
Other	98	.434	.342
All Northeast	66	.618	.479
Southeast	13	—	—
Other	112	.438	.478
Midwest	31	—	.521
Plains	7	—	.643

Significance above .001 not noted; between .002 and .099 is in parentheses; less than .099 is excluded.
Source: Tenth U.S. Census, Frederick Wines, *The Defective, Dependent, and Delinquent Classes* (Washington, D.C.: GPO, 1888), Table CXXXVI. Number of cases with complete data: 125.

Table D.4. *Annual number of lost children returned to parents by the NYSPCC compared to those returned by the New York police*

Year	NYSPCC	Police	Year	NYSPCC	Police	Year	NYSPCC	Police
1875	11	—	1886	138	3,750	1897	2,810	—
1876	25	—	1887	115	3,360	1898	2,884	3,457
1877	58	5,976	1888	187	3,078	1899	3,803	3,000
1878	81	—	1889	167	2,968	1900	3,532	3,157
1879	79	—	1890	298	3,049	1901	2,728	2,262
1880	109	4,993	1891	365	3,137	1902	4,031	2,661
1881	149	—	1892	497	2,758	1903	6,106	2,814
1882	106	—	1893	1,166	2,581	1904	4,299	2,260
1883	180	—	1894	1,859	2,580			
1884	161	—	1895	2,261	2,305			
1885	150	4,308	1896	2,749	2,397			

Source: Annual Reports of the New York Society for the Prevention of Cruelty to Children, New York police.

Appendix E *Synopsis of crime rates from previous studies*

Table E.1. *Synopsis of crime rates from previous studies*

Place	Offense category	Trends	Peaks
Massachusetts			
Entire state		Declining, 1871–92	
Boston	Murder	Declining most, 1871–92	
Other cities		Declining, 1871–92	
Rural		Declining least, 1871–92	
Boston	Overall	Rising, 1703–1967	
	Drunkenness	Rising to 1917	1890, 1917
	"Major"	Rising to 1870, then declining	1870–1920
Salem	Drunkenness	Declining, 1853–1920	1880, 1910
Salem	Assault and larceny	Declining, 1853–1920	1870s
State	"Serious"	Rising, 1834–1901	
	"Minor"	Declining, 1834–1901	
	All felonies	Rising, 1836–73	1855
Philadelphia	Overall	Stable, 1791–1937	
	Public order	Rising, 1791–1937	
Buffalo	Minor	Stable, 1856–1919	1870s
	Personal violence	Stable, 1856–1905, then rising	
	Property	Stable, 1856–1919	1870s
Ohio	Murder	Stable, 1867–91	
	Theft	Declining, 1867–91	1867
Columbus	All felonies	Stable, 1859–85	1863, 1867
	Murder	Stable, 1859–85	1860–5
	Assault, theft	Stable, 1859–85	1870
Rockford	Violent	Stable, 1880–1920	1902
	Petty	Stable, 1880–1920	
	Public order	Stable, 1880–1920	1900
Iowa	All felonies[a]	Stable, 1860–1910, rising to 1920	1860, 1870s

Table E.1. *Synopsis of crime rates from previous studies*

Place	Offense category	Trends	Peaks
Missouri	All felonies	Rising, 1850–1920	1860, 1870s, 1890s
San Francisco	All arrests Public order	Rising, 1863–1920 Rising to 1905, declining, 1920	1863
Oakland	All arrests	Climbing, 1870–1920	1875, 1890, 1920

[a]Higher level urban, same trends.
Source: See Chapter 2, notes 1–15.

Appendix F *Lagged police correlated with criminal arrests, by city*

Table F.1. *Lagged police correlated with criminal arrests, by city*

City	1860–1920	1860–90	1890–1920	Increase in R
New York	.92	.56	.88	yes
Philadelphia	.97	.67	.94	yes
Brooklyn	.43	.64	—[a]	
Chicago	.86	.89	.62	no
Boston	.89	.61	.92	yes
St. Louis	.67	.59	−.25[b]	
Baltimore	.79	−.84	.71	yes
Cincinnati	.74	.75	.36	no
San Francisco	.64	.48	.77	yes
New Orleans	—	—	—	
Cleveland	.77	.13[b]	.58	
Buffalo	.82	.04[b]	.63	
Washington, D.C.	.82	.09[b]	.74	
Newark, N.J.	.91	.14[b]	.91	
Louisville, Ky.	.40	−.01[b]	.47	
Detroit	.85	.70	.95	yes
Milwaukee	.89	.26[b]	.94	
Providence, R.I.	.53	−.41	.84	yes
Rochester, N.Y.	.24*	—	.24[b]	
Pittsburgh	.46*	—	.32[b]	
Richmond, Va.	.91	.68	.91	yes
New Haven, Conn.	.69	.09[b]	.86	
Lowell, Mass.	.70	.72	.37[b]	

[a]A dash signifies insufficient data.
[b]Significance less than .05.

Notes

Introduction

1 Between 1816 and 1848, for instance, at least 2,563 persons had been killed by steamboat explosions alone. See John G. Burke, "Bursting Boilers and the Federal Power," *Technology and Culture* (Winter 1966), 18.

2 For a summary of mobility rates in the colonial era, see Linda A. Bissell, "From One Generation to Another: Mobility in Seventeenth Century Windsor, Connecticut," *William and Mary Quarterly* (Jan. 1974), 102, Table 7. For the nineteenth century, see Stephan Thernstrom, *The Other Bostonians: Social Mobility in a Nineteenth Century City* (Cambridge, Mass.: Harvard University Press, 1973), 234, Table 9.4.

3 See the historians included in Hugh D. Graham and Ted R. Gurr, *Violence in America: Historical and Comparative Perspectives,* A Report to the National Commission on the Causes and Prevention of Violence, June 1969 (New York: New American Library, 1969). Robert M. Fogelson, an urban historian, is the author of *Who Riots? A Study of Participation in the 1967 Riots,* A Report to the United States National Advisory Commission on Civil Disorders (Washington, D.C.: GPO, 1968); more recently Fogelson has published *Big City Police* (Cambridge, Mass.: Harvard University Press, 1977).

4 Roger Lane, *Policing the City: Boston, 1822–1885* (Cambridge, Mass.: Harvard University Press, 1967); James Richardson, *The New York Police: Colonial Times to 1901* (New York: Oxford University Press, 1970); Wilbur R. Miller, *Cops and Bobbies: Police Authority in New York and London, 1830–1870* (Chicago: University of Chicago Press, 1976); Samuel Walker, *A Critical History of Police Reform: The Emergence of Professionalism* (Lexington, Mass.: Heath, 1977); Fogelson, *Big City Police.*

5 Roger Lane, "Urbanization and Criminal Violence in the Nineteenth Century: Massachusetts as a Test Case," *Journal of Social History* (Winter 1968), 156–63, and also "Crime and the Industrial Revolution: British and American Views," *Journal of Social History* (Spring 1974), 287–303; Theodore N. Ferdinand, "The Criminal Patterns of Boston Since 1849," *American Journal of Sociology* (July 1967), 84–9; Eric H. Monkkonen, *The Dangerous Class: Crime and Poverty in Columbus, Ohio, 1860–1885* (Cambridge, Mass.: Harvard University Press, 1975); Michael S. Hindus, "Black Justice Under White Law: Criminal Prosecutions of Blacks in Antebellum South Carolina," *Journal of American History* (Dec. 1976), 575–99, and "Contours of Crime in Massachusetts

183

and South Carolina, 1767–1878," *American Journal of Legal History* (July 1977), 212–37, and "The History of Crime: Not Robbed of Its Potential, But Still on Probation," in Egon Bittner and Sheldon Messinger, eds., *Criminology Review Yearbook* (Beverly Hills, Calif.: Sage, 1979), 217–41. See also the special issue of *Annals of the American Academy of Political and Social Science: Crime and Justice in America, 1776–1976* (Jan. 1976), for a collection of essays on the history of crime. I do not deal with organized crime and vice in this book becasue of my interest in accounting for the largest parts of police behavior. Substantial work has already been done on organized crime and vice in the United States: See, for further citations, Mark H. Haller and John V. Alviti, "Loansharking in American Cities: Historical Analysis of a Marginal Enterprise," *American Journal of Legal History* (April 1977), 125–56, and Humbert Nelli, *The Business of Crime: Italians and Syndicate Crime in the United States* (New York: Oxford University Press, 1976). James A. Inciardi, Alan A. Block, and Lyle A. Hallowell, *Historical Approaches to Crime: Research Strategies and Issues* (Beverly Hills, Calif.: Sage, 1977), includes material on organized crime and cowboy outlaws.

6   Kenneth C. Land and Marcus Felson, "A General Framework for Building Dynamic Macro Social Indicator Models: Including an Analysis of Changes in Crime Rates and Police Expenditures," *American Journal of Sociology* (Nov. 1976), 565–604; Charles Tilly and David Snyder, "Hardship and Collective Violence in France, 1830 to 1960," *American Sociological Review* (Oct. 1972), 520–32; Robert V. Percival, "Municipal Justice in the Melting Pot: Arrest and Prosecution in Oakland, 1872–1910," manuscript (Stanford, Calif.: Stanford University Law School). For the current controversy over capital punishment, see Isaac Ehrlich, "The Deterrent Effect of Capital Punishment: A Question of Life or Death," *American Economic Review* (June 1975), 397–417; see the critiques of Ehrlich in Hugo A. Bedau and Chester M. Pierce, eds., *Capital Punishment in the United States* (New York: AMS Press, 1975); for a more sophisticated critique, see Brian E. Forst, "The Deterrent Effect of Capital Punishment: A Cross-State Analysis of the 1960's," *Minnesota Law Review* (May 1977), 743–67.

7   The following list of social control history books and articles suggests the substantive and methodological variety of works utilizing the social control thesis: Kai Erikson, *Wayward Puritans: A Study in the Sociology of Deviance* (New York: Wiley, 1966); David Rothman, *The Discovery of the Asylum: Social Order and Disorder in the American Republic* (Boston: Little, Brown, 1971); Anthony Platt, *The Child Savers: The Invention of Delinquency* (Chicago: University of Chicago Press, 1969); Michael Katz, *Class, Bureaucracy and the Schools* (New York: Praeger, 1971); Stanley Buder, "Pullman: Town Planning as Social Control," *Journal of the American Institue of Planners* (Jan. 1967), 2–10; Lois W. Banner, "Religious Benevolence as Social Control," *Journal of American History* (June 1972), 23–41; Marvin Gettleman, "Charity and Social

Classes in the United States, 1874–1900, II," *American Journal of Economics and Sociology* (July 1963), 417–26, and "Philanthropy as Social Control," *Societas* (Winter 1974–5), 49–59; Peter A. Hall, "Boston Charity: A Theory of Charitable Benevolence and Class Development," *Science and Society* (Winter 1974–5), 464–77; Sidney Harring and Lorraine McMullin, "The Buffalo Police, 1872–1890: Labor Unrest, Political Power and the Creation of the Police Institution," *Crime and Social Justice* (Fall–Winter 1975), 5–14; Sidney Harring, "The Development of the Police in the United States," *Crime and Social Justice* (Summer 1976), 54–9; Keith Melder, "Mask of Oppression: The Female Seminary Movement," *New York History* (July 1974), 261–79; William A. Muraskin, "Regulating the Poor," *Contemporary Sociology* (Nov. 1975), 607–13, and "The Social Control Theory in American History: A Critique," *Journal of Social History* (Summer 1976), 559–68; Timothy J. Naylor, "Responding to the Fire: The Work of the Chicago Relief and Aid Society," *Science and Society* (Winter 1975–6), 450–64; Richard M. Rollins, "Words as Social Control: Webster's Dictionary," *American Quarterly* (Fall 1976), 415–30.

8   One historian has carefully scrutinized the shaky conceptual foundations of the social control synthesis. See Muraskin, "Social Control Theory." See also Don S. Kirschner, "The Ambiguous Legacy: Social Justice and Social Control in the Progressive Era," *Historical Reflections* (Summer 1975), 85, n. 52. However, I do not wish to overdraw the critique of the social control thesis, as Diane Ravitch has done in her provocative, *The Revisionists Revised: A Critique of the Radical Attack on the Schools* (New York: Basic Books, 1978). One should be alert to the "latent function" of social control, but this awareness should not substitute for analysis.

9   On Buffalo, see Harring and McMullin, "Buffalo Police." Also see Alan Dawley, *Class and Community: The Industrial Revolution in Lynn* (Cambridge, Mass.: Harvard University Press, 1976), 105–10. Samuel Walker, "The Police and the Community: Scranton, Pennsylvania, 1866–1884, A Test Case," *American Studies* (Spring 1978), 79–90, provides a case study critique of Harring and McMullin.

10   Bruce C. Johnson, "Taking Care of Labor: The Police in American Politics," *Theory and Society* (Spring 1976), 89–117. For a recent study of the subtleties of police–labor relations, see Daniel J. Walkowitz, *Worker City, Company Town: Iron- and Cotton-Worker Protest in Troy and Cohoes, New York, 1855–84* (Urbana: University of Illinois Press, 1978), 194–218, 233–8.

11   Erikson, *Wayward Puritans*; Rothman, *Discovery of the Asylum*; Platt, *The Child Savers*. Steven L. Schlossman, *Love and the American Delinquent: The Theory and Practice of "Progressive" Juvenile Justice, 1825–1920* (Chicago: University of Chicago Press, 1977), is a considerable improvement over Platt and has several pointed critiques of Platt's social control thesis.

12　Peter Gould and Rodney White, *Mental Maps* (New York: Penguin, 1974).

13　See Michael Frisch, *Town Into City: Springfield, Massachusetts, and the Meaning of Community, 1840–1880* (Cambridge, Mass.: Harvard University Press, 1972), and especially his article, "The Community Elite and the Emergence of Urban Politics: Springfield, Massachusetts, 1840–1880," in Stephan Thernstrom and Richard Sennett, eds., *Nineteenth Century Cities* (New Haven, Conn.: Yale University Press, 1969). See also Sam B. Warner, Jr., *The Urban Wilderness* (New York: Harper & Row, 1972), Chaps. 3 and 4, for his analysis of this phenomenon.

14　Douglas Hay, "Property, Authority and the Criminal Law," in Douglas Hay, et al., *Albion's Fatal Tree: Crime and Society in Eighteenth Century England* (New York: Pantheon, 1975), 33.

15　In the 1890s, one reform administration in Denver had creases sewn into uniform pants, assuring neatness and order.

16　Stephan Thernstrom and Peter Knights, "Men in Motion: Some Data and Speculations on Urban Population Turnover in Nineteenth Century America," *Journal of Interdisciplinary History* (Autumn 1970), 7–35; Richard S. Alcorn, "Leadership and Stability in Mid-Nineteenth Century America: A Case Study of an Illinois Town," *Journal of American History* (Dec. 1974), 685–702; Robert H. Wiebe, *The Search for Order, 1877–1920* (New York: Hill and Wang, 1967).

17　Sam B. Warner, Jr., *The Private City: Philadelphia in Three Periods of Its Growth* (Philadelphia: University of Pennsylvania Press, 1968).

18　Jerome H. Skolnick, *Justice Without Trial: Law Enforcement in Democratic Society* (New York: Wiley, 1966). For a discussion of nineteenth-century detective work, see David R. Johnson, *Policing the Urban Underworld: The Impact of Crime on the Development of the American Police, 1800–1887* (Philadelphia: Temple University Press, 1979), ch. 2.

19　This is not to deny that people attacked one another, took one another's property, or became drunk in public before such behavior was criminalized or before there were police responsible to the law; but the study of victims and offenses under such circumstances would have to be conceived differently.

20　Herman Schwendinger and Julia Schwendinger, "Defenders of Order or Guardians of Human Rights," in Ian Taylor, Paul Walton, and Jock Young, eds., *Critical Criminology* (London: Routledge and Kegan Paul, 1975), 113–46.

21　Here I am speaking in twentieth-century terms: In the early, pre-uniformed-police era, victims paid prosecution costs. Relating crime to the state, this definition is also in explicit conflict with the anthropological view. See, for instance, Sally F. Moore, *Law as Process: An Anthropological Approach* (Boston: Routledge and Kegan Paul, 1978).

22　James F. Stephen, *A History of the Criminal Law of England* (London: Macmillan, 1883), 1:184–5.

23 Frederick Pollock and Frederick W. Maitland, *The History of English Law*, 2d ed. (Cambridge: Cambridge University Press, 1952; 1st ed., 1898), 1:45.

24 Pollock and Maitland, 2:464.

25 Nigel D. Walker, "Lost Causes in Criminology," in Roger Hood, ed., *Crime, Criminology, and Public Policy: Essays in Honour of Leon Radzinowicz* (London: Heineman, 1974), 47–61, argues that such a causal notion is an Aristotelian use of a final cause and that it is tautological. He is correct, of course, but my point here is to ask the reader to suspend the leap into the vexing analysis of criminal motivation in the past until this book has provided a theoretical and empirical description of crime and police. See Walker, *Explaining Misbehavior* (Cambridge: Cambridge University Press, 1974), as the outline for a philosophically sophisticated approach to the causal analysis of crime.

26 See, for example, Jerome Hall's analysis of Carrier's case in *Theft, Law and Society* (Boston: Little, Brown, 1935), 315–46.

27 For other overviews of theories of crime, see Travis Hirschi and David Rudisill, "The Great American Search: Causes of Crime, 1876–1976," *Annals of the American Academy of Political and Social Science* (Jan. 1976), special ed.; Graeme R. Newman, *Crime and Justice in America: 1776–1976*, 14–22; or see Ian Taylor, Paul Walton, and Jock Young, *The New Criminology: For a Social Theory of Deviance* (London: Routledge and Kegan Paul, 1973). For the anthropological perspective on crime, which I have not discussed here as it is little employed by criminologists or historians, see Robert B. Edgerton, *Deviance, A Cross-Cultural Perspective* (Menlo Park, Calif.: Cummings, 1976).

28 Frederick H. Wines, Tenth U.S. Census, *Report on the Defective, Dependent, and Delinquent Classes of the Population of the United States* (Washington, D.C.: GPO, 1888), observed that the preponderance of male prisoners "is partly because women are better than men . . . ," p. xlviii.

29 Schwendinger and Schwendinger; also see Manual Lopez-Rey, "A Criminological Manifesto," *Federal Probation* (Sept. 1975), 18–22.

30 Robert Dugdale, *The Jukes: A Study in Crime, Pauperism, Disease and Heredity* (New York: Arno, 1970).

31 Marvin Wolfgang, "Cesare Lombroso," in Hermann Mannheim, ed., *Pioneers in Criminology* (London: Stevens, 1960), 168–227.

32 Stein Rokkan and Mattei Dugan, eds., *Quantitative Ecological Analysis in the Social Sciences* (Cambridge, Mass.: MIT Press, 1969).

33 For instance, Harvey J. Graff, "'Pauperism, Misery, and Vice'; Illiteracy and Criminality in the Nineteenth Century," *Journal of Social History* (Winter 1977), 245–68.

34 As an example that employs labeling theory, see David Matza, *Becoming Deviant* (Englewood Cliffs, N.J.: Prentice-Hall, 1969); for structural conflict, see Marvin Wolfgang and Franco Feracutti, *Subculture of Vio-*

lenco: Towards an Integrated Theory of Criminology (New York: Tavistock, 1967). For an overview, see Walter R. Gove, ed., *The Labelling of Deviance: Evaluating a Perspective* (Beverly Hills, Calif.: Sage, 1975); more to the point, see the review of this book by Ken Plummer in *British Journal of Criminology* (Jan. 1977), 79–81.

35 David K. Farrington, "The Effects of Public Labelling," *British Journal of Criminology* (April 1977), 112–25.

36 The term "Desperate class" was used in a Denver newspaper in the 1860s; cited by Rider, p. 86; "A Sermon of the Perishing Classes in Boston," in Theodore Parker, *Collected Works*, v. 7: "Discourses of Social Science" (London: Trübner, 1864), 34–59. For a thorough discussion of the "dangerous class," see Christopher G. Tiedman, "Police Control of Dangerous Classes, Other Than By Criminal Prosecutions," *American Law Review* (July–Aug., 1885), 547–70.

37 Both quotes from Marx are cited by Paul Hirst, "Marx and Engels on Law, Crime and Morality," in Taylor, Walton, Young, 215–16.

38 See Taylor, Walton, and Young for the classic work of "new criminology."

39 One excellent piece of research has been published by a new criminologist: see Ian Taylor, "Soccer Consciousness and Soccer Hooliganism," in Stanley Cohen, ed., *Images of Deviance* (Harmondsworth, Eng.: Penguin, 1971), 134–64. Hirst, 203–32.

40 Ian Taylor, "Soccer Consciousness," shows how the apparently random and meaningless violence of British football riots has its origins in nineteenth-century working-class, community football rivalry.

41 For a diagrammatic example of deviance amplification, see Jock Young, "The Role of Police as Amplifiers of Deviance, Negotiators of Reality and Translators of Fantasy: Some Consequences of Our Present System of Drug Controls as Seen in Notting Hill," in Cohen, 34. Labeling continues to generate controversy: See Gove and Plummer.

42 Roger Lane, *Violent Death in the City: Suicide, Accident, and Murder in Nineteenth-Century Philadelphia* (Cambridge, Mass.: Harvard University Press, 1979), opens up several new avenues of social history through its use of coroners' records.

43 Ernest S. Griffith, *A History of American City Government: The Conspicuous Failure, 1870–1920* (New York: Praeger, 1974), 235–45, briefly discusses separation of powers and city government, as does William B. Munro, *The Government of American Cities* (New York: Macmillan, 1920), 315.

44 See John C. Teaford, "Special Legislation and the Cities, 1865–1900," manuscript (Lafayette, Ind.: Purdue University, n.d.), for evidence that through special legislation, cities virtually had carte blanche power in state legislatures.

45 Thernstrom and Knights, "Men in Motion."

46 John Rawls, *A Theory of Justice* (Cambridge, Mass.: Harvard University Press, 1971).

47 Currently, anthropologists tend to hold a contrary position to mine, finding law and crime in all societies. See Edgerton: also see Moore.
48 Eric H. Monkkonen, "States Rights vs. Corporate Rights: Bank of Augusta vs. Earle 1836," *Alabama Quarterly* (Summer 1973), 113–30.
49 Herein lies the problem in Erikson's *Wayward Puritans:* He sees crime as defining behavioral boundaries or social norms, but ignores its inherently political nature.
50 Pollock and Maitland, 1:52, 53.

1. The historical development of the police

1 Roger Lane, *Policing the City: Boston, 1822–1905* (Cambridge, Mass.: Harvard University Press, 1967); James F. Richardson, *The New York Police: Colonial Times to 1901* (New York: Oxford University Press, 1970); George A. Ketcham, "Municipal Police Reform: A Comparative Study of Law Enforcement in Cincinnati, Chicago, New Orleans, New York, and St. Louis, 1844–1877," Ph.D. dissertation (Columbia: University of Missouri, 1967); John K. Maniha, "The Mobility of Elites in a Bureaucratizing Organization: The St. Louis Police Department, 1861–1961," Ph.D. dissertation (Ann Arbor: University of Michigan, 1970); Jerald E. Levine, "Police, Parties, and Polity: The Bureaucratization, Unionization, and Professionalization of the New York City Police, 1870–1917," Ph.D. dissertation (Madison: University of Wisconsin, 1971); Eugene F. Rider, "The Denver Police Department: An Administrative, Organizational, and Operational History, 1858–1905," Ph.D. dissertation (Denver: University of Denver, 1971); David R. Johnson, "The Search for an Urban Discipline: Police Reform as a Response to Crime in American Cities, 1800–1875," Ph.D. dissertation (Chicago: University of Chicago, 1972); Wilbur R. Miller, "Legitimization of the London and New York City Police, 1830–1870," Ph.D. dissertation (New York: Columbia University, 1973), published as *Cops and Bobbies: Police Authority in New York and London, 1830–1870* (Chicago: University of Chicago Press, 1976); Kenneth G. Alfers, "The Washington Police: A History, 1800–1886," Ph.D. dissertation (Washington, D.C.: George Washington University, 1975); Allan E. Levett, "Centralization of City Police in the Nineteenth Century United States," Ph.D. dissertation (Ann Arbor: University of Michigan, 1975); Maximilian I. Reichard, "The Origins of Urban Police: Freedom and Order in Antebellum St. Louis," Ph.D. dissertation (Saint Louis: Washington University, 1975); Louis B. Cei, "Law Enforcement in Richmond: A History of Police Community Relations, 1737–1974," Ph.D. dissertation (Tallahassee: Florida State University, 1975); Charles F. Tracy, "The Police of Portland, 1840–1870," Ph.D. dissertation (Berkeley: University of California, 1978); Louis I. Marchiafava, "Institutional and Legal Aspects of the Growth of Professional Urban Police Service: The Hous-

ton Experience, 1870–1940," Ph.D. dissertation (Houston: Rice University, 1976). Johnson, Ketcham, Levett, and Miller all bring more than one city into their analyses.

2   Roger Lane, "Comments," Organization of American Historians Annual Meeting, Saint Louis, April 8, 1976. James Q. Wilson, *Varieties of Police Behavior: The Management of Law and Order in Eight Communities* (Cambridge, Mass.: Harvard University Press, 1968), finds four different "styles" of policing in the modern United States.

3   Thomas A. Critchley, *A History of Police in England and Wales, 1900– 1966* (London: Constable, 1967), 11–13.

4   Ketcham, 48, citing the *Louisiana Gazette*, August 5, 1808. The suggestion here is that the watch substitutes were recruited from the "dangerous class," rather than just being ancient and decrepit. If so, this forecasts the general character of the night police during the mid nineteenth century.

5   Levett, 42, says that in the United States, some constables could raise the *posse comitatus*.

6   William A. Morris, *The Frankpledge System* (New York: Longmans, Green, 1910), cited by Critchley, 3.

7   Rider, 31.

8   Lane, *Policing the City*, 10–11.

9   Ketcham, 51.

10 Rider, 19.

11 Rider, 249, citing the *Rocky Mountain News* (Jan. 19, 1883). This duty was not unique to Denver. The similar marshal system of Charlotte, North Carolina, had orders to shoot all unlicensed dogs. (*Charlotte Observer*, June 1876).

12 Lane, *Policing the City*, cites an instance where the Boston watch was ordered to "prevent and suppress" night disturbances; although this is not the same as the general idea of a mission to prevent crime, it does suggest that the notion of prevention was present in the conception of the night watch, with its regular patrol.

13 There is some evidence that this may have been a difference of degree rather than kind: Theodore N. Ferdinand, "Criminality, the Courts and the Constabulary in Boston: 1703–1967," manuscript (1973), claims to show that "between 1824 and 1860–69, drunkenness became the single most important offense in Boston" (p. 11). The amount to which these arrests climbed would be a measure of the increased initiative taken by a preventive police. Nevertheless, it is clear that the constable–watch system of Boston was primarily conceived as acting after offenses and upon complaints: For instance, arguing against a unified preventive police as late as 1863, Thomas C. Amory stated, "'It is the duty of the police officer to serve . . . warrants, when directed to him. It is nowhere made his duty to initiate prosecutions'" (Lane, *Policing the City*, 130). As an example of the variety of social welfare chores freely assigned to constables, in 1860 the marshal of

Denver was given the care of Chihuahua, a lunatic, by the city (Rider, 27–8).

14 Historians usually repeat the judgments of contemporaries complaining about the constable–watch system, but both Levett and Ferdinand make arguments for the effectiveness of the constable–watch. Because of the measurement problems involved in comparing the arrest rates of the two different systems, this argument can probably never be resolved.

15 Lane, *Policing the City*, 10.

16 It is interesting in this connection that major employers of detectives today are insurance companies. See the *New York Times Magazine* (March 12, 1972), 36–7, 114–18.

17 Richardson, 304, n. 38, citing Charles H. Haswell, *Reminiscences of an Octogenarian* (New York: Harper & Row, 1896), 510.

18 Ketcham, 50, 68.

19 Johnson, 176–7.

20 Adrian Cook, *The Armies of the Streets: The New York City Draft Riots of 1863* (Lexington: University of Kentucky Press, 1974). This incident illustrated a pattern still common today: Police mobilize against a rioting group, escalating the level of violence and confrontation, shifting the target of the mob to the police themselves; police discipline fails, resulting in more violence on both sides, and finally political leaders call in the military or militia. Although police today have reached new levels of weaponry, riot control tactics, and technological sophistication, the same scenario will no doubt recur.

21 Norman Gash, *Mr. Secretary Peel: The Life of Sir Robert Peel to 1830* (Cambridge, Mass.: Harvard University Press, 1961), 109.

22 Cited by Gash, 175.

23 Quoted by Gash from a speech by Peel, June 23, 1814, 179.

24 Gash, 185; see also Robert Curtis, *The History of the Royal Irish Constabulary* (Dublin: Moffat, 1869), 2–51.

25 Gash, 184.

26 Miller, 64.

27 Richardson, 64.

28 Unfortunately, Miller's sources tend to bias his results – for London he uses departmental correspondence and memos, whereas for New York he relies upon external sources. In a sense, then, he has the inner views of what the London police were trying to do, as opposed to the outsiders' views of the New York police.

29 Herbert Asbury, *The Gangs of New York: An Informal History of the Underworld* (New York: Knopf, 1927), 237.

30 Leon Radzinowicz, *Ideology and Crime: A Study of Crime in its Social and Historical Context* (London: Heinemann, 1966), 6–14.

31 Miller, 112; Johnson, 173; Rider, 100; James W. Gerard, *London and New York: Their Crime and Police* (New York: W. C. Bryant, 1853).

32 Miller, 64.

33 Perhaps the preventive detention part of the D.C. Crime Bill suggests
    the next step in the prevention concept – imprisoning potential of-
    fenders, rather than speedily trying them for offenses in fact commit-
    ted. James Franklin, Benjamin's older brother, established the freedom
    of the press from prior restraint with the New England *Courant*, early
    in the eighteenth century. See Edwin Emory, *The Press and America: An
    Interpretive History of Journalism* (Englewood Cliffs, N.J.: Prentice-Hall,
    1962), 48–51.
34 Gerard, 1, 6, 17.
35 Levett argues that urban elites consciously created the police to control
    the "dangerous class."
36 Essentially, the arrest power of the constable did not differ from that of
    a private citizen until the late eighteenth century, when differing defi-
    nitions began to emerge in England, coincident with the beginnings of
    the uniformed police. These differences remained unsettled and in
    constant flux until two years before Peel's London police were created.
    At this point, in 1827, the issue finally became clarified, when it was
    decided that a police officer might arrest when there were reasonable
    grounds to suspect that a felony had been committed, whereas a pri-
    vate citizen could only arrest upon proof that a felony had been com-
    mitted. See Jerome Hall, "Legal and Social Aspects of Arrest Without a
    Warrant," *Harvard Law Review*, (Feb. 1936), 566–92, for a clear discus-
    sion of this matter.
37 See Richardson, 102–8, for a more detailed account.
38 Rider, 371–88.
39 Rider, 398.
40 For instance, police in Denver, through telegraphic call-boxes, had a
    communciations network by 1885 (Rider, 271, 276, 471): again, other
    larger cities provided the model. See Seymour Mandelbaum, *Boss
    Tweed's New York* (New York: Wiley, 1965), for an interesting analysis
    of bosses and communication networks.
41 Richardson, 106, quoting George Templeton Strong, *The Diary of
    George Templeton Strong*, ed. Allan Nevins and Milton H. Thomas
    (New York: Macmillan, 1952).
42 Gerard, 17, 18.
43 Lane, *Policing the City*, 105; also, Lane, "Comments."
44 Alfers, 53.
45 Lane, *Policing the City*, 105.
46 Richardson, 65, citing the *New York Times* (June 30, 1854).
47 Johnson, 172, citing the *Chicago Tribune* (March 19, 1855).
48 Johnson, 173–6, citing the Philadelphia *Public Ledger* (Feb. 28 and
    March 5, 1855).
49 Incident described in Howard O. Sprogle, *The Philadelphia Police, Past
    and Present* (Philadelphia: n.p., 1877), 103–22.
       The proposed uniforms for the San Francisco police in 1855 were
    mocked by an editorial in the *Weekly Journal* (Sept. 29, 1855) that

heaped abuse on the "monkey show" and then went on to ask for full military regalia and "'fuss and feathers'": "Then let no man be appointed as a policeman who has not a countenance full of war." As late as 1878, the issue of police uniforms in San Francisco was the butt of editorial jokes. A proposal to change the color of the uniforms from grey to blue and to copy the style of the New York police was the subject of a cartoon in the *Wasp* (May 25, 1878) and, later, an article describing how the new color ran in the first rainstorm (Oct. 26, 1878). Similarly, the New Bedford, Massachusetts, police uniforms were greeted with laughter, apparently because the city had a tradition of officers creating their own outfits (*Sunday Standard*, Feb. 5, 1911).

The point, however, should be made clear that the visibility of uniforms and change in uniforms, rather than their implicit meaning, created controversy. And the new uniforms were not always resisted by the police officers. For instance, the officers of the Bridgeport, Connecticut, police force petitioned the city to be uniformed on Nov. 4, 1861; n.a., *History of the Police Department, of Bridgeport, Conn.* (Bridgeport: Relief Book Publishing, 1892), 35. For over a century, this aspect of policing has attracted attention; see, for instance, the story about Houston police resistance to replacing cowboy boots with shoes; Nicholas C. Chriss, "Police Toe Line, Turn in Boots for Wing-Tips," *Los Angeles Times* (Jan. 27, 1975), 1.

50 Rider, 120, citing the *Rocky Mountain Times*; also 425.
51 For more detail, see Lane, *Policing the City*, 9–101.
52 Lane, *Policing the City*, 17.
53 Alfers, 16.
54 See Jerome H. Skolnik, *Justice Without Trial: Law Enforcement in Democratic Society* (New York: Wiley, 1966); Rider, 346–7; Lane, 148; Richardson, 282; Alfers, 192.
55 Lane, *Policing the City*, 34.
56 Lane, *Policing the City*, 6. See also Rider, 100, 213, 272; or Ketcham, 143, 152–7, for similar intercity communications.
57 Ketcham, Walker, and Levett have the best national surveys of police changes.
58 See Gudmund Hernes, "Structural Change and Social Processes," *American Journal of Sociology* (Nov. 1976), 520, for a good brief expression of this notion.
59 Richard Wade, *Slavery in the Cities: The South, 1820–1860* (New York: Oxford University Press, 1964).
60 See Hernes, 520, and also 513–47, for a longer discussion of these models and their relationship to social structure.
61 There has been a good deal of literature on the methodological implications of the ecological fallacy since the term was introduced by W. S. Robinson in a famous article, "Ecological Correlations and the Behavior of Individuals," *American Sociological Review* (June 1950), 351–7. More recently, a collection of pieces on the subject, Stein Rokkan and

Mattei Dugan, eds., *Quantitative Ecological Analysis in the Social Sciences* (Cambridge, Mass.: MIT Press, 1969), has shown how research based on relating large units can be pursued without being crippled by the logical problems of the ecological fallacy.

62 See Johnson, *Policing the Urban Underworld*, whose thesis is that the police were modernized to fight rising crime.

63 Thorsten Sellin, *Slavery and the Penal System* (New York: Elsevier, 1976), shows how the penal response to crime came from models of slavery. Police do not enter his interesting and provocative discussion.

64 For instance, see Miller, *Cops and Bobbies*, 43, on the resistance to the Metropolitan Police in London.

65 Allan Silver, "The Demand for Order in Civil Society: A Review of Some Themes in the History of Urban Crime, Police, and Riot," in David J. Bordua, ed., *The Police: Six Sociological Essays* (New York: Wiley, 1967).

66 See Note 1.

67 Levett, 25.

68 For the Marxist version of Buffalo, see Sidney Harring and Lorrain McMullin, "The Buffalo Police, 1872–1900: Labor Unrest, Political Power and the Creation of the Police Institution," *Crime and Social Justice* (Fall-Winter 1975), 5–14. For the Durkheimian approach, see Elwin Powell, "Crime as a Function of Anomie," *Journal of Criminal Law, Criminology and Police Science* (June 1966), 161–71.

69 See Everett M. Rogers, *Diffusion of Innovations* (New York: Free Press, 1962), 21–56, for a succinct discussion of the major areas of diffusion research. For a more mathematical analysis, see James G. Coleman, *Introduction to Mathematical Sociology* (Glencoe, Ill.: Free Press, 1964) 492–517; and with Elihu Katz and Herbert Menzel, *Medical Innovation: A Diffusion Study* (Indianapolis: Bobbs-Merrill, 1966), 103, n. 5 for a good brief discussion of the S curve. Chapter 11, "Spatial Diffusion: Meshing Space and Time," in Ronald Abler, John S. Adams, and Peter Gould, *Spatial Organization: The Geographer's View of the World* (Prentice-Hall: Englewood Cliffs, N.J., 1971), 389–451, has a thorough and well-written summary of the geographer's version of innovation diffusion. This includes a good section, 437–47, on various geographical studies of diffusion across the nineteenth-century United States, which shows a transition in the middle of the century from a diffusion pattern that followed water transport routes to one flowing through the urban hierarchy. This chapter also makes clear how a diffusion process may often contain both hierarchical and contagious patterns. For a suggestive analysis of diffusion through an urban system in an underdeveloped nation, an important characteristic of which is the adaptation of innovations from other nations (thus making this recent study similar to the adoption of the English policing model in the United States), see Poul O. Pederson, "Innovation Diffusion Within and Between National Urban Systems," *Geographical Analysis* (July 1970),

203–54. For a rather disappointing treatment of nineteenth-century
diffusion of innovations adopted by state governments, see Jack L.
Walker, "The Diffusion of Innovations Among the American States,"
American Political Science Review (Sept. 1969), 880–99. Walker tends to
ignore time and space consideration for a multivariate analysis of propensity to innovate; his footnotes are extensive. Almost the whole first
issue of *Geographical Analysis* (Jan. 1969) was devoted to diffusion
analysis – all of the articles are relevant, but of special interest is G. P.
Pyle, "The Diffusion of Cholera in the United States in the Nineteenth
Century," 59–75.

70 Rogers, 13–19.
71 St. Louis evolved from a constable (city marshal)–watch system, to a
separate day and night police (1846), to a unified police in 1861. Chicago, on the other hand, changed directly from the constable–watch
system to a unified police in 1853. (Ketcham, 120–33).
72 Silver, 12–13; Miller, 113–14.
73 Jack J. Preiss and Howard J. Ehrlich, *An Examination of Role Theory:
The Case of the State Police* (Lincoln, Neb.: University of Nebraska
Press, 1966), 20. Thus, there were usually one of three reasons given for
the uniform: that of the contemporary police officer cited here, the
hope of deterrence, or the need to control the police themselves. The
Norfolk (Va.) *Journal* (December 20, 1866) expected that the newly uniformed police would make "life and property . . . more secure hence-
forth, than it has in the past." In addition to deterrence and control
over officers, the Worcester, Massachusetts, marshal pointed out that
"strangers visiting our depots and other public places, and needing
the services of a Police officer" would appreciate the visibility of a
uniform. *Report of the City Marshal* (Worcester, Mass., 1864), 172.
    Nursing outfits provide one comparable example, although they
came somewhat later in the nineteenth century than police uniforms.
Caps were the first formalized part of the nurse outfit, those in the
United States apparently imitating European precedents from the early
nineteenth century. The earliest caps appeared, with a uniform, in
New York City (Bellevue) in the early 1870s, and were shortly followed
in Boston and Philadelphia in 1878. Later adopters directly imitated
these early innovators. The Good Samaritan hospital in Portland, Ore-
gon, copied Bellevue; the Cincinnati Nursing School copied Blockly
Hospital in Philadelphia; and St. Luke's in Denver copied St. Luke's in
Chicago. The relevant point here is that, like police departments, nursing organizations followed the precedents set in larger urban places.
See n.a., *Why a Cap? A Short History of Nursing Caps from Some Schools
Organized Prior to 1891* (Philadelphia: Lippincott, 1940).
74 Hernes, 513–47, relates these two models to theories of social structure
and social change.
75 The shape of the curve is for all practical purposes identical to that of
the normal curve expressed additively, and has often been interpreted

as the graph of diffusion in a system where resistance to innovation is normally and randomly distributed. See Earl H. Pemberton, "The Curve of Cultural Diffusion Rate," *American Sociological Review* (Aug. 1936), 550, for a classic statement on this. The implication is that the speed of diffusion is simply determined by randomly distributed and unspecified traits among, in this case, a population of cities: This notion is neither theoretically nor substantively satisfying, and can be readily rejected in this study by the analysis of the order in which cities uniformed their police, an order which clearly was nonrandom and hierarchical.

76 For an explanation of the model of precipitants and preconditions, see Harry Eckstein, "On the Etiology of Internal Wars," *History and Theory*, 4 (1965), 133–64. The problem of explaining the creation of uniformed police solely as a response to urban riots may be highlighted by the patterns of major riots in New York City. The following list of dates show those years that historians have identified as occasions for major riots from 1800 to 1900. Note that the list in itself provides no guide as to a likely point for changing the police system. For convenience I have stopped the list at 1900, although it could be extended:

Year	Riot
1806	Irish Catholic
1826	New Year's Eve
1834	Abolitionist, election
1837	Flour
1849	Astor Place
1855	Seventeenth Ward beer riots
1857	Police, dead rabbits, bread (all following the creation of the police)
1863	Draft
1870–1	Orange
1874	Tompkins Square
1900	Irish–Negro

Source: Richardson, 14–16, 28, 68, 105, 109–10, 166, 195, 276, and Joel T. Headley, *The Great Riots of New York: 1712–1873* (New York, 1873; Indianapolis: Bobbs-Merrill, 1970), 97, 134, 289. To more clearly test the hypothesis that riots precipitated police change, one would have to mount a study similar to that of Charles Tilly documented by R. A. Schweitzer, "A Study of Contentious Gatherings in Early Nineteenth-Century Great Britain," *Historical Methods* (Spring 1979), 123–6.

77 Pyle, Figures 1a, 2a, and 3a. As New York and Boston copied the police of London (a single point), smaller cities copied New York and Boston. The police of Lowell, Massachusetts, copied their badges from those of Boston in 1887 (*City Documents* [Lowell, Mass.: n.p., 1888], 19). The Providence, Rhode Island, police modeled their whole uniform on Bos-

ton's in 1865 (Henry Mann, ed., *Our Police*, [Providence, R.I., n.p., 1889]). The buttons of the Utica, New York, uniform were copied from the New York City police in 1859 – and the uniforms were paid for by the proceeds from a ball! (*Utica* [N.Y.] *Morning Herald* [Oct. 26, 1859]). The material of the uniform of the Paterson, New Jersey, police was the same as that of the New York uniforms in 1871 (n.a., *History of the Fire and Police Departments of Paterson, New Jersey*, "General Rules" [Paterson, N.J.: n.p., 1893], 163). *The Norfolk* (Va.) *Journal* (Dec. 20, 1866) proudly announced the new uniform would be made in Baltimore, but "is the same as worn by the police of New York, Baltimore and Washington. . . ."

78 Nelson W. Polsby, "The Institutionalization of the U.S. House of Representatives," *American Political Science Review* (March 1968), 144–68.

79 See Eugene Watts, "(One Dimension of the) Social Dynamics of 'Cop' Careers: The St. Louis Police, 1899–1970," paper presented at the Organization of American Historians Annual Meeting, April 8, 1976.

80 See Bruce C. Johnson, "Taking Care of Labor: The Police in American Politics," *Theory and Society* (Spring 1976), 89–117, for a discussion of progressives and police reform.

81 Both Levine and David Johnson argue that conflicting demands placed on the individual police officers by politicians, the public, and the police command structure forced police to professionalize and develop their own norms.

82 Alix J. Muller, *History of the Police and Fire Departments of the Twin Cities* (Minneapolis: Minneapolis, St. Paul, American Land and Title Registration Association, 1899), incorrectly stated that the Minneapolis police got their uniforms in 1874 (p. 41).

83 *Minneapolis Tribune* (Nov. 15, 1874). The *Tribune* of March 20, 1874, noted that the Saint Paul police wore new uniforms, but these apparently were not their first, as the council had paid for new "outfits" on June 4, 1872. (*Proceedings of the Common Council, 1872–1874* [St. Paul, 1874]).

84 *Proceedings of the City Council, 1876*, June 21, 1876 (Minneapolis, 1876), 41.

85 *Proceedings of the Common Council, 1872–1874*, June 4, 1872 (St. Paul, 1874), 66.

86 *Proceedings of the City Council, 1876*, Oct. 20, 1875 (Minneapolis, 1876), 77.

87 *Minneapolis Tribune*, April 18, 1872.

88 *Proceedings of the City Council, 1876*, April 11, 1876 (Minneapolis, 1876), 3.

89 *Minneapolis Tribune*, April 14, 1876.

90 *Minneapolis Tribune*, May 19, 1876.

91 *Proceedings of the City Council, 1876*, Oct. 20, 1875 (Minneapolis, 1876), 77.

92 *Proceedings of the City Council, 1877*, Dec. 20, 1876 (Minneapolis, 1877).

93 *Annual Report of the Chief of Police, 1879* (Minneapolis, 1879), 94–5.
94 *Proceedings of the Common Council, 1871–1872* (St. Paul, 1872), 2.
95 See Bruce Laurie's article on fire gangs in Allen F. Davis and Mark H. Haller, eds., *The Peoples of Philadelphia: A History of Ethnic Groups and Lower Class Life, 1790–1940* (Philadelphia: Temple University Press, 1973). See also Richard B. Calhoun, "New York City Fire Department Modernization, 1865–1870: A Civil War Legacy," *New–York Historical Society Quarterly* (Jan./April 1976), 7–34, who argues that Civil War military organizational experience provided a model for reorganizing the New York City fire department.
96 Wade, 98, citing Frederick L. Olmsted, *A Journey in the Back Country* (New York: Mason Brothers, 1860), 280; one suspects Olmsted may have been looking for tyranny. Lane, *Policing the City*, 129, quotes a Bostonian who compared the Southern police to those of Cuba and Europe: The date, 1861, suggests such sentiment again reflects anti-Southern bias rather than accurate analysis.
97 Alfers, 47–130.
98 Richard H. Haunton, "Law and Order in Savannah, 1850–1860," *Georgia Historical Quarterly* (Spring 1972), 14. Leonard P. Curry, "Urbanization and Urbanism in the Old South: A Comparative View," *Journal of Southern History* (Feb. 1974), 53–4, emphasizes the similarity of the Northern and Southern police.
99 Eugene J. Watts, "The Police in Atlanta, 1890–1905," *Journal of Southern History* (May 1973), 165–82.
100 Ketcham, 213.

2. Arrest trends, 1860–1920

1 Roger Lane, "Crime and Criminal Statistics in Nineteenth-Century Massachusetts," *Journal of Social History* (Winter 1968), 156–63.
2 The use of sentencing or convictions poses several measurement problems, not the least of which is shown by Charles N. Burrows, *Criminal Statistics in Iowa, University of Iowa Studies in the Social Sciences*, 9 (1931) n. 2, p. 110, who found a greater fluctuation in convictions than in sentences over a seventy-five-year period. Theodore N. Ferdinand, "Criminality, the Courts, and the Constabulary in Boston, 1703–1967," manuscript (De Kalb: Northern Illinois University) n. 6, p. 23; "The Criminal Patterns of Boston Since 1849," *American Journal of Sociology* (July 1967), 84–99; "Politics, the Police and Arresting Policies in Salem, Massachusetts, since the Civil War," *Social Problems* (Spring 1972), 572–88; "From a Service to a Legalistic Style Police Department: A Case Study [of Rockford, Illinois]," manuscript (De Kalb: Northern Illinois University). An earlier study, Leonard V. Harrison, *Police Administration in Boston* (Cambridge, Mass.: Harvard University Press, 1934), found patterns conflicting with those reported by Ferdinand. Robbery

arrests were stable, 1860–1930, while assault and battery, breaking and entering, and drunkenness declined, 1860–1900. Different categories may account for these contradictions.

3 Waldo L. Cook, "Murders in Massachusetts," *Journal of the American Statistical Association* (Sept. 1893), 357–8. The table in Appendix E briefly summarizes these previous studies.

4 Ferdinand, "Criminality, Courts and Constabulary;" Sam Bass Warner, *Crime and Criminal Statistics in Boston* (Cambridge, Mass.: Harvard University Press, 1934), 27.

5 Ferdinand, "Criminal Patterns."

6 Ferdinand, "Politics and Arresting Policy."

7 Lane, "Crime and Criminal Statistics." Michael S. Hindus, "Prison and Plantation: Criminal Justice in Nineteenth-century Massachusetts and South Carolina," Ph.D. dissertation (Berkeley: University of California, 1975), 102.

8 Arthur H. Hobbs, "Criminality in Philadelphia: 1790–1810 Compared with 1937," *American Sociological Review* (Feb. 1943), 198–202.

9 Elwin H. Powell, "Crime as a Function of Anomie," *Journal of Criminal Law, Criminology and Police Science* (June 1966), 161–71.

10 Eric H. Monkkonen, *The Dangerous Class: Crime and Poverty in Columbus, Ohio, 1860–1885* (Cambridge, Mass.: Harvard University Press, 1975), 30–1, 50–1.

11 Ferdinand, "From Service to Legalistic Style."

12 Burrows, *Criminal Statistics*, 106–9.

13 Augustus F. Kuhlman, "Crime and Punishment in Missouri: A Study of the Social Forces in the Trial and Error Process of Penal Reform," Ph.D. dissertation (Chicago: University of Chicago, 1929), Table 1, p. 96.

14 Monkkonen, "Toward a Dynamic Theory of Crime and the Police: A Criminal Justice Systems Perspective," *Historical Methods* (Fall 1977), 157–65.

15 Robert V. Percival, "Municipal Justice in the Melting Pot: Arrest and Prosecution in Oakland, 1872–1910," manuscript (Stanford, Calif.: Stanford University), Fig. 1, Table 4, and p. 24.

16 Monkkonen, "Municipal Reports as an Indicator Source: The Nineteenth-century Police," *Historical Methods* (Spring 1979), 57–65.

17 I concur with V. A. C. Gatrell and T. B. Hadden, "Criminal Statistics and Their Interpretation," in E. A. Wrigley, ed., *Nineteenth Century Society: Essays in the Use of Quantitative Methods for the Study of Social Data* (Cambridge: Cambridge University Press, 1972), 362, rule 4. They feel national data may successfully cancel out local deviations. But see their complete discussion, 336–96. For a good, if somewhat too discouraging, analysis of the use of arrests as a measurement statistic, see Sam B. Warner, *Survey of Criminal Statistics in the United States for the National Commission on Law Observance and Enforcement* [Wickersham

Commission], 32–40, in the National Commission on Law Observance and Enforcement, *Report on Criminal Statistics* (Washington, D.C.: GPO, 1931), 19–147. The President's Commission on Law Enforcement and Administration of Justice, *The Challenge of Crime in a Free Society* (New York: Avon, 1968), deals with this problem in several places, for instance, 96–107. More recently, the Law Enforcement Assistance Administration has several local crime victimization surveys under way in an attempt to determine what criminologists refer to as the "dark number" of unreported crimes: See, for example, the National Crime Panel Survey Report, *Criminal Victimization in the United States*, vol. 1 (May 1975). The literature on criminal statistics and arrest rates in particular is extensive, but two articles stand out: John I. Kitsuse and Aaron V. Cicourel, "A Note on the Use of Official Statistics," *Social Problems* (Fall 1963), 131–9; and A. Keith Bottomley and Clive A. Coleman, "Criminal Statistics: The Police Role in the Discovery and Detection of Crime," *International Journal of Criminology and Penology*, 4 (1976), 33–58. And for a brief, useful discussion of arrest as stigma, see Jack D. Douglas, *American Social Order: Social Rules in a Pluralistic Society* (New York: Free Press, 1971), 316–17.

18   Fred Kohler, *Annual Report of the Chief of Police* (Cleveland, 1910), 13–14.

19   Raymond Fosdick, et al., *Criminal Justice in Cleveland* (Cleveland: Cleveland Foundation, 1910), 323–4.

20   Actual annual homicide arrests for 1905–15 in Cleveland were as follows: 32, 21, 31, 36, 28, 35, 37, 30, 44, and 57. They correlate positively with actual initiative arrests, $R^2 = .47$, significance greater than .01.

21   Murder here includes all forms of criminal homicide, including vehicular; when vehicular (estimated) is excluded, the trend remains the same. The advantage of using murder as an indicator of criminal behavior, rather than of police behavior, is that it is a crime very often cleared by arrest; at least it is today, when we know both the number of offenses known to the police as well as the number cleared by arrest. See the President's Commission on Law Enforcement and Administration of Justice, *Challenge of Crime*. The reason for the high clearance rate for murder is that often there is a witness, and often the murderer is a friend, relative, or acquaintance of the victim. Further, murder has long been regarded as a serious matter, whereas other, more numerous offenses may not have been regarded as such. For the purposes of historians, it would be more useful to know the number of thefts that actually occurred in a given place as an index of actual criminal behavior, but murder may be a reasonable substitute for an index to violence. For consistency, and to overcome the possible results of some preliminary plea bargaining, I have combined all categories in which there was an arrest made for a death by violence. This includes nonin-

tentional homicide charges, not a large category before the mass usage
of automobiles. The reason for including nonintentional homicides is,
again, to take into account the possibility of some form of plea bargaining between the person charged and the police, and also because there
is good reason to conceive homicide by vehicle as similar to death by
other weapons. See Raymond J. Michalowski, Jr., "Violence in the
Road: The Crime of Vehicular Homicide," *Journal of Research in Crime
and Delinquency* (Jan. 1975), 30–43. The arrest series for homicide generated in this manner can be asserted to reflect actual homicides, but it
can only be crudely validated for the last twenty-one years of the series. *Historical Statistics of the United States: Colonial Times to 1970*, Pt. 1
(Washington, D.C.: GPO, 1975), 414, Ser. H 971–986, gives annual
homicide data for 26% to 80% of the statewide population of the
United States from 1900 on. Although not directly comparable to the
urban arrest data of this study, the two series show some parallel. The
simple Pearsonian R between the two (both in rates per population) is
.635, significant at .001. This is not as high as one could desire, but
considering the different bases for the data (whole states versus urban
areas; coroner reported homicide versus homicide arrests), the results
suggest the general validity, if not absolute precision, of the arrest series.
22 Slope = − .508; significance = .00001.
23 Ted R. Gurr et al., *The Politics of Crime and Conflict: A Comparative
History of Four Cities* (Beverly Hills, Calif.: Sage, 1976).
24 The homicide arrest series indicates an upturn in homicide arrests occurring around 1880. Roger Lane's *Violent Death in the City: Suicide,
Accident, and Murder in Nineteenth-Century Philadelphia* (Cambridge,
Mass.: Harvard University Press, 1979), 60, indicates that an upturn in
Philadelphia did not occur until later − some time in the early twentieth century. A comparison of the data also shows about 30% more
homicide arrests than actual homicides. This creates two issues, one
concerning the use of arrests as a measure of homicide and the other
about the timing of the upturn. I included negligent homicides, many
arrests for which probably did not result in indictment or in indictable
offenses. Further, the police often made dragnet arrests for one homicide, which artificially inflated the arrest rate. Also, given the argument of this whole book on the changing role of policing, it is likely
that throughout the period under study, but especially after 1890, the
police focus on crime control produced proportionately more arrests
for homicide.Lane makes this argument more forcefully in "Violent
Death and Homicide: Patterns, Rates, and Speculation Over Time," a
paper presented at the Social Science History Association annual meeting, Cambridge, Mass., Nov. 3, 1979, 4–5. This would have the effect
of spuriously moving the upturn back in time. It is also possible the
Philadelphia experience did not mirror that of other cities. The ques-

tion of the relationship of arrest practice to prosecution to actual homicide clearly is an important topic needing more work.

25 See Hindus, 102, Fig. 1, for the wave of 1855.

26 Both notions expounded by Edith Abbott, "The Civil War and the
    Crime Wave of 1865–70," *Social Service Review* (June 1927), 212–34.
    See J. M. Beattie, "The Pattern of Crime in England, 1660–1800," *Past
    and Present* (Feb. 1974), 47–95, for a useful discussion of war and crime
    waves in England.

27 John C. Schneider, "Detroit and the Problem of Disorder: The Riot of
    1863," *Michigan History* (Spring 1974), 5.

28 Powell.

29 Kai T. Erikson, *The Wayward Puritans: A Study in the Sociology of Devi-
    ance* (New York: Wiley, 1966).

30 See John C. Schneider, "The Spatial Organization of Crime in De-
    troit," paper presented at the annual meeting of the Social Science His-
    tory Assn., Oct. 22, 1977, Ann Arbor, Mich.

31 Monkkonen, *Dangerous Class*, 53–4.

32 Fred Shannon, *The Organization and Administration of the Union Army,
    1861–1865*, 2 vols. (Cleveland: Arthur H. Clark, 1928). Eugene C. Mur-
    dock, *One Million Men: The Civil War Draft in the North* (Madison: His-
    torical Soceity of Wisconsin, 1971), 356, shows the biggest draft bite to
    have been in 1864.

33 Abbott, 212–34.

34 Abbott, 229.

35 For instance, there was no statistically significant relationship between
    tramps and felony rates in Columbus, Ohio, 1867–81, although there
    was a slight correlation between tramp and petty theft rates ($R = .38$,
    sig. $= .08$). Monkkonen, *Dangerous Class*, 126.

36 Thorsten Sellin, *Research Memorandum on Crime in the Depression* (New
    York: Social Science Research Council, 1937).

37 This, in a sense, is a corrolary to Weber's argument concerning the rise
    of Protestantism and the internalization of norms and goals.

38 Sheldon Hackney, "Southern Violence," in Ted Gurr and Hugh Gra-
    ham, *Violence in America: Historical and Comparative Perspectives* (New
    York: New American Library, 1969), 479–500. Although provocative,
    Hackney is substantively wrong; see Colin Loftin and Robert H. Hill,
    "Regional Subculture and Homicide: An Examination of the Gastil-
    Hackney Thesis," *American Sociological Review* (Oct. 1974), 714–24.

39 Thomas Byrnes, *1886, Professional Criminals in America* (New York,
    1969), 34, cites an incident when all "known" pickpockets in New York
    were arrested on suspicion, then discharged the next day, allegedly to
    stop crimes during the visit of a president.

40 Suspicion and vagrancy arrests, combined, decreased 67% from 1860
    to 1920, whereas dismissals, from 1891 to 1920, fell by 78%.

41 Correlations of harrassment measures with arrests (Pearson's R):

	All arrests	Drunkenness	Offenses with victims	Suspicion
Dismissals (N = 46)	−.128(n.s.)	−.026(n.s.)	−.171(n.s.)	.126(n.s.)
Suspicion (N = 46)	.379(.001)	.246(.021)	−.111(n.s.)	—

Significance in parentheses. All variables are rates based on simple linear interpolations of population.

42   Ted R. Gurr, "Development and Decay: Their Impact on Public Order in Western History," paper given at Conference on Historical Approaches to Studying Crime, Oct. 10–11, 1979, Washington, D.C., 5.

3. Tramps and children: the decline of police welfare

1   Eric H. Monkkonen, *The Dangerous Class: Crime and Poverty in Columbus, Ohio, 1860–1885* (Cambridge, Mass.: Harvard University Press, 1975), Chap. 7.
2   For an overview of tramping, see Kenneth Allsop, *Hard Travellin': The Hobo and His History* (New York: New American Library, 1967). For tramps, reformers, and an excellent bibliography, see Paul T. Ringenbach, *Tramps and Reformers, 1873–1916: The Discovery of Unemployment in New York* (Westport, Conn.: Greenwood, 1973), and Frank Leonard, "Helping the Unemployed in the Nineteenth Century: The Case of the American Tramp," *Social Service Review* (Dec. 1966), 429–34. See also Clark C. Spence, "Knights of the Tie and Rail – Tramps and Hoboes in the West," *Western Historical Quarterly* (Jan. 1971), 5–19. For a provocative historical analysis of vagrancy, see William J. Chambliss, "A Sociological Analysis of the Law of Vagrancy," *Social Problems* (Summer 1964), 67–77.
3   Alice Willard Solenberger, *One Thousand Homeless Men: A Study of Original Records* (New York: Russell Sage Foundation, 1911), 6, describes how different kinds of transients sought aid at different kinds of agencies. Those who were mobile workers, the great majority no doubt, did not often get into the formal charity net, which most often dealt with the feeble-minded or otherwise incapacitated.
4   For a discussion of life course that does not specifically mention tramping as a part of the work cycle, but implies how it might be included, see Glen H. Elder, "Family History and the Life Course," *Journal of Family History* (Winter 1977), 279–304. Clyde Griffen and Sally Griffen, *Natives and Newcomers: The Ordering of Opportunity in Nineteenth-Century Poughkeepsie* (Cambridge, Mass.: Harvard University Press, 1977), 22–3, mention a person who leaves town apparently to tramp, during periods of unemployment. They also discuss local employment condi-

tions, which presumably produced tramps with regularity (pp. 186–7, 224–5).

5 John D. Seelye, "The American Tramp: A Version of the Picaresque," *American Quarterly*, 15 (Winter 1963), 535–53.

6 Essentially the same lodging incident is mentioned by Jacob A. Riis in *The Making of an American* (New York: Macmillan, 1901), 71–7, 232–62, and in *The Battle with the Slum* (New York: Macmillan, 1902), 48–50, 168–70. See also Walter Wyckoff, *The Workers: The West* (New York: Scribner, 1898), 22–43, 86–93. Carleton Parker, *The Casual Laborer and Other Essays* (New York: Harcourt, 1920), 120, mentions the large number of lodgers in Chicago.

7 Josiah Flynt [Willard], *Tramping with Tramps: Studies and Sketches of Vagabond Life* (New York: New York Century, 1899). Flynt's main interest was in the nonworking homeless, and his work excludes the wandering workers, who were far more numerous. His bias and own personal problems may have influenced the focus of his aunt, by whom he was raised, Alice W. Solenberger. The most typical perspective on nineteenth-century tramping remains filtered through the image of the jungle, usually located at a transfer point or slow point on the railroad line. See the story by H. C. Bunner, "The Lost Child," *Scribner's Magazine* (Jan.-June 1896), 342–52, for a sympathetic portrayal of tramps who care for a lost child in their jungle.

8 Blanche D. Coll, *Perspectives in Public Welfare: A History* (Washington, D.C.: GPO, 1969), 20.

9 Wyckoff, 36–7.

10 Wyckoff, 42.

11 Wyckoff, 41–2.

12 Alvin F. Sanborn, "A Study of Beggars and Their Lodgings," *Forum* (April 1895), 200.

13 Leah H. Feder, *Unemployment Relief in Periods of Depression: A Study of Measures Adopted in Certain American Cities, 1857 through 1922* (New York: Russell Sage Foundation, 1936), 65–6.

14 Edward H. Savage, *Police Records and Recollections: Or, Boston by Daylight and Gaslight* (Boston: J. P. Dale, 1873), 106.

15 Sanborn, 207–8.

16 "Reports From Delegates," *Proceedings of the National Conference of Charities* (Boston, 1877), xxiv.

17 Riis, *Making of an American*, 71–4.

18 Riis, *Making of an American*, 76.

19 John J. McCook, "A Tramp Census and Its Revelations," *Forum* (August 1893), 753–66.

20 McCook, 760.

21 Calculated from Third Precinct Lodgers Register, 1891–5, Washington, D.C., Police, U.S. National Archives.

22 Monkkonen, 160.

23 McCook, 753, 756. There are two probable sources of bias in McCook's
    "census": the police officers who administered the questionnaire and
    the high unemployment rate during the depression.
24 Solenberger, 6.
25 Feder, 166.
26 Feder, 166.
27 James F. Richardson, *The New York Police: Colonial Times to 1901* (New
    York: Oxford University Press, 1970), 60–1.
28 Richardson, 152.
29 Richardson, 265.
30 McCook, 761.
31 Feder, 163.
32 Monkkonen, 114.
33 "Superintendent's Report," "Report of the Police Department," *An-
    nual Reports of the City Departments of the City of Cincinnati, 1876* (Cin-
    cinnati, 1877), 27.
34 "Report of the Chief of Police," *Providence City Documents, 1891* (Prov-
    idence, R.I., 1892), 20–21.
35 "Report of the Chief of Police," *Providence City Documents, 1889* (Prov-
    idence, R.I., 1890), 12. A somewhat sympathetic attitude also appeared
    in the *History of Alleghany Police Department, Published by and for the
    Benefit of the Patrolmen's Benevolent Association* (Alleghany, Pa., 1901):
    "The great business depression [1893] which prevailed throughout the
    country threw many men out of employment and as a conequence
    [*sic*] thieving became general, but was not exceptionally noticed in Al-
    leghany owing to the precautions taken. Many workingmen traveling
    about the country in search of work applied for lodging, as a system of
    giving each a good breakfast of bread and coffee was introduced and
    continued throughout the year. Each lodger was given all that he could
    desire, and as a consequence begging was eliminated. Of course,
    many that were unworthy took advantage of the breakfasts, but no
    discrimination was shown" (p. 61).
36 *Report of Major and Superintendent of Police for Fiscal Year 1884* (Wash-
    ington, D.C., 1884), 15, 17.
37 See Arthur Stinchcombe, "Institutions of Privacy in the Determination
    of Police Administrative Practice," *American Journal of Sociology* (Sept.
    1963); 150–60.
38 Monkkonen, 157–9.
39 It should be pointed out that although the use of drunkenness and
    suspicion and vagrancy categories as a measure holds more appeal
    than total arrests, the issue of intercity comparability for aggregating
    cities holds greater difficulty, because occasionally cities for short per-
    iods of time used other categories as the catchall offense for police-ini-
    tiated arrests – trespassing, for instance. Nevertheless, I have included
    the results obtained by using these categories. Neither rate, it must be

emphasized, is the number of cases that came to trial nor for which a guilty plea was entered. The figures are for arrests, and no attempt has been made to calculate conviction rates, partly because such figures relate more to police efficiency, court proceedings, and sometimes to police harassment practices. Most people arrested on suspicion, for instance, were discharged before any action was taken because the charge was simply a way to get people off the streets and into the station houses. (See, for example, Thomas Byrnes, *1886, Professional Criminals of America* [New York: Chelsea House, 1969], 34.) The emphasis here is on arrests as a measure of police behavior, whether on the officer's own initiative or as a response to a complaint.

40 *Proceedings of the National Conference of Charities* (1877), xxiv.
41 Wyckoff, 92, mentions that individual Chicago police officers helped people find jobs or at least expressed individual concern.
42 For details of the attack on boarding, see John Modell and Tamara K. Hareven, "Urbanization and the Malleable Household: An Examination of Boarding and Lodging in American Families," *Journal of Marriage and the Family* (Aug. 1973), 467–79. See Ringenbach, 83, for a discussion of Josephine Lowell and the criticism of outdoor relief. One non-police-authored discussion of charity, "A Police Department in Charitable Work," n.a., *Municipal Affairs* (Sept. 1897), 572, abstracted an article from *Open Court* (June 1897) that discussed the efficiency with which Chicago police had distributed charity during the harsh winter of 1896–7. The article took pains to indicate that the costs of distribution had been nothing.
43 Feder, 164.
44 Riis, *Making of an American*, 232–3. See also Rosalie Butler, "Separation of Charities and Correction," *Charities Review* (1892), 164–70.
45 Riis, *Making of an American*, 259.
46 Edward T. Devine, "The Shiftless and Floating City Population," *Annals of the American Academy of Political and Social Science* (Sept. 1897), 153.
47 Devine, 159.
48 Riis, *Battle with the Slum*, 170.
49 Riis, *Making of an American*, 260–1.
50 T. F. Ring, "The Boston Wayfarers' Lodge," *Proceedings of the National Conference of Charities and Corrections* (Boston, 1885), 325. Leonard, 430, discusses some of the more bizarre suggestions for work tests, such as a drowning tank where vagrants had to bail to stay alive.
51 Henry McBride, "The Lost Children of New York," *Harper's Weekly* (Jan. 5, 1895), 16–17. Both this and Riis's article may have been efforts to improve the image of the New York police after the devastating Lexow investigation, slightly earlier. A short article had appeared in *Frank Leslie's Illustrated Newspaper* (Aug. 26, 1882), 7, with a large illustration. This article detailed the work of the department, with little comment other than brief praise for its administration. It does corrobo-

rate the wide range of children lost, the several reasons for getting lost, and the details for handling them at the station house. It also mentions that a matron, Mrs. M. Webb, had for ten years dealt with the children. Whether she was the first matron to be used for lost children, or whether this was her sole responsibility, is left unclear.

52 Monkkonen, 86, 113.

53 For the Pittsburgh sample, 50% of the lost children were below three years old, suggesting that for most lost children, their home language was a relatively minor factor in getting lost or found. Ethnic child-rearing differences and attitudes toward the use of public services clearly played a role in determining whose children got lost; the difficulty is in estimating what and how large these differences were. An article in *Die Abendpost* (Sept. 8, 1891), a Chicago German-language newspaper, compared German to American child-rearing practices: "In reality the lack of the democratic spirit in many families is to be construed as the basic factor for the laxity in child training. Parents fail to meet their responsibility towards society. They expect too much from the school and the government and do very little themselves. They desire that their own children as well as all the others should be trained by the paid teachers and guided in the path of virtue and moderation by the policemen's club." (Translation from the Chicago Foreign Language Press Survey.)

54 An analysis using rank-order correlations (Spearman's rho) for each different region was also performed to confirm the results of the regression, as it is arguable whether population is an ordinal or interval variable. The results are given in Appendix D, Table D.3.

For the Southern police, see Richard Wade, *Slavery in the Cities: The South, 1820–1860* (New York: Oxford University Press, 1964), 98–101. See also Louis Cei, "Law Enforcement in Richmond: A History of Police–Community Relations, 1737–1974," Ph.D. dissertation (Tallahassee: Florida State University, 1975), and Richard H. Haunton, "Law and Order in Savannah, 1850–1860," *Georgia Historical Quarterly* (Spring 1972), 1–24.

55 *New York Daily Times* (June 16, 1857), 8. The Philadelphia *Public Ledger* (April 2, 1839) stated: "Almost every family in this city has been distressed by the loss of some of its little flock." The article asserted there was a band of kidnappers operating in the city, returning the children for ransom, a practice similar to that in operation with thief catchers. (Roger Lane has been kind enough to provide me with this and several other citations concerning lost children in Philadelphia.) Another incident concerning a lost child in Reading, Pennsylvania, around 1869 confirms the impression given by the New York account, though it is difficult to date with accuracy. Related by James H. Maurer in *It Can Be Done* (New York: Rand School Press, 1938), the account emphasizes the communications vacuum of the prepolice city. When Maurer stayed out late playing with friends, his father "ordered all the bell ringers.

These men would walk about ringing their bells and crying 'Lost Child! Lost Child!' until they had covered the whole city if necessary" (p. 5). Although presumably an efficient way of mobilizing a small community, the bell ringers still lacked a central communication hierarchy, one that the reorganized, uniformed police would be able to provide. (I wish to thank David Waterhouse for bringing this incident to my attention.)

56 Early police reports, published in the *New York Daily Times*, do not mention lost children. See Jan. 23, 1852; Oct. 9, 1852; Jan. 8, 1853.

57 Jacob Riis, "Out of the Book of Humanity," *Atlantic Monthly* (March 1896), 699.

58 In speaking of the other organizations that provided children with assistance, the president of the New York Society for the Prevention of Cruelty to Children (NYSPCC) pointed out, "It is not within their province to seek out and to rescue from the dens and slums of the city these little unfortunates whose childish lives are rendered miserable. . . ." He claimed existing laws were adequate, but that "The police and prosecuting officers of the people are necessarily engaged in securing the conviction and punishment of offenders of a graver legal stripe." NYSPCC, *Second Annual Report* (New York, 1877), 5–6.

59 The 1877 NYSPCC annual report lists seven societies formed on the model of New York City in 1875–6 (Rochester; Newburgh, N.Y.: Buffalo; Cleveland; San Francisco; Portsmouth, N.H.; and Philadelphia). By 1887, 72 societies had been formed across the country, and by 1897 the number had climed to 180. Source: annual reports of the NYSPCC.

60 NYSPCC, *Thirteenth Annual Report* (New York, 1887), 7.

61 NYSPCC, *Thirteenth Annual Report*, 19, 26.

62 Table D.4 in Appendix D shows the annual number of lost children returned to their parents by the NYSPCC compared to the number for the same year by the police for years when NYSPCC data are available.

4. A narrowing of function

1 This model is a production function. Because lodging was "produced" by the police in addition to arrests, it is necessary to include lodging as a dependent variable. As a graph of the lodging rates in Chapter 3 makes clear, most of the variation in these rates came from variation in demand for lodging, determined almost completely by unemployment, if the peaks of lodging during depression years are at all meaningful. Thus the model of the police production of lodging can be expected to be inadequate. A more intuitively satisfying model would include lodging as an independent variable, acting as an indicator of unemployment: This model produces considerably higher $\bar{R}^2$s but, more importantly, parallel and stronger results than the restricted and conservative model used in the early parts of this chapter. See, for instance, the results reported in Eric H. Monkkonen, "Systematic

Criminal Justice History: Some Suggestions," *Journal of Interdisciplinary History* (Winter 1979), 451–64, and "Municipal Reports as an Indicator Source: The Nineteenth-Century Police," *Historical Methods* (Spring 1979), 57–65. I am grateful to Lance Davis for bringing the implicit production function model to my attention.

2   Although especially appropriate and powerful for use with interval time series data, multiple regression does contain some pitfalls for the unwary, mainly the problem of serially correlated errors. If the error terms, that is, the differences between the value predicted and the actual value for each observation, are serially correlated, then one of the mathematical assumptions of the regression calculation has been violated. Econometricians have developed both a statistic (the Durbin-Watson test) to indicate the presence of serial correlation, as well as a means of eliminating the serial correlation. It turns out that most time series data will have serially correlated errors because most of these data have trends. If one's model specifies inclusion of the lagged dependent variable as an independent variable or using first differences rather than annual values, then the data have been effectively detrended.

Another potential problem with multiple regression is the presence of intercorrelated independent or predictor variables. There is no consensus on the solutions to this problem, because whereas the presence of such variables may give unreliable coefficients, the model that specifies their inclusion cannot simply be discarded. I have chosen to include those few variables that seem appropriate and necessary to the model: As most of the purposes of this analysis can be achieved simply by correctly estimating the sign of a variable's coefficient, absolute precision is not a high priority here.

For a sensible, if somewhat compressed, discussion of both these problems, see Potluri Rao and Roger L. Miller, *Applied Econometrics* (Belmont, Calif.: Wadsworth, 1971), 121–6, 46–52. Also, for one of the first discussions alerting historians to the serial correlation problem, see Laura I. Langbein, "The Transformation of Time-Series Data to Meet Least Squares Assumption," Social Science History Association, *Newsletter: Methodology Network* (1978).

The point of view presented here should not be taken as an indication that these statistical problems have been resolved, for although my point of view is conventional, there is still much controversy, both over the use of first differences as well as over using population as the denominator in rate or ratio variables. See Brian F. Pendleton, Richard D. Warren, and H. C. Chang, "Correlated Denominators in Multiple Regression and Change Analysis," *Sociological Methods and Research* (May 1979), 451–74.

3   All statistics referred to are included in Appendix C.

4   Ted R. Gurr et al., *The Politics of Crime and Conflict: A Comparative History of Four Cities* (Beverly Hills, Calif.: Sage, 1976).

5   I wish to thank Colin Loftin for suggesting this method of testing for spatial autocorrelation.

6   For a useful survey of published information on U.S. cities, see U.S. National Resources Committee, Research Committee on Urbanism, Supplementary Report No. 1, *Federal Reporting of Urban Information*, (Washington, D.C.: GPO, 1938), 161–74.

7   This bureaucratic change paralleled similar developments in other urban institutions. See Steven L. Schlossman, *Love and the American Delinquent: The Theory and Practice of "Progressive" Juvenile Justice, 1825–1920* (Chicago: University of Chicago Press, 1977), particularly Chaps. 4–8. Michael B. Katz found a bureaucratic growth and crystallization in educational institutions occurring slightly earlier, in the 1880s. See his *Class, Bureaucracy, and Schools: The Illusion of Educational Change in America* (New York: Praeger, 1975), 53, 60, 105.

8   This interpretation of the consequences of bureaucratization for institutional growth corresponds with the summary of related theory presented by W. Richard Scott, "Organizational Structure," in Alex Inkeles, ed., *Annual Review of Sociology* (Palo Alto, Calif.: Annual Reviews, 1975), 1–20. See particularly his summary of a study by Freeman and Hannan, which shows "that the size of the administrative component increases along with the size of the organization during periods of growth, but that during periods of decline the size of the administrative component does not diminish along with the total organizational size" (p. 16) (John Freeman and Michael T. Hannan, "Growth and Decline Processes in Organizations," *American Sociological Review* [April 1975], 215–28). This creates problems with any cross-sectional study that combines both growing and declining organizations. In the case of the cross-sectional analyses presented in this chapter, such a problem does not appear, but for studies of policing later in the twentieth century, this would indeed be an analytic problem.

9   First pointed out to me by Eugene Watts. See Samuel Walker, *A Critical History of Police Reform* (Lexington, Mass.: Heath, 1977), 63–4, for a discussion of the two- and three-platoon shifts.

10   This general decline conforms to the best estimate of English offenses, which also finds a nineteenth-century decline. See V. A. C. Gatrell and T. B. Hadden, "Criminal Statistics and Their Interpretation," in E. A. Wrigley, ed., *Nineteenth Century Society: Essays in the Use of Quantitative Methods for the Study of Social Data* (Cambridge: Cambridge University Press, 1972), 374.

11   In certain ways, even the lost-children data support this notion of narrowed police service. Although Chapter 3 emphasized how the decline in the return rate related to the introduction of uniformed police forces in each particular city, the diffusion of policing had nearly concluded by the mid 1880s. The net effect on the national rates of lost children returned was a decrease between 1880 and 1890, when all cities are

aggregated. In 1880, 2.451 children per 1,000 total population were returned by the police. In 1890, the rate had dropped to 1.758 (1880 based on 120 cities, 1890 on 235. Source: Tenth U.S. Census, *Report on Defective, Dependent, and Delinquent Classes* [Washington, D.C.: GPO, 1888], Eleventh U.S. Census, *Report on Crime, Pauperism, and Benevolence* [Washington, D.C.: GPO, 1895].)

Conclusion

1 Robert Fogelson, *Big City Police* (Cambridge, Mass.: Harvard University Press, 1977), Chap. 1.
2 "The Dangerous Class," *New Republic* (May 8, 1915), 7–8, reference supplied by Lynne Wiener. The most explicit definition of the earlier concept of the "dangerous class" I have found is in an article by the noted nineteenth-century constitutional scholar, Christopher G. Tiedman. In the article, he discussed the "dangerous class, other than criminal, – persons whose unrestrained freedom involves elements of danger to the State and Society." These included the diseased, insane, alcoholics, vagrants, and beggars. And even this broad definition represented a narrowing of earlier definitions, which included the impoverished and sometimes all working-class people. See his "Police Control of Dangerous Classes, Other Than By Criminal Prosecutions," *American Law Review* (July-Aug. 1885), 547–70.
3 See Wilbur Miller, *Cops and Bobbies* (Chicago: University of Chicago Press, 1977), and James P. Gifford, "The Celebrated World of Currier and Ives: In Which Heroic Fire Laddies Raced to Battle Conflagrations While the Police Disappeared in the Most Amazing Way," *New–York Historical Society Quarterly* (Oct. 1975), 348–65. I have found one suggestive reference that goes beyond the media nonimage. Mrs. Andrea Marie Kornmann, *Our Police . . . By A Policeman's Wife* (New York: J. J. Little, 1887), wrote a strange and almost paranoid book defending the moral character of police officers: She commented, "There seems to be a species of social ostracism exercised against the police. They seem to be cut off from association with other people outside the Department, and this ostracism seems to extend to their families" (p. 79). She continues with incidents of tenants in apartment buildings resenting the moving in of a police officer's family, that tenants considered police "a very coarse, rough class of people," but notes that police families paid their rent promptly, as opposed to mechanics who get "behindhand" in rent in "dull seasons" (p. 80).
4 Barbara Hanawalt, "Conflict Theory and Medieval Criminal Justice: Is There Really Community Justice?" Social Science History Association Annual Meeting, Oct. 21–3, 1977, Ann Arbor, Mich., criticizes the notion of community justice. See also her *Crime and Conflict in English Communities, 1300–1348* (Cambridge, Mass.: Harvard University Press, 1979). David H. Flaherty, *Privacy in Colonial New England*

(Charlottesville: University Press of Virginia, 1972) notes, "Since colonial towns did not have persons who made a real career of law enforcement, the pressures were great to let sleeping dogs lie" (p. 218). Flaherty also cites the incident of a New Haven, Connecticut, postmaster who in 1773 was afraid to inform on offenses of post riders: He would rather have suffered himself than lose friends. And Douglas Greenberg, *Crime and Law Enforcement in the Colony of New York, 1691–1776* (Ithaca, N.Y.: Cornell University Press, 1976), 89, 180–1, discusses the substantial evidence of popular feelings of hostility toward the constables.

5   Lawrence M. Friedman, "The Long Arm of the Law," *Reviews in American History* (June 1978), 227.

6   Michael H. Frisch, *Town into City: Springfield, Massachusetts, and the Meaning of Community, 1840–1880* (Cambridge, Mass.: Harvard University Press, 1972).

7   Samuel Hays, "The Changing Political Structure of the City in Industrial America," *Journal of Urban History* (Nov. 1974), 12–28.

8   Seymour Mandelbaum, *Boss Tweed's New York* (New York: Wiley, 1965).

9   See Fogelson, 20–35, for a graphic description of corrupt police practices.

10   Hays uses the term "centrifugal" to describe the urban path of expansion. Alan Anderson, *The Origin and Resolution of an Urban Crisis: Baltimore, 1890–1930* (Baltimore: Johns Hopkins University Press, 1977), 38–40, notes the relatively early centralization of Baltimore's police and fire service compared to other city activities.

11   Hays, 18.

12   See Bruce C. Johnson, "Taking Care of Labor: The Police in American Politics," *Theory and Society* (Spring 1976), 89–117, on the working class and the police.

13   Jerald E. Levine, "Police, Parties, and Polity: The Bureaucratization, Unionization, and Professionalization of the New York City Police, 1870–1917," Ph.D. dissertation (Madison: University of Wisconsin, 1971), explicitly focuses on job consciousness and rank and file unionization efforts.

14   Dwight F. Davis, "The Neighborhood Center – A Moral and Educational Factor," *Charities and Commons* (Feb. 1, 1908), 1505–6; cited by Don S. Kirschner, "The Ambiguous Legacy: Social Justice and Social Control in the Progressive Era," *Historical Reflections* (Summer 1975), 81. The active intervention of the New York Society for the Prevention of Cruelty to Children, and other similar agencies elsewhere, although focused on child abuse, also relieved police from such heavy child care activities as the late 1860s and early 1870s saw.

15   Harold Pepinsky suggests that the decline in initiative arrests resulted from the increase in bureaucratization: Fewer officers spent their time on the street and thus were unable to produce these street-based ar-

rests. "Comments," Social Science History Association Annual Meeting, Oct. 1977, Ann Arbor, Mich.

16 John T. Ringenbach, *Tramps and Reformers, 1873–1896: The Discovery of Unemployment in New York* (Westport, Conn.: Greenwood, 1973), gives a thorough discussion of the various tramp-reform ideologies.

17 "A National Police Convention in St. Louis," *New York Times* (Aug. 24, 1871), 1. For a convenient collection of materials on the growth of the International Association of the Chiefs of Police (IACP), see Donald C. Dilworth, ed., *The Blue and the Brass: American Policing: 1890–1910* (Gaithersburg, Md.: IACP, 1976).

18 See the U.S. House of Representatives, Report 429, *National Bureau of Criminal Identification* (Feb. 7, 1902), U.S. Serial Set 4401, for a mention of this bureau. From 1898 on, the IACP's semi-official publication, *The Detective*, provided national communications for police fugitive notices. For an example from 1906, see Dilworth, *Blue and Brass*, 42–3. Another IACP volume edited by Dilworth, *Identification Wanted: Development of the American Criminal Identification System, 1893–1943* (Gaithersburg, Md.: IACP, 1977), traces the vagaries of the efforts of the police chiefs to create their National Identification Bureau. See also John L. Thompson, "National Identification Bureau is IACP Pioneers' Legacy," *Police Chief* (Jan. 1964), 10–41. As a parallel to this national development, the earliest manufacturer's catalog I have been able to identify with police equipment is that of the John P. Lovell Arms Company in 1893: This catalog lists equipment patented between 1874 and the 1880s. It seems reasonable to date national mail-order availability between 1874 and the mid 1880s. The Ridabock and Company catalog (New York, 1880) included, along with military goods, police hats, caps, belts, and clubs (pp. 12, 41). I am grateful to Robert W. Lovett of the Baker Library, Harvard University, and Marjorie G. McMach of the Eleutherian Mills Historical Library for this information.

19 Richard Sylvester, "Report of the Standing Committee on Police Forces in Cities," *Proceedings of the Annual Congress of the National Prison Association of the United States* (1902), 329 (reprinted New York: Arno, 1971).

20 The National Bureau of Criminal Identification became the Federal Bureau of Identification in 1924 and a part of the newly created Federal Bureau of Investigation in 1930. See Thompson, 40–2.

21 Sylvester, 338.

22 The assertion that police crime-control efforts converged in the different cities can be substantiated by examining the Pearsonian correlation coefficients between the estimated criminal offense arrest rates and the police strength per capita in the previous year. This should capture the consequences of police strength variation in a cumulative manner. By dividing the 1860–1920 era into two periods at 1890, we can examine the change in this relationship for the individual cities

that have been combined to make up the aggregate data here for this study. In Table F 1 (p. 182) the Rs for the whole period, and for the pre- and post-1890 eras, are displayed. Of the ten cities with sufficiently complete data for analysis in both eras, only two, Chicago and Cincinnati, show a decrease in the strength of association between lagged police and crime arrests. Adding in the cities where the R was not statistically significant produces two more nonconforming cities, Saint Louis and Lowell, Massachusetts; but at least seven more conforming cities. Thus the behavior of police in individual cities, with four exceptions out of twenty-two, conformed to the model established for all large cities.

23 Fogelson, 2–10.
24 Paul Murphy, *The Constitution in Crisis Times, 1918–1969* (New York: Harper & Row, 1971), 434–9. Also *World War I and the Origin of Civil Liberties in the United States* (New York: Norton, 1980).
25 Kenneth Fox, *Better City Government: Innovation in American Urban Politics, 1850–1937* (Philadelphia: Temple University Press, 1977).
26 Paul Boyer, *Urban Masses and Moral Order in America, 1820–1920* (Cambridge, Mass.: Harvard University Press, 1978), 154.
27 Melvin G. Holli, "Urban Reform in the Progressive Era," in Lewis L. Gould, ed., *The Progressive Era* (Syracuse, N.Y.: Syracuse University Press, 1974), 133.

Index